Does Local Government Matter?

Globalization and Community
Susan E. Clarke, series editor
Dennis R. Judd, founding editor

VOLUME 19

Does Local Government Matter? How Urban Policies Shape Civic Engagement
Elaine B. Sharp

VOLUME 18

Justice and the American Metropolis
Clarissa Rile Hayward and Todd Swanstrom, editors

VOLUME 17

Mobile Urbanism: Cities and Policymaking in the Global Age
Eugene McCann and Kevin Ward, editors

VOLUME 16

Seeking Spatial Justice
Edward W. Soja

VOLUME 15

Shanghai Rising: State Power and Local Transformations in a Global Megacity
Xiangming Chen, editor

VOLUME 14

A World of Gangs: Armed Young Men and Gangsta Culture
John M. Hagedorn

VOLUME 13

El Paso: Local Frontiers at a Global Crossroads
Victor M. Ortíz-González

VOLUME 12

Remaking New York: Primitive Globalization and the Politics of Urban Community
William Sites

(continued on page 234)

Does Local Government Matter?

How Urban Policies Shape Civic Engagement

Elaine B. Sharp

Globalization and Community, Volume 19

University of Minnesota Press
Minneapolis
London

The University of Minnesota Press gratefully acknowledges financial assistance provided for the publication of this book from the Department of Political Science at the University of Kansas.

A version of chapter 1 was previously published as "Local Government, Social Programs, and Political Participation: A Test of Policy-Centered Theory," *State and Local Government Review* 41, no. 3 (2009): 182–92; reprinted by permission of Carl Vinson Institute of Government, University of Georgia.

Published by the University of Minnesota Press
111 Third Avenue South, Suite 290
Minneapolis, MN 55401-2520
http://www.upress.umn.edu

Library of Congress Cataloging-in-Publication Data
Sharp, Elaine B.
Does local government matter? : how urban policies shape civic engagement /
Elaine B. Sharp.
(Globalization and community ; v. 19)
Includes bibliographical references and index.
ISBN 978-0-8166-7708-5 (hc : alk. paper)
ISBN 978-0-8166-7718-4 (pb : alk. paper)
1. Local government—United States. 2. Municipal government—United States. 3. Political planning—United States. 4. Urban policy—United States. 5. Political participation—United States—States. I. Title.
JS331.S46 2012
320.8′50973—dc23

2011031778

Printed in the United States of America on acid-free paper

18 17 16 15 14 13 12 10 9 8 7 6 5 4 3 2 1

Contents

Acknowledgments

I thankfully acknowledge Professor Anne Schneider for the invaluable insights and suggestions she provided for this project. I also thank Andrea Vieux; her laborious reading and coding of articles about neighborhood associations in numerous cities was essential for the content analysis in chapter 4. Finally, I thank Susan Clarke for her support and encouragement. She helped me see how the policy feedback applications of interest to me in this volume fit into the larger picture of local adaptations to globalization challenges.

Introduction

Government Programs Matter

Political Learning, Policy Feedback, and the Policy-Centered Approach

Does government matter? To many people, the answer to this question may seem obvious, especially if the focus is on either the federal or the state government. When officials in power take us into war, there are major consequences with respect to national security, the image of the nation in the world, the country's relationships with various foreign powers, spending commitments, and for those who serve in the nation's military and their families, the largest of personal consequences. Efforts to reform health care in America reveal that despite their flaws and problems, Medicare and Medicaid are crucial programmatic anchors for making health care accessible to many Americans. At the state level, the restrictiveness of a state government's policies with respect to abortion has a substantial bearing on the number of abortions performed in the state and on access to reproductive health services. And although no government policy can claim to solve the problem of crime, state governments' policy choices and programs with respect to crime and punishment have enormous consequences on everything from whether individuals are executed for serious crimes, to the size of the prison population, to the recidivism rates for various categories of offenders.

This is not to say that the causal logic linking federal or state government action to specific outcomes that are of consequence to citizens is either simple or undisputed. In the realm of fiscal policy, for example, tremendous battles rage over the impacts of tax cuts for higher-income taxpayers, with proponents of supply-side economics claiming the approach enhances economic growth and critics of that approach arguing tax cuts exacerbate spending deficits rather than stimulating investment or indirectly shrinking the size of total government spending (Jones and Williams 2008). Few would deny government programs can fail to have the desired impacts or sometimes can have quite nasty unintended consequences.

But the policy impacts or consequences that are typically the focus of public debate and scholarly analysis are consequences having to do with the overt function of government programs in enhancing the public's health, safety, and economic well-being. With rare exceptions (e.g., government policies or programs dealing with civil rights, those dealing with voting procedures, or policies specifically intended to enhance citizen participation) neither public debate nor scholarly analysis typically focuses on the consequences of government policies and programs *for the quality of democracy,* that is, the magnitude and effectiveness of ordinary citizens' political engagement. Until fairly recently, policy evaluation has mostly meant assessing whether government programs raise reading levels, decrease teen pregnancy rates, improve air-quality levels, decrease drunk-driving rates, or achieve any of the other things that government programs are ostensibly created to do. Whether such programs also have consequences with respect to future demands for government action on the part of various types of citizens and whether government programs can heighten citizen involvement in civic activities or, contrarily, have a chilling effect on political participation of some types of citizens are questions that typically are not asked.

This book is about just such questions, as applied to local government. It shows the policies and programs of local governments do have consequences with respect to citizens' political participation. For example, though they are not ostensibly designed for the purpose, means-tested programs administered by county governments diminish the civic engagement of those who use them; by contrast, many health and hospital programs of county governments enhance levels of civic engagement among the rest of the population. This book also shows community policing and other, broader neighborhood empowerment efforts explicitly designed to foster citizen involvement in local public affairs actually diminish residents' participation in neighborhood associations and their propensity to work on community projects. Meanwhile, policies designed to make businesses more accountable for the subsidies they receive actually empower enhanced business involvement in economic development policymaking, especially in smaller cities. Evidence of these impacts of local government on political participation, along with information on how and why they occur, is presented in chapters 1–5.

This is by no means the first investigation of the consequences that government programs have for civic or political engagement. Rather, this book was inspired by and builds on the work of a group of scholars who developed a framework for analysis featuring that very topic, albeit with primary emphasis on federal government programs rather than local government. The work of these policy-centered theorists reverses the prevailing view that patterns of political engagement influence what policies and programs government adopts; instead, these scholars take seriously the possibility that the policies and programs that the government adopts influence subsequent patterns of political engagement. Because the policy-centered framework guides the analytical approach used in this book and introduces important concepts applied in each of the chapters, the remainder of this introduction lays out that theoretical framework, highlighting both its potentially powerful application to local government and its limitations.

Emergence of a Policy-Centered or Policy Feedback Approach

Policy-centered theory emerged from important scholarly developments in the 1990s. Ingram and Smith's (1993) edited volume and Schneider and Ingram's *Policy Design for Democracy* (1997) both forced attention to the impacts that public policy can have on citizenship, political empowerment, and democracy. Drawing inspiration from Lowi's (1964, 1972) insight that the character of public policy shapes the nature of politics surrounding it, Ingram and Schneider (1993, 72) developed a thesis that public policies can have varied impacts on political participation and democracy, depending on key elements of policy design. These policy design elements include the definition and prevailing view (or social construction) of target populations, whether the policy distributes benefits or burdens, what kinds of tools the policy relies on to activate target populations (authority, incentives, capacity building, etc.), the rationales used to justify the policy (e.g., merit, need, and efficiency), and the messages implied by the policy. Primary emphasis was given to the social construction of target groups, with four main types differentiated on the basis of the level of political power held by the group and the "cultural valence" of the group, which is to say whether the group is generally viewed by society as being deserving, virtuous, and likable or undeserving, lacking in virtue, and unlikable (73). The four ideal types of target groups yielded by these two dimensions are the advantaged (high power and positive valence), the contenders (high power and negative valence), the dependents (low power and positive valence), and the deviants (low power and negative valence) (73–85).

Ultimately, Schneider and Ingram (1997, 5) argued that government policy is "strongly implicated in the current crisis of democracy," because instead of providing "institutions and symbols to ensure that the self-correcting mechanisms of pluralist democracy will be operative, policies deceive, confuse, and in other ways discourage active citizenship, minimize the possibility of self-corrections, and perpetuate or exacerbate the very tendencies that produced dysfunctional public policies in the first place." Schneider and Ingram's critique of public policy is not based on arguments that public policies often fail to solve public problems. Rather, their critique is focused on the corrosive effect that public policies can have on democracy itself because of the way that type of target population interacts with other design elements.

Essential to this critique is the notion that public policies carry important messages. "Citizen orientations toward government, their participation patterns, and the extent to which they trust and respect fellow citizens are all affected by the messages and experiences with public policy" (Schneider and Ingram 1997, 5–6). And from Schneider and Ingram's perspective, an all-too-common type of policy design is the "degenerative" policy design, with design elements that are biased toward advantaged target populations, and to some extent contenders, and against dependents and deviants. For example, when benefits are being distributed by public policy, universal provision with high funding typifies policies targeted to the advantaged, whereas particularistic (i.e., means-tested) provision with low funding typifies policies targeted to dependents and deviants. Or, when burdens such as regulations or restrictions on behavior are being distributed by public policy, authority and sanctions are the typical tools when dependents and deviants are the targets, whereas positive inducements and self-regulation are more common tools when advantaged groups are the targets (125–34). Schneider and Ingram argued that as a result of these and similar biases in the way that other elements of policy design are directed to different target groups, degenerative policy designs "send messages to people about whether their interests are legitimate and how much (or little) they are valued by the society. These policy designs serve to reinforce the stereotypes of 'deserving' and 'undeserving people' so that policies afford privilege to some and stigmatize and disenfranchise others" (6).

Other scholarly developments quickly amplified the importance of Schneider and Ingram's focus on the impacts of public policy on democracy. Several high-profile studies offered empirical evidence that social policies can either enhance or diminish the political activities of affected citizens, depending on the policy's design elements. For example, Soss (1999) analyzes the unusually low levels of political participation of welfare recipients, whose important stake in public policy might logically have led us to expect heightened political mobilization. Drawing on both arguments about the social control functions of welfare programs and Schneider and Ingram's work on the social construction of target populations, Soss developed a thesis that attributes diminished levels of political participation among welfare recipients to political learning from the experience of the welfare program itself. He argued,

> As clients participate in welfare programs they learn lessons about how citizens and governments relate, and these lessons have political consequences beyond the domain of welfare agencies. Program designs structure clients' experiences in ways that shape their beliefs about the effectiveness of asserting themselves at the welfare agency. Because clients associate the agency with government as a whole, these program-specific beliefs, in turn, become the basis for broader orientations toward government and political action. (364)

Soss (1999) found that even after key factors such as education, age, income, and partisanship are taken into account, recipients of public assistance from the Aid to Families with Dependent Children (AFDC) program, the nation's main "welfare" program until the reform legislation of 1996, were less likely to vote than members of the population as a whole; by contrast, recipients of Social Security Disability Insurance (SSDI) were no less likely to vote than comparable members of the public who were not SSDI recipients. According to Soss, program design elements are responsible for these differences. AFDC involved intensive casework relationships that required recipients to repeatedly show their means-tested eligibility and placed them under the thumb of caseworkers who had substantial discretion over clients and the power to demand private information from them. Drawing on intensive interviews with AFDC clients and some direct observation of welfare recipients in group settings, Soss was able to show that experiencing these program features had a "chilling effect" on demand making by welfare clients. Moreover, welfare clients generalized their experience with the welfare bureaucracy to all of government, and the lesson they generalized is that government does not care about their input and is so unlikely to be responsive to their demands as to make political involvement a pointless and even counterproductive exercise.

By contrast, the design of the SSDI program "does not include mandatory reviews, SSDI clients initiate most of their dealings with the agency instead of responding to directives. . . . [And] because they do not have caseworkers, they typically fend for themselves when they need agency actions" (Soss 1999, 366). As a result, these program recipients learn that they can actively shape their experience with the program. Not surprisingly, they do not learn to expect government to ignore them—and there is no chilling effect on political participation.

In contrast with the AFDC program that is the primary focus of Soss's study, Mettler's (2002, 351) study of the impact of the GI Bill on veterans' civic engagement focused on "one of the most generous and inclusive social entitlements the federal government has ever funded and administered." In addition, GI Bill beneficiaries

> experienced a program administered according to standardized, routinized procedures applied uniformly to all veterans regardless of socioeconomic background. The absence of invasive procedures and the universality of coverage elevated the status of less privileged beneficiaries, rather than stigmatizing them in the manner associated with targeted programs for the poor. (360)

Mettler found a veteran's use of the GI Bill's educational benefits was a significant and positive predictor of both the number of memberships that a veteran had in civic organizations in the 1950–64 period and the veteran's level of participation on a broad index of political participation that included joining political organizations, contacting political officials, working on a campaign, serving on a government board, contributing money to a campaign, and participating in protests. The explanatory power of GI Bill usage held even when factors suggested by other theories of participation were taken into account—factors such as the levels of education and civic activity of the veteran's parents and the family's standard of living before World War II.

Both Mettler's (2002) and Soss's (1999) empirical work and their later work (2004) took up an important distinction about policy feedback suggested by Pierson (1993). Pierson emphasized two major avenues by which public policy can shape political participation: resource effects and interpretive effects. Resource effects have to do with the material stakes created by public policies—material stakes that shape both the incentives for political participation by various groups and the political capabilities of those groups. In Skocpol's (1985, 2007) work, for example, the character of early social policy choices was shown to have important political consequences by virtually creating interest groups that arise to defend the largesse that public policy has bestowed on them. Resource effects can involve other sorts of phenomena, such as countermobilizations by those opposed to policies that have been enacted and creation of political "niches" or opportunities for entrepreneurs to play a role in mobilizing interest groups. In addition, resource effects include a variety of policy-produced resources that enhance certain groups' *capacity* for mobilization. These range from funding to enhanced access to decision makers (Pierson 1993, 601–2).

But resource effects are only one avenue by which public policy can affect political participation and democratic processes. In addition, there is the possibility of interpretive effects—that is, the "impact of policies on the cognitive processes of social actors" (Pierson 1993, 610). Pierson emphasized the possibility that particular features of public policies may shape the reaction of the public to broad public policies but does not elaborate on the interpretive effects of policy on the public. But Soss's (1999) work on welfare recipients and Mettler's (2002) work on users of the GI Bill showed the importance of a specific kind of interpretive effect: the political learning that comes from clients' direct experience with a government program.

Drawing on the work of Schneider and Ingram (1997) and others, along with their own previous studies, Mettler and Soss (2004) developed a theoretical framework that they refer to as a "policy feedback" approach. They and others also refer to this as a "policy-centered" perspective because, in contrast with "society-centered" explanations of political participation, it focuses on the political consequences of public policy (Hacker, Mettler, and Soss 2007). This approach specifies various mechanisms by which public policy can be hypothesized to affect political behavior. Some mechanisms clearly operate through resource effects, some clearly operate through interpretive effects that better fit the notion of "political learning," and some involve both resource and interpretive effects.

One category of mechanisms that primarily involve resource effects focuses on the ways in which public policies build or undermine civic capacity. Specifically, Mettler and Soss (2004, 62) argued six points. Their first three arguments were (1) "Resources extended by policies may create material incentives for mobilization," (2) public policies can build and distribute civic skills ranging from formal education to skills in "how to deal effectively with government," and (3) "policies may supply resources for political mobilization" even beyond the material incentives already noted, such as when policies are specifically devoted to enhancing the political participation of various groups. Two other categories ("forging political community or delineating groups" and "framing policy agendas, problems, and evaluations") primarily highlight interpretive effects. Specifically, (4) public policies frame the meaning and origins of societal problems by identifying target groups for government actions and defining solutions, and in a related vein, (5) policies "influence patterns of group identity" via symbolic content that not only can affect how various groups are viewed in the society but also can shape "how group members perceive and evaluate one another—a feedback effect that has major consequences for the likelihood that group members will want to join together in collective political action" (61). In addition, (6) "because public policies are expressive, they also have the power to shape public evaluations of governments and their actions" (63).

Resource effects and interpretive effects are not divorced from each other. Indeed, the same element of public policy that creates resource effects can create interpretive effects, as shown by Mettler's (2002) work on the GI Bill. The GI Bill's provision of generous benefits for pursuing higher education had resource effects via the higher levels of educational attainment and subsequently enhanced civic capacity that it created; those same benefits also yielded interpretive effects, because the GI Bill's generous benefits signaled appreciation and welcoming inclusiveness to veterans, who in turn developed reciprocal feelings of obligation to society.

However, the distinction between the two kinds of effects is important for several reasons. First, insights derived from the resource effects side of policy feedback theory are more straightforward, less original, and hence less interesting than the insights from the interpretive effects side. Those who have self-consciously pushed for development of policy feedback theory acknowledge well-established insights about how government programs create political activism by creating stakeholders and interest groups centered on the protection of program benefits (Lowi 1972; Wilson 1973; Heclo 1978). The more original and still potentially controversial side of policy-centered theory is on the interpretive effects side, with its inherently interesting and subtler claims about the meanings conveyed to program recipients (and to the broader public) about program recipients' value to and expected role in the polity. This aspect of policy-centered theory provides an important microfoundation for studies of broad, aggregate-level trends in political participation in the United States—trends that policy-centered theorists wish to attribute to changes in the mix of programs comprising U.S. social welfare policy and the messages embodied in those programs (Mettler 2007b).

Interpretive effects are also of special interest because they may have amplifying consequences in what Campbell (2007, 124) described as a "participation–policy" cycle. In such a cycle, a public policy that undermines (or conversely, empowers) the participation of a particular segment of the population leads to subsequent policymaking that further undermines (or conversely, empowers) that segment of the population. As a result, policies "can put programs and their client groups on upward or downward trajectories that change the face of political inequality and policy outcomes in the United States." The fate of government programs is, however, based on the views and political behavior of both the client groups and the broader public (128). Although many kinds of resource effects may be expected to affect program clientele, *interpretive effects have the capacity to influence both client groups and broader public opinion.* In this way, interpretive effects could have more substantial impacts on patterns of civic engagement and on prospects for policy reform than do resource effects. In this vein, recent work by Soss and Schram (2007) on the public's views of welfare and welfare recipients suggested government programs can so powerfully lock in the public's negative view of a client group that even a major overhaul of the program cannot change that view.

Limitations of Policy-Centered Theory

Theory and empirical research in the policy-centered tradition have already made major contributions to the study of American politics and policy. In particular, this tradition is important in the way in which it provides a new kind of link between the study of public policy and the study of political participation—two subareas that have developed apart from each other (Mettler and Soss 2004). This link gives added conceptual breadth to both policy studies and studies of political participation. Nevertheless, there are several important limitations of the policy-centered approach as developed so far.

For one thing, empirical research in this genre has generally been narrower than might be expected from the theoretical framework from which it is derived. It is narrow in the sense that empirical research has tended to focus on the contrast between means-tested and universal programs. Relatively little attention has been given to variation in more nuanced elements of program design and variation in implementation. The original focus on multiple and subtle details of program design—as in Schneider and Ingram's (1997) long list of design elements and in Soss's (1999) detailed listing of how SSDI differed from AFDC—has in subsequent work been largely collapsed into a simpler focus on a key program design distinction between means-tested and universal (or non-means-tested) programs.

In part, this collapsing into a simpler means-tested versus universal distinction may be because many of the other differences in program design elements line up with this more fundamental design difference (Campbell 2007, 121). For example, the various program design elements that Soss (1999) showed as differentiating the SSDI experience from the AFDC experience may all be viewed as a function of AFDC being a means-tested program whereas SSDI is not. In part, it may simply be the means-tested versus universal distinction is more prominent and potent and is of long-standing relevance to scholars. As Mettler and Stonecash (2008, 275) noted,

> Scholars have long surmised that means-tested programs convey very different messages to citizens than non-means tested programs. Universal eligibility criteria may help incorporate beneficiaries as full members of society, bestowing dignity and respect on them. Conversely means-tested programs may convey stigma and thus reinforce and expand beneficiaries' isolation.

However, it is possible that other program design features can trump the significance of the distinction between means-tested and universal programs. This is evident from the results of Soss's (1999) investigation of the Head Start program, a means-tested program that also has strong client participation elements, resulting in higher levels of external political efficacy (and hence participation) among poor Head Start parents than among equally poor welfare clients. Campbell (2007, 127) highlighted this result to argue that "means-tested programs do not necessarily undermine client participation" and that the addition of participation design elements to a means-tested program "engenders positive citizenship learning and empowerment."

Despite this possibility, work in the policy-centered mode has been dominated by research that is less attuned to policy design elements, such as client participation requirements. Instead, policy-centered theory has yielded its strongest and most prominent findings in its showing of highly contrasting impacts on participation depending on whether a policy is means tested or universal, with means-tested programs consistently having a demobilizing effect on clients and universal programs having mobilizing effects.

In addition to the relative neglect of other program design features, the heavy emphasis on the means-tested versus universal program distinction overlooks the target population types that are so important in Schneider and Ingram's (1997) work. Schneider and Ingram (1997) argued that the impact of design features like means testing versus universal programming depends on the target population at issue. For example, they argued that universal and generous programs directed at dependent populations will over time increase the political participation of dependent populations by assuring them of their own worthiness and helping them understand their interests are important to the broader public. By contrast, universal programs directed at advantaged populations are not expected to have participation-enhancing effects. Part of the reason is that participation levels of advantaged groups are already by definition high. In addition, the receipt of government largesse sends no transformative message that binds such individuals to the state; instead, the advantaged already believe they deserve at least as much as they are getting, if not more. But the advantaged *can* be mobilized to even higher levels of political participation by public policies that impose burdens on them (e.g., regulations) or are threatening in other ways (e.g., reduction of benefits).

A second limitation of the policy-centered approach to date is its dominant focus on the impact of individual policies and programs on recipients. But if, as policy-centered theory suggests, government policies and programs shape citizens' attitudes and political involvements, then citizens who are touched by more than one government program are presumably influenced by all of them. That influence could be *reinforcing* if the programs have similar design elements that send similar messages to similar target groups. Alternatively, there could be contrasting design elements and conflicting messages, yielding *contradictory* influences that either cancel one another out or at least dilute the impact of any particular programmatic impact.

Recently, policy-centered theorists have begun to attend to this limitation by exploring the scope of citizen experiences with government programs overall. Mettler and Milstein (2007) produced an ambitious chronology of the development of major federal programs and policies influencing citizens' economic security and well-being in the United States from 1860 to 2000. By tracking the development and expansion or contraction of programs ranging from veterans' pensions to Social Security and from the Fair Labor Standards Act to food stamps and various forms of welfare, Mettler and Milstein (2007, 129–30) provided a detailed depiction of the "waxing and waning of government's influence in citizens' lives" over a long period. This policy history thus provides the basis for future longitudinal studies that would explore the political participation effects of the waxing and waning of the federal governments' influence in the lives of various categories of citizens. Some initial elements of this enterprise are already evident (Pierson and Skocpol 2007).

Although studies linking aggregate trends in political participation with patterns of change in aggregate federal social policy over time are beginning to emerge, Mettler and Stonecash (2008) have taken another step to overcome the one-at-a-time program focus that limits most policy-centered work. Using a 2005 poll asking respondents whether they had ever received benefits from any of 18 federal social programs—some means tested and some not—Mettler and Stonecash were able to show that political participation in the form of voting is enhanced by the number of non-means-tested programs utilized but diminished by the number of means-tested programs used by the individual, even once the effects of education, age, income, and a variety of other traditionally used explanatory factors are taken into account (287).

Promising as these developments are for overcoming the single program limitation of policy-centered studies, they underscore yet another limitation of the approach—the dominant focus on large identity-making federal social programs in which the individual is a client. Thus, the initial development of the policy-centered tradition is narrowly based because it is built not only largely on studies of single programs or pairs of programs but also on studies of special kinds of programs having the following features: (1) *cash benefits* or their near equivalent (e.g., in the case of the GI Bill, payment of education costs) are provided *to individuals,* (2) the *value of the program benefit is large* enough to be of life-altering significance to the beneficiary, and (3) there are relatively *high levels of program visibility* nationally (i.e., most citizens have some awareness of Social Security and "welfare"; in their heyday, the same could be said of the GI Bill, and Head Start).

These program characteristics mean that policy-centered studies have largely been focusing on programs that are so important to recipients as to become a part of their identity. Individuals can be expected to define themselves as Social Security recipients once they go through the formal process of signing up for retirement benefits, and being "on welfare" is clearly an identity status, albeit one with a different valence. Research on Head Start suggested that having been a Head Start student or parent is also something with which one personally identifies (Ames 1997), and being a GI Bill recipient is an important part of many vets' identities. Research showing that such identities subsequently shape individuals' levels of political engagement is undeniably of breakthrough importance. But could the same be said of other kinds of government programs that do not have identity-defining characteristics? Mettler and Stonecash's (2008) study of citizens' aggregate experience with federal programs included not only programs such as Social Security, the GI Bill, and welfare but also programs such as federal mortgage deduction, unemployment compensation, and workers' comp—programs less likely to have the power to define a recipient's identity. But it is unclear from their study whether citizens' experience with the latter type of program is patterned in the same way as citizens' experience with major, identity-defining programs or whether the aggregate patterns observed are largely driven by identity-defining programs.

The third limitation of the policy-centered approach is that, with few exceptions, empirical work in the genre has tested the impact of government programs on a narrow range of forms of political participation. Most commonly, voting in national elections is the focus, as in research on citizens' aggregate experience with federal programs (Mettler 2007b; Mettler and Stonecash 2008) and Soss's (1999) work on the impact of the AFDC and disability insurance (SSDI) programs. There is also some policy-centered work that looks at political participation as claim making, either in the form of applying for welfare (Soss 2000) or in the form of applications and appeals with respect to disability insurance and supplemental security income program eligibility (Soss and Keiser 2006). Finally, Skocpol's (1985, 2007) work introduced a focus on organized interest groups, examining how changes in the character of federal social policy over time are linked with "the reorganization of American civic democracy" (2007, 39) in the form of change in the number of organized interest groups of various types.

Voting in national elections, claims on federal programs, and the activities of organized interests in the national arena are all important forms of participation. However, other forms of political participation may be even more relevant than voting, especially if interpretive rather than resource effects are of interest. Voting on the basis of stakeholder interests in a program is a matter that has long been studied and is a phenomenon that would be pointed to by rational choice theory as well as policy-centered theory. But interpretive effects, which are theorized to send messages about an individual's worth, would presumably be especially relevant when considering various forms of local and face-to-face political participation, such as involvement in community organizations, participation in community projects, or the kinds of cooperative work with government agencies that are entailed by coproduction of government services (Marschall 2004). However, only two foundational studies in the policy-centered tradition have focused on a broader range of forms of participation—Campbell's (2003) work on the Social Security retirement program's empowerment of the elderly and Mettler's (2002) study of the GI Bill. Only one of these (Mettler 2002) included locally oriented and face-to-face forms of civic engagement, such as joining neighborhood associations and school support groups and serving on a local government board or council. These forms of civic engagement may be especially relevant for understanding interpretive effects.

A fourth limitation of the policy-centered approach to date is its emphasis on political participation impacts of experience with government programs that are ostensibly unrelated to political empowerment or demobilization. It might be argued that what gives policy-centered theory its "pop" as a breakthrough line of work is this notion of unintended (or perhaps we should say subtly disguised) consequences. However, this leaves unaddressed the tantalizing question of how policy-centered theory applies when the policy in question is one with the ostensible purpose of enhancing citizen participation in general or enhancing political involvement of otherwise disempowered groups in particular. In their review of the policy feedback approach, Mettler and Soss (2004, 62) explicitly acknowledged that among the resource effects policies can have are the direct mobilizing effects that accrue from programs such as the federal Community Action Program of the 1960s that provided resources for neighborhood-based participation in local governance. However, the line of more contemporary work under the policy-centered theory banner has largely ignored policies with the overt purpose of political mobilization.

In some programs, the two kinds of purposes (empowerment and either social welfare or other nonempowerment purposes) are intermingled. Head Start, for example, was built on the twin premises that (1) early childhood programs involving a mix of nutrition, health care, socialization, and educational experiences could take impoverished children off the path of lagging educational attainment and (2) empowerment of the parents of these impoverished children in defining the proper mix of program elements and helping run the Head Start centers was as important as the resources being provided for health services and nutrition. Similarly, the Community Development Block Grant program, at least in some phases of its existence, required citizen involvement in implementation based on the premise that redevelopment of impoverished areas will be most effective if the ideas and priorities of the residents in affected areas are incorporated into decision making about the uses of the funds.

Beyond these are policies and programs whose ostensible purpose *only* involves political engagement. These include motor voter registration, for example, as well as civil rights legislation. The impacts of some of these programs have been investigated without an explicit policy-centered theoretical perspective. Using programs of this type to test the range of policy-centered theory may demand a rethinking of the kinds of program design elements that are important, the array of messages that may be sent to citizens by such programs, and the meaning of both resource and interpretive effects.

Finally, while the target populations of the programs featured in the foundational studies of the policy-centered approach include the important contrast between the advantaged (e.g., Social Security retirees) and those in Schneider and Ingram's (1997) dependent category (e.g., welfare recipients), work in this tradition has tended to overlook programs aimed at the other two categories in their typology of negative versus positive social construction and high versus low power. In particular, the crucial category of contenders, featuring high-power groups that are nonetheless negatively socially constructed, has been largely overlooked in policy-focused, empirical studies.

In some sense then, the policy-centered approach developed on the basis of empirical study of a unique sample of programs. The characteristics of those programs are such that the likelihood of observing resource effects and interpretive effects is maximized. But this leaves us without information about the scope and limitations of policy-centered theory. Does it apply to programs that do not provide life-defining benefits to individuals? Does it apply to programs for which the target is not a category of individuals with program-defined characteristics but collectivities, such as neighborhoods? Apart from means testing, what program design elements affect the participation levels of recipients? And are various forms of participation at the community level shaped by government program experience in the same ways as voting and other forms of national-level political involvement? These and other issues loom large when we consider the prospect of applying policy-centered theory to local government policies and programs.

Policy-Centered Theory and Urban Politics

There are two important reasons for applying policy-centered theory to the policies and programs of local governments. One has to do with the need to test the range of the theory to get beyond the limitations outlined previously. The second points to the potential for the policy-centered approach to enrich our understanding of urban politics.

Testing the Range of Policy-Centered Theory

The reach or range of applicability of policy-centered theory can only be assessed by applying it in diverse policy contexts. That could mean other periods, a possibility that is already being explored in the development of long-term, longitudinal studies of federal social policy by key contributors in the policy-centered tradition (Mettler 2007b; Mettler and Milstein

2007). Application to subnational governments would also be a useful test of the range of the theory. So far, however, policy-centered theory has had limited application even to state governments, and the work done in that area focuses only on state implementation of the sorts of federal social programs that have been heavily studied in this genre (Soss and Keiser 2006).

Local government provides a promising venue for testing the limits of policy-centered theory because urban policies and programs have features that differentiate them in important ways from the identity-forming social programs featured in policy-centered empirical studies so far. A substantial portion of what local governments do involves allocational policy (Peterson 1981)—that is, the provision of city services such as policing, fire protection, and street repair. These programmatic activities do not involve providing cash benefits, and the "target populations" are neighborhoods (police beats, fire substation zones, etc.) rather than individuals. A substantial part of the ordinary citizen's experience with urban government therefore comes not as an individual client of a government program for which that person must distinctly qualify but as one of many recipients of benefits, services, or attention provided to everyone. Issues and controversies over allocational policy have to do with real or perceived differences in the quality or quantity of services provided to different neighborhoods. This provides the potential to explore whether the subtle dynamics of the interpretive side of policy-centered theory apply when we are dealing with how governments handle neighborhoods rather than individual clients.

A second major category of local government activity is developmental policy (Peterson 1981)—the enactment and implementation of programs designed to sustain private sector investments in the local economy by keeping the community attractive to businesses and higher-than-average taxpayers. Programmatic activities in this category include investments in facilities such as airports, major highways, research, or industrial parks, as well as tax and land-use decisions. As with allocational policy, these programs have collective targets (some spectrum of businesses), rather than individual clients. Yet another set of policies in the developmental category involves subsidies (e.g., loans, loan guarantees, tax abatements, and tax increment financing project status) being given to specific businesses that might then be considered clients. Because of the controversy surrounding such subsidies, the relevant target group for local governments' economic development policies would, in a number of cities, fall into Schneider and Ingram's (1997) contender category—that is, businesses have high power, but controversies over "corporate welfare" mean that the broader community may view them negatively in terms of deservingness. Hence, in contrast with the advantaged, deviant, and dependent target groups featured in the touchstone empirical studies of policy-centered theory, applying policy-centered theory to city governments' economic development policy provides the opportunity to expand the theory to the understudied contender group.

Local governments, especially county governments, provide redistributive social services as well. However, their activities in this sphere are primarily those of implementing agents for federal programs, such as public housing; federal–state programs, such as Medicaid—the joint federal–state program for medical care for low-income individuals—or the nation's welfare program (AFDC, and later Temporary Assistance to Needy Families); or the various federal and state programs in the health category that county governments administer, such as state child health insurance programs, hospital construction, STD testing and family planning services, and the special supplemental nutrition program for low income women, infants, and children.

These social service programs bring us back to the terrain most central to development of policy-centered theory. However, with the partial exception of Soss's (1999) work, studies in the policy-centered tradition have not attended to the significance for political mobilization of how *local* agents "deliver" federal- and state-funded programs to clients. Even in Soss's work, the focus is on the clients' perceptions rather than the potential significance of variation in what local governments and their personnel do. Hence, as Sidney (2003, 13) argued, "The policy design framework can be fruitfully extended to incorporate intergovernmental relationships." Policy-centered study of local governments' redistributional policy activity provides that opportunity. In addition, like recent policy-centered studies of the impact of aggregate social policy on political participation in national elections (Mettler 2007b; Mettler and Stonecash 2008), local governments can be compared to one another with respect to their overall means-tested and universal program activity in the redistributive policy realm, and the impacts of variation in aggregate program activity on the participation levels of both the target populations and the overall public can be assessed. More importantly, impacts can be assessed on a broader array of forms of political participation than on just voting in national elections.

In sum, the very challenges of applying policy-centered theory to urban programs are, in another sense, opportunities to test the range of that theory. Empirically assessing the applicability of policy-centered theory to urban government means assessment of programs with collective, as well as individual, clients; programs involving local involvement in federal and state policies; programs involving important design elements, in addition to the distinction between means tested and universal; programs involving a target group in the understudied category of contender; and multiple social programs whose aggregate impact on citizens should be assessed. Empirically assessing the applicability of policy-centered theory also means assessing the impact of government programs on a range of locally oriented forms of political participation. In these ways, the urban venue provides a ready opportunity to overcome the existing limitations of policy-centered theory.

Enriched Understanding of Urban Politics via a Policy-Centered Approach?

There is a second reason for testing policy-centered theory on the policies and programs of local governments. Such an application has the potential to provide many of the same kinds of breakthrough insights for urban politics that policy-centered theory has provided for studies of federal policy and national-level political participation.

In some ways, testing policy-centered theory in the context of city government would not be entirely new to the scholarship of urban politics. As the dominant writers in the policy-centered tradition readily acknowledge (Mettler and Soss 2004, 60), their approach grows in part out of work by Lowi (1964, 1972), showing how different types of policies engender different types of politics. That breakthrough insight about policy shaping politics turned conventional thinking about politics shaping policy on its head, inviting an emphasis on policy-centered explanations of political participation rather than society-centered explanations of policy.

In much the same way, Lowi's work helped inspire Peterson's (1981) classic study of urban politics. Taking up the notion that the character of public policy shapes the character of politics, rather than the other way around, Peterson argued that business elites would be dominant, participation by ordinary citizens would be limited, and politics would be consensual when economic development matters were at issue in cities;

by contrast, in the realm of allocational policy, his thesis depicted the hurly-burly of heightened participation by a variety of nonbusiness groups, along with the numerous conflicts that are a part of pluralism. Redistributional policy is depicted as a nonparticipatory sphere for local governments because the imperatives of remaining economically competitive create agenda-setting barriers to consideration of much in the way of welfare programming.

However, neither in Peterson's work nor in subsequent research in the urban field did this "policy shapes politics" theme develop into a full-blown policy-centered tradition, complete with specifications of policy design elements that could empower or disempower citizens via resource and interpretive effects.[1] Instead, with a couple of important exceptions that are acknowledged in due course, urban research in all three arenas (developmental, allocational, and redistributive) has been so dominated by *society-centered* theory and empirical research that a policy-centered approach has yet to take strong root.

Understanding the Economic Development Politics and Policy

With respect to the politics and policies of economic development, for example, urban research has been dominated by regime theory. Pioneering work on regime theory (Stone 1987b, 1989) resisted Peterson's claims about economic development policy influencing the character of politics in that realm. Instead, regime theory takes a society-centered viewpoint, stressing that "regime character shapes policy" (Stone 1987a, 271). Regime theory ultimately features depictions of how informal but stable governing coalitions, or regimes, determine what developmental policies cities will pursue (Stone 1989).

Though it has been subjected to occasional critiques (Imbroscio 1998; Dowding et al. 1999; Mossberger and Stoker 2001), regime theory has been a focal point for the study of urban politics, sparking an explosion of regime theory–based case studies of cities' development policymaking (see DeLeon 1992 and Kantor, Savitch, and Haddock 1997, among many others). However, neither the various critiques of the theory nor the applications that have stretched its conceptualization have challenged the essentially society-centered character of regime theory.[2] Research in the policy-centered tradition could take the predominantly society-centered work in this area to the next level by showing how the interaction of particular design features of development policy and changing social constructions of business and development interests influence the political mobilization of those interests.

Understanding Redistributional Policy and Politics

Existing research on redistributional activity by cities and counties is fairly limited and takes an almost exclusively society-centered approach, focused on explaining the reasons for variation in local governments' redistributive spending (Peterson 1981; Schneider 1987; Sharp and Maynard-Moody 1991; Craw 2006, 2010). The consequences of redistributional spending are rarely considered apart from some attention to the welfare-magnet thesis (Craw 2006). The possible impact of local governments' redistributional policy on the level and distribution of political activity in the community is completed neglected.

Apart from research on redistributional spending, urban scholars have generated research on particular programs in the urban social welfare category. For example, there is an avalanche of work on the nation's public housing program, largely outlining various problems with that program. To the extent that program impacts are considered, they largely focus on the ways in which public housing either assists individuals toward economic self-sufficiency or segregates them in concentrated poverty locations that interfere with long-term economic success (Newman and Harkness 2002; Goering and Feins 2003). However, it is in this area of research on specific urban programs involving the poor that a policy-centered approach has begun to establish a toehold, thereby revealing some of the kinds of insights that could be gained from broader use of this framework. For example, Sidney (2003) examined local implementation of the Fair Housing Act of 1968 and the Community Reinvestment Act of 1977 with explicit attention to the ways in which policy design elements of these two programs have shaped the strategies and the political strength of local fair housing activists. She suggested that the "resources within community reinvestment policy have a demobilizing effect on local movements over time" (127). By contrast, "fair housing policy design offers advocacy groups a wider range of resources than the community reinvestment design offers" (129) and provides them with a legitimate position in bringing discrimination claims to court. Although the focus is on nonprofit activist groups rather than on the ultimate clients of these programs, Sidney's book nevertheless is able to make sense of differing patterns of local political activism on housing based on the specifics of these two contrasting policy designs.

Yet another example is provided by Lawless and Fox (2001), who used Soss's (1999) work as a springboard for examining whether poor urban residents' experiences with welfare workers and the police shape their levels of political participation, without the effects of the political attitudes and demographic factors that are staples of society-centered explanations of participation. They found that the better the quality of experiences that individuals had with welfare case workers, the higher their levels of political participation; by contrast, the more negative their experience with police officers, the higher their levels of political participation. Again we see the intriguing findings that can emerge when the policy-centered approach is applied to distinctly urban phenomena.

Understanding Allocational Policy and Citizen Participation

Like the work on development and redistributional policy, urban research on matters in the allocational policy realm is largely society centered. Research on the determinants of cities' decisions to contract out for service delivery or to engage in interlocal collaboration for service delivery treats government policies and programmatic decisions as *outcomes* of sociopolitical pressures and institutional arrangements (Hefetz and Warner 2004; Feiock 2007); the consequences of these decisions for citizens' political activity are largely ignored. Studies with a focus on forms of citizen participation, such as direct contacting of city officials, that are distinctive to routine urban service delivery programs are also dominated by society-centered explanations (Hirlinger 1992; Thomas and Melkers 1999), though a surge in attention to the impact that e-government has on citizen contacting (Thomas and Streib 2003) introduced at least one policy-centered element.

By contrast, a substantial body of empirical work assesses the impact of urban policies and programs that are *overtly designed to try to empower otherwise underinvolved citizens* in local governance processes involving routine city services. Although these works are not explicitly framed by policy-centered theory, they nonetheless provide some important evidence about the impacts of local government efforts to empower citizens and the program design elements that yield those effects. In *The Rebirth of Urban Democracy* for example, Berry, Portney, and Thomson (1993) investigate programs in five cities that enacted elaborate programs for enhancing citizen involvement in urban governance at the neighborhood level. Their study showed the importance to successful citizen participation programs of several key design elements, such as the provision of city staffing resources and establishing opportunities to affect citywide budget priorities. Similarly, Fung (2004) described a pair of participatory governance experiments in Chicago, using them to argue that successful neighborhood democracy initiatives require neighborhood groups to have external support from city government (in the form of financing, expertise, etc.), coupled with accountability to central authority.

In some ways, then, there is already a nascent policy-centered focus in urban scholarship. But it primarily involves programs with the overt and exclusive purpose of empowering participation, along with limited treatment of the empowering or disempowering effects of a few other programs. Exploring the extent to which participation is shaped by the messages that programs send—that is, interpretive effects—rather than the more obvious matter of resource effects is also an underdeveloped area. Therefore, although testing policy-centered theory on urban programs allows us to extend, refine, and establish the range of that theory, it also provides a potentially important framework for better understanding political participation in all realms of local governance.

Overview of the Book

Chapter Overview

Chapter 1 begins the application of policy-centered theory to urban phenomenon on the programmatic terrain that is closest to the foundational work in the policy-centered tradition: social welfare policy. Because county governments are more important in this regard than city governments, they are the local governments at issue in this chapter. The links between individual residents' political participation and counties' spending on means-tested and universal, or non-means-tested, social welfare programs are assessed. The chapter features several forms of local political participation and a look at how the meaning of social welfare programs' target population needs to be expanded.

Chapter 2 assesses the political participation impact of city governments' actions with respect to urban neighborhoods. The chapter examines both cities that have formal systems for involving neighborhood residents in governance activities and cities that do not. It also provides a broad basis for gauging city governments' responsiveness to neighborhood concerns and the potential empowerment impacts of such responsiveness, even in places without formal programs for neighborhood-based participation. The chapter yields a surprising and counterintuitive finding about the link between city government responsiveness to neighborhoods and levels of neighborhood activism—a finding that showcases the need to modify policy-centered theory when neighborhood groups rather than individuals are the program "clients."

Chapter 3 follows the neighborhood participation chapter with another urban program that is ostensibly focused on neighborhood-based, *collective* empowerment: community policing. Community policing is a multifaceted innovation adopted by numerous police departments in the 1990s and still prevalent at the end of the 2000s. It involves enhanced emphasis on police officers' role in crime prevention relative to their traditionally dominant law enforcement role, enhanced collaboration between neighborhood-based police officers and neighborhood residents, and acknowledgment that problems of social order (e.g., graffiti, vandalism, and public drunkenness) can make neighborhoods vulnerable to criminal elements and thus should be a priority for problem-solving collaborations involving police, neighborhood residents, and other city agencies. Like neighborhood empowerment more generally, community policing provides an excellent opportunity to explore the applicability of policy-centered theory when the policy at issue involves collective rather than individual clients. In addition, this policy provides an opportunity to consider (1) the consequences of specific program design elements, apart from the means-tested versus universal distinction that has dominated policy-centered research to date; (2) the theoretical implications of program design elements that send *conflicting* rather than consistent messages to citizens; and (3) the possibility that even the same design element can send different messages to different kinds of individuals living in urban neighborhoods.

Chapter 4 turns to the realm of urban developmental policy, focusing on the possible link between city governments' development subsidy policies and political activation of businesses in the community. In particular, the chapter examines whether city policies designed to make business subsidy programs more accountable affect business involvement in community politics. The chapter's quantitative analysis of survey data from a nationwide sample of cities reveals a complex relationship between cities' development subsidies and empowerment of the business community, but one consistent with policy-centered theory.

Chapter 5 extends the investigation of the impact of cities' development policies via a case study of a particular city's adoption of first one and then several other accountability controls on tax abatements for businesses. The case study's historical detail and firsthand narrative from businesses affected by the city's changing tax abatement policy allow for stronger inferences about the interpretive effects that such policy changes have on businesses and on the complexity of business reaction to these program design elements.

Chapter 6 concludes with an overview of the ways in which the book's results both reinforce and call for modifications to policy-centered theory as it has been developed to date and a discussion of the global–local implications of the findings. The chapter introduces contingent views of policy-centered theory that have recently been suggested (Soss and Schram 2007; Patashnik and Zelizer 2009) and shows the pattern of local government's policy feedback effects is largely in accord with these contingent views. At the same time, the evidence from this study of local government's policy feedback on democracy yields additional considerations that should be pondered by policy-centered scholars.

Research Methods and Evidence

Strong tests of policy-centered theory with respect to local government programs require (1) pooled time series designs, with detailed data across both places and times on variation in program characteristics for a representative sample of local governments, as well as corresponding aggregate data for each jurisdiction on a variety of political participation measures, from voting to neighborhood organization involvement, or (2) cross-sectional designs, with data on both individuals' experience with or exposure to various government programs of theoretical interest and their level of political participation at a time no earlier than their exposure to those programs. Ideally, these forms of evidence would be supplemented by qualitative data, such as evidence from in-depth interviews with recipients of various government programs about their experiences with the program, their reactions to those experiences, and the ways in which those experiences send messages that the recipients use as reasons for either civic engagement or withdrawal from civic affairs.

However, as forerunner scholars in the policy-centered tradition have noted, such data is typically not available, even for federal government programs. Instead, surveys including questions on political participation typically do not include questions about usage of government programs, and surveys of the recipients of particular government programs typically do not ask about political participation (Mettler 2002).

The premier empirical studies of policy-centered theory at the national level have gotten around these problems in several ways. They have used the two exceptional surveys that *do* ask about federal program usage and political participation, at least in the form of voting behavior (Soss 1999; Mettler and Stonecash 2008). For studies of the GI Bill, the AFDC program, and SSDI, original surveys and in-person interviews of members of relevant target populations were done (Soss 1999; Mettler 2002). Still others used aggregate trend data on political participation vis-à-vis the timing of policy adoption to make inferences about the impact of the Social Security retirement program on the political empowerment of the elderly (Campbell 2003). Original, long-term trend data on the changing character of American social policy as a whole has also been developed toward the ultimate goal of matching it with evidence on long-term trends in participation (Mettler 2007b; Mettler and Milstein 2007). And data on the prevalence of voluntary associations by type has been compiled and linked with information about federal policy changes to draw inferences about how changing patterns of federal policy have influenced the face of civic democracy in the form of organized interest group activity (Skocpol 2007).

In short, policy-centered work on federal programs has advanced through use of a multimethod, opportunistic approach. This means (1) using existing data where relevant, even when it means using a research design that is less than the ideal for drawing inferences; (2) collecting original data where possible, especially on the microfoundations of the theory (i.e., individual experiences with and reactions to government programs); and (3) amassing a diverse set of studies, focusing on theoretically important types of policies and programs and using different data sources and research methods. Scholars can then judge the merit of the policy-centered approach based on the weight of the evidence.

For empirical testing that would extend the policy-centered theory to local government programs, data availability problems are even greater. Survey data on participation at the local level is even rarer, especially for samples of respondents in numerous cities that differ from one another with respect to a government program of theoretical interest. Aggregate data on *either* political participation levels or program characteristics across cities and over time (let alone on both) is extremely limited, and systematic data on which citizens are exposed to which programs is virtually nonexistent.

These difficulties make it even more important to use a multimethod, opportunistic approach. Hence, the chapters that follow use a variety of sources of evidence. One key source is data from the Social Capital Benchmark Community (SCBC) survey—a set of surveys of individuals in 40 communities conducted by Putnam (2000) and focused on an array of forms of civic engagement. The survey also provides information on a variety of individual characteristics (e.g., demographic attributes and attitudes) that are needed to control for rival explanations of what influences political participation.

To match these respondents' political behavior with local government policies or programs of theoretical importance, the SCBC data set was supplemented with information about the characteristics of programs at issue for this study. Survey respondents were given scorings on these characteristics based on the scoring of the community in which they live. Data on county governments' spending on social service programs in both the means-tested and the universal categories is drawn from the Census Bureau's Census of Governments (1997). Data on city governments' responses to neighborhoods is based on original content analysis of newspaper articles about neighborhoods in each of the SCBC cities. Data on the existence and character of each city's community policing program is drawn from the annual survey of local police departments conducted by the U.S. Department of Justice (1999). Quantitative analysis of the impact of city governments' economic development program characteristics on the local political involvement of businesses is drawn from the International City Management Association's national surveys (1999, 2004) of economic development practices by cities, which also provide data on business activities in the community.

The follow-up case study of the history of business development subsidies in Lawrence, Kansas, is based on documentary sources and in depth interviews with businesses conducted by the author in 2008.

All of these data sources have their limitations, and none allow for a perfect research design. Taken together, however, the results from multiple analyses using different data sources and research methods allow us to get a sense of whether the weight of the evidence is supportive of the core elements of the policy-centered framework.

1

The Participatory Impacts of County Governments' Means-Tested and Universal Social Programs

As noted in the introduction, policy-centered theory with its emphasis on the ways in which public programs shape subsequent political participation developed primarily in studies of major, national-level social welfare programs. The most dramatic empirical support for policy-centered theory involves the finding that experience with means-tested programs has a chilling effect on political participation whereas experience with universal social welfare programs encourages political involvement. This chapter begins the task of applying policy-centered theory to *local* government with a test of whether local government involvement in social welfare programs of the two types (means tested and universal) has the same pattern of contrasting effects on local political participation.

City governments have been depicted as functioning in a realm apart from social welfare programs—especially as relates to the redistributive programs that are the essence of what most Americans mean by "welfare." Peterson's (1981) classic treatment highlighted that local governments must compete with one another for private economic investment. Such competition constrains them so that they cannot undertake redistributive social programs that would adversely affect their tax rate without providing distinct benefits for higher-than-average taxpaying residents and businesses, whose presence is presumed to be essential for economic development.

Local governments spend a much smaller percentage of their revenue on social programs than does the federal government. But there are important reasons for bringing local government back into the picture when considering the impact of such programs on citizens' involvement in the local polity, especially if the focus is on counties. Although they are still largely the forgotten governments of urban scholarship, county governments have expanded their roles in large metropolitan areas (Schneider and Park 1989) while sustaining their traditional roles, which include the provision of welfare, health, and hospital services. Their increasing role in economic development presumably makes them subject to some of the competitive pressures that cities face, but they remain heavily involved in the implementation of both federal welfare programs and federal and state programs for providing health and hospital services.

As a result, county governments spend nontrivial sums of money on redistributive programs (Craw 2006). In 1996–97, counties spent $60.7 billion (or about 30 percent of all their expenditures) in the U.S. Census Bureau categories of welfare, hospitals, and public health programs (U.S. Bureau of the Census 1997). Although these categories still accounted for roughly 30 percent of their spending, by 2001–2 counties were spending more than $78 billion, including $33.5 billion for welfare, $23.1 billion for hospitals, and $21.4 billion for public health programs (U.S. Bureau of the Census 2002).[1]

Scholarship on local government involvement in such social programs largely focuses on accounting for variation in such spending (Sharp and Maynard-Moody 1991; Craw 2006; Minkoff 2008), rather than investigating the impact of that spending. Furthermore, that literature conceptually treats local government involvement in welfare, hospitals, and public health (and sometimes other categories) as an undifferentiated "redistribution" category—a category made theoretically relevant for scholars of local government by Peterson's (1981) thesis. Whether variation in local government involvement in means-tested social program spending and in universal social program spending influence civic engagement, but in different directions, is an issue that has not been addressed in a literature that lumps both forms of social program spending into a redistribution category and that looks to causes rather than consequences of that spending. Applying policy-centered theory to local government means focusing on county government, but it also requires a disaggregation of redistributive social program spending into the means-tested and universal categories that are relevant and requires a reorientation of the analysis toward the outcomes of that spending.

Application of policy-centered theory to county government involvement in social programs also requires an additional consideration, one that stems from the intergovernmental character of county government involvement in those programs. As the following sections make clear, county governments are enmeshed in complex partnerships with state governments and the federal government as they engage in spending and administration for both means-tested and universal social programs. This does not necessarily mean that county governments are neutral administrators of programs formulated elsewhere. Partly because of the choices that state governments make about centralized versus localized administration of major federal social programs, there is considerable variation in the extent to which the federal government's devolution of policy authority has been extended to provide counties with the capacity to make policy choices about the social programs that they administer. Furthermore, even in states that have opted to minimize counties' power to make policy choices about these programs, the inevitable discretion that local caseworkers wield in handling program applicants means that counties may have a meaningful role in shaping citizens' welfare experience.

But does this mean that counties that choose to play such a role can transform the essential character of these programs, perhaps such that the stigmatizing and demeaning aspects of programs such as welfare are no longer present? If so, the distinction between means-tested and universal programs would blur, and policy-centered theory's core thesis of contrasting participatory effects of involvement in welfare versus universal social programs would be undercut. The central hypothesis of this chapter, however, is based on the assumption that despite the potential for discretion, county government involvement in administering intergovernmental social programs makes such governments participants in providing the key message that is entailed in those programs' core design element. That element is means-testing rather than universal provision—a design element distinction that is not open to local override.

Therefore, variation in counties' involvement in administering *means-tested* programs should, à la policy-centered theory, be *inversely* related to political participation, at least for those individuals who are in the target groups for such programs. This is because counties that are more enmeshed in such means-tested programs are presumably the agents for sending demeaning messages to recipients—messages that policy-centered theory posits will discourage recipients' political engagement. By contrast, variation in counties' involvement in *universal* social programs should be *positively* related to political participation if the lessons from Mettler's (2002) study of the GI Bill are generalizable to this form of universal program. Counties that are more involved in universal social programs are presumably the agents for sending messages about the worthiness and importance of recipients to the community. The result should be encouragement of political engagement. Schneider and Ingram's (1997) theorizing, however, would suggest that the universal social program spending of county governments will only have such participation-enhancing effects for individuals with low levels of political power, whereas more powerful target populations (the advantaged and contenders) will largely take such programs for granted.

This chapter focuses exclusively on county governments and tests these hypotheses about the impact of county involvement in the two kinds of social programs on the political participation of individual citizens. An ideal test of the hypotheses would require (1) large samples of individuals drawn from counties that vary greatly with respect to means-tested and universal social program activity, (2) survey data to determine which individuals have been recipients of benefits from the two kinds of social programs in their county of current residence, and (3) survey data on those same individuals' political participation, not only in voting at the national level but also in a variety of local forms of political participation.

Scholarship in the policy-centered tradition has had to confront the problem that even the second and third of these requirements are rarely available. Standard surveys for the study of mass-based political participation usually do not have information about individuals' involvement in government programs (Mettler 2002, 354), so empirical research in the policy-centered tradition has either relied on original surveys of special populations (Mettler 2002) or used those few national sample surveys that have variables that tap respondents' reported usage of certain major social programs and political participation data, typically about voting in national elections (Soss 1999; Mettler and Stonecash 2008). The challenge becomes even greater in attempting to apply policy-centered theory at the local level. No available surveys provide both data on political participation at the local level and data on individual usage of various social programs administered by county government. Even comparable data on local political participation for a substantial number of different communities is extraordinarily rare.

Fortunately, Putnam's Social Capital Benchmark Community (SCBC) survey, administered in 2000, at least provides the necessary political participation variables for substantial samples of citizens from different communities. Political participation questions were asked not only about voting in the last U.S. presidential election but also about attending a public meeting discussing school or town affairs; working on a community project; signing a petition; attending a political meeting or rally; participating in a demonstration, protest, or march; and many forms of group involvement. The survey was administered in more than forty "community samples" of at least five hundred respondents each. But many of the community samples were large metropolitan areas or even whole states, yielding respondents sprinkled (sometimes rather thinly) across multiple counties. Given the need to link individuals' political behavior with the social program spending of their county government, the analysis that follows hones in on respondents from the core county of each of the metropolitan areas in the SCBC survey.

There is no information in the SCBC survey results on whether or not the individual respondent is a recipient of any county-administered social programs of interest. However, this chapter shows that counties in the United States, and SCBC counties in particular, vary dramatically in their levels of involvement in means-tested and universal social programs. Hence, county involvement in the two types of programs, measured via county expenditures in relevant Census Bureau categories, provides information about the county government social welfare program context for individual survey respondents. This, coupled with the SCBC survey's information on each respondent's income, provides a proxy measure of respondents' likely exposure to or experience with means-tested and universal social programs administered by their county government. To provide some evidence that the causal direction is from county activity to political behavior, rather than the other way around, data on county governments' social program spending is taken from the 1997 Census of Governments that preceded the survey on individuals' political behavior conducted in 2000.

County Government Involvement in Means-Tested and Universal Social Programs

County Governments and Means-Tested Programs: Welfare and Medicaid

The substantial sums that county governments collectively spend in the Census Bureau's category of welfare expenditures include only spending on means-tested programs (U.S. Bureau of the Census 1997), primarily the federal–state welfare program—previously called Aid to Families with Dependent Children (AFDC) (and, after a major 1996 reform, called Temporary Assistance to Needy Families, or TANF)—as well as Medicaid, the federal–state program of medical assistance for the poor. County involvement in means-tested social programs is almost exclusively via devolution of these two key federal–state programs to the local level. The analysis in this chapter relies on the county spending data reported in the 1997 Census of Governments—data predominantly reflecting calendar year 1996 spending. Hence, though the nation's current welfare program is TANF, the remainder of the chapter refers to the AFDC program that was in its final year when the spending data at issue here was collected.

There is substantial variation across the United States in the extent to which county governments were involved in AFDC. Even before the passage of major welfare reform legislation in 1996, some fifteen states had chosen to have the AFDC program administered by counties, while the other thirty-five had state-administered AFDC. In thirteen of the fifteen states that had county-administered AFDC, the county government had to bear at least a share of the cost of administration; in six of the state-administered states, counties contributed to administrative costs of the AFDC program. In ten of the fifteen county-administered states, as well as in state-administered Indiana, counties were also expected to share in the costs of benefits being paid to welfare recipients (Gainsborough 2003, 606–8). Although the local share of benefit costs was typically quite low (e.g., 4 percent in Ohio), New York and North Carolina were notable for their imposition of a local cost share of 50 percent (Zedlewski and Giannarelli 1997). Thus, although at first blush it might seem that counties that spend more on welfare are more generous, these mandates and divisions of program responsibility and costs between state and local governments suggest that devolution has simply forced many counties into greater expenditures. This is a key reason for rejecting any assumption that higher county welfare spending reflects heightened generosity and the use of devolution to shape an essentially different message for welfare recipients. Rather, the devolution and mandated spending dynamic is at least as likely to translate into local program administration that reinforces the aspects of a means-tested social program that, from a policy-centered theory perspective, send demeaning, politically demobilizing messages.

There is also variation in the extent of county involvement in the other means-tested program at issue here: Medicaid. Medicaid is a joint federal–state program of health-care services for the needy. There are broad federal guidelines about eligible populations, services to be covered, and other matters, but states essentially run their own Medicaid programs within those parameters. The federal government provides funds to match those spent by states on services for Medicaid recipients, but the match rate varies from state to state (from 50 to 77 percent as of 2005), depending primarily on state income levels (with lower income states having higher match rates) (Kaiser Commission on Medicaid and the Uninsured 2005). As with the welfare program, some states administer Medicaid centrally, but others have chosen local administration of Medicaid. As of the early 1990s, six states even gave "substantial administrative discretion" to their localities in administering the program (Weissert 1992, 96). Given that huge growth in Medicaid spending has threatened state budget stability for some time, it is not surprising that an increasing number of states require a local financial match. In the early 1990s, localities (primarily county governments) in fifteen states helped fund the program (Weissert 1992, 94); a decade later, twenty states had some type of local financial matching requirement. The required local contributions are not huge (one of the largest is New York's requirement that counties provide half the state's share of costs for acute care under Medicaid), and federal legislation limits the local portion of the state share to 60 percent (Kaiser Commission on Medicaid and the Uninsured 2005).

In some ways, Medicaid might be viewed as less appropriate than AFDC expenditures for placement in the welfare spending category. Beginning in the 1980s and extending into the 1990s, the federal government mandated a variety of expansions of Medicaid eligibility and covered services (Weissert 1992, 102), a process that has opened the door to the possibility that Medicaid could be the "path to a more universal health care system" in the United States—of interest to middle-class America rather than just a medical care program for the poor (Grogan and Patashnik 2003, 822). However, especially from the standpoint of evaluating county activities in 1996, Medicaid belongs in the welfare category. The federal government did not decouple Medicaid eligibility and enrollment from AFDC until the passage of welfare reform in 1996. And, "Medicaid is still a means-tested program that carries the moral stigma of welfare in the eyes of many" (Grogan and Patashnik 2003, 823). Evidence for this is found in the results of a study of levels of enrollment of eligible children in Medicaid in the late 1990s. The study by Kronebusch (2001) found declining enrollments from 1995–98 despite federal mandates intended to sustain children's Medicaid coverage in the face of welfare reform; it also found that at least one-third of children in very low income families were not enrolled in Medicaid despite these mandates. The study's conclusions about the reasons for lagging enrollment underscore the ways in which Medicaid had always been and still remained a program with precisely the kinds of elements that policy-centered theorists point to as typical of means-tested welfare programs:

> Potential enrollees must surmount a number of barriers including misunderstandings and lack of information about programs and their rules, burdensome applications and documentation requirements, complicated redetermination requirements, language difficulties, intrusive questions, demeaning experiences in the enrollment process, as well as the historic connections to welfare, which create the possibility that negative feelings and perceptions about welfare receipt will inhibit Medicaid participation as well. (Kronebusch 2001, 108)

If these elements characterized Medicaid in the years immediately after welfare reform in 1996, they certainly would have characterized it up to and including 1996. These are the very elements that policy-centered theorists point to as inhibiting the political participation of participants who endure the difficulties of entering the Medicaid program. Both Medicaid and the AFDC program were classic, means-tested programs in 1996. The experience of being determined eligible for Medicaid services or AFDC benefits—an experience featuring intrusive and embarrassing questions, complex rules, and burdensome documentation requirements that demonstrate suspicion of applicants—sends participants a strong message that they are second-class citizens who are not trusted, valued, or expected to be politically relevant. To the extent that county government officials were the agents of this message, we should expect that political participation at the local level is diminished for the target populations of these programs.

Consistent with the portrait just painted of national variation in county-level involvement in the AFDC and Medicaid programs, the twenty-eight counties from which respondents were drawn for this analysis[2] consisted of three counties (Yakima, Washington; Kanawha, West Virginia; and Androscoggin, Maine) with no welfare expenditures, several with substantial sums in the welfare expenditures category, and others with smaller amounts.

Some counties have larger populations than others and, more importantly for means-tested programs, more poor people than others. Their welfare expenditures might be thought to reflect only this. However, even when welfare expenditures are adjusted for the size of the county's population in poverty,[3] there is great variation among the study counties. Welfare expenditures per poor person range from only a little over $13 in New Castle County, Delaware; to $27 in Chicago's Cook County; to $40 in Seattle's King County; to more than $4,000 in two New York counties: Monroe (Rochester area) and Onondaga (Syracuse). Minnesota counties are notably high as well, with St. Paul's Ramsey County at $3,245 and Minneapolis's Hennepin County at $2,129.

County Governments and Non-Means-Tested Programs

In addition to the means-tested programs outlined previously, county governments are heavily involved in universal (i.e., non-means-tested) social programs. These fall primarily in either the Census Bureau's public health spending category, covering an array of counties' traditional responsibilities in the public health area (e.g., immunization and other outpatient clinics, research and education, ambulance service, and mosquito abatement in some areas), or the Census Bureau's hospitals spending category (including the construction, maintenance, and operation of public hospitals and in some cases public support provided to private hospitals).

As an illustration of the array of health- and hospital-related social programs provided by county government, consider the health and hospital services handled by Hennepin County. In 2002, 32.8 percent of the county's entire budget, or $557.55 million, was spent in the public health category. By far the largest element in this category was the Hennepin County Medical Center, at a little more than $408 million. Like all medical centers, that facility presumably provides some indigent care. But it largely provides services to all comers, although their access to the facility may be via private insurance, Medicare, private payment, or indigent care. The county also funds several clinics, including the Red Door Clinic that provides testing for human immunodeficiency virus and other sexually transmitted diseases, pregnancy prevention services, and other intervention and prevention programs. The clinic's services are available to all and are charged on a sliding scale based on the client's ability to pay. Another clinic provides a full range of medical and dental services, regardless of an individual's insurance status. In addition, the county's public health clinic offers diagnosis and treatment of tuberculosis (TB) and treatment of latent TB infection in high-risk individuals, and there is a program for baby immunization information and services. The county also provides assessment, treatment, case management, and other support services for those with alcohol and drug abuse problems, either through regular intake or through referral by a court unit with which the health department collaborates. The health department provides inspections of septic systems and beaches, licensing and inspections related to the food service industry, investigations related to infectious disease outbreaks, education and prevention programs of many kinds, and development of public health databases and emergency planning (Hennepin County 2009).

In contrast with the means-tested programs that are in the Census Bureau's category of welfare spending, these various components of the public health and hospitals expenditure categories are largely universal spending programs. Although individuals may pay different amounts or access these services in different ways and some may be able to use the programs without paying, the programs themselves mostly are not literally means tested and the health-care professionals providing services do not necessarily know or provide differential service based on who is insured and who is not or who is a paying client and who is indigent.

Just as there is national variation in county-level expenditures on means-tested social programs, there is also substantial variation in such expenditures in these public health and hospitals categories. These expenditures are for universal programs, although they may be more important for lower-income residents than for wealthier residents, who are more likely to rely on private sector equivalents for many services provided in the category. For comparability with the welfare spending outcomes, expenditures in the combined public health and hospitals categories are also adjusted for the size of the county population in poverty. For the twenty-eight counties from which respondents were drawn for this analysis, one (Androscoggin, Maine) has no health or hospital spending, several (Boulder, Colorado; New Castle, Delaware; Ramsey, Minnesota; and Yakima, Washington) have only a few hundred dollars of this type of spending per poor person, many spend between $1,000 and $2,000 per poor person, and the largest spenders weigh in at $2,944 (Cuyahoga County, Ohio) and $5,304 (Hennepin County) per poor person.

Testing Policy-Centered Hypotheses about County Social Program Spending

In this section, analysis of the impact of county government involvement in means-tested and universal social programs on the civic engagement of county residents proceeds in several steps. First, a model is presented that is "baseline" in two respects: (1) it includes an array of individual characteristics that are well-established predictors of political participation from a society-centered theoretical perspective (Mettler 2002), and (2) it focuses, like the bulk of the empirical research in the policy-centered tradition, on voting in a U.S. presidential election rather than alternative forms of more locally oriented participation. Next, these results are compared with the results obtained when the same, standard set of individual-level explanatory variables is used to account for other, more locally oriented forms of political participation that are of interest here. This exercise reveals the limitations of the standard, society-centered model in accounting for these alternative, locally oriented forms of participation. Third, variables representative of a policy-centered approach—in this case, two categories of social program expenditures (means tested and universal) for each individual's county of residence—are added to the model to determine whether, net the effects of individual-level characteristics, the extent of county government involvement with each type of program affects the political participation of residents.

Table 1.1 shows the baseline model and reveals that a suite of individual-level characteristics that have traditionally been part of a standard model of participation does a reasonable job of explaining participation in a U.S. presidential election, either for respondents generally or for the very poor. As expected via a literature that is well established by now, voting propensity is higher among older individuals, better-educated people, more frequent churchgoers, homeowners, and those who have lived in the community longer. Also consistent with the broad literature is the finding that women are more likely to vote than men; once variables such as education and income are taken into account, racial differences in voting turnout for U.S. president are negligible (Conway 2000). Having children living at home is not part of the suite of variables typically incorporated in models of voting, and for the population overall, it is not an important predictor. It is included to make this baseline model comparable to the follow-up presented later for the impact of welfare on more locally oriented forms of participation (for which having children at home is relevant).

TABLE 1.1

A baseline explanatory model: Accounting for voting participation in the last U.S. presidential election

	ALL	<$20K ONLY
Age	.044**	.040**
	(.002)	(.004)
Education	.490**	.548**
	(.021)	(.058)
Race (0 = white, 1 = nonwhite)	−.176	.033
	(.110)	(.171)
Homeownership	.595**	.367**
	(.053)	(.122)
Church attendance (higher values = less frequent)	−.127**	−.094*
	(.021)	(.041)
Time in community	.121**	.188**
	(.022)	(.050)
Gender (1 = male, 2 = female)	.119*	.263*
	(.053)	(.117)
Have kids over age 6	.084	.449#
	(.075)	(.253)
Constant	−3.019**	−4.213**
	(.215)	(.405)
N	12,226	1,633
Pseudo-R^2	.20	.21

(Source: Data from 2000 Social Capital Benchmark Community survey)
Note: The numbers presented are logistic regression coefficients (robust standard error).
**$p < .01$
*$p < .05$
#$p < .10$

As Table 1.1 indicates, this variable approaches significance for the poorest segment of the community even when voting in a presidential election is at issue.

Table 1.2 presents the results when the standard, individual-level characteristics of the baseline model are used to explain variation in forms of political engagement that are of particular importance for local governance.

TABLE 1.2

The baseline explanatory model applied to two forms of local political participation

(a) Worked on a community project in last 12 months

	ALL	<$20K ONLY
Age	−.012**	−.014**
	(.001)	(.003)
Education	.296**	.314**
	(.016)	(.039)
Race (0 = white, 1 = nonwhite)	−.009	.083
	(.068)	(.153)
Homeownership	.344**	.224
	(.052)	(.147)
Church attendance (higher values = less frequent)	−.207**	−.235**
	(.014)	(.034)
Time in community	.091**	.061
	(.017)	(.051)
Gender (1 = male, 2 = female)	.116**	.035
	(.033)	(.113)
Have kids over age 6	.350**	.423#
	(.068)	(.285)
Constant	−1.486**	−1.488**
	(.126)	(.285)
N	12,885	1,744
Pseudo-R^2	.08	.06
(b) Engaged in at least one of five forms of local political participation		
Age	−.008**	−.006**
	(.001)	(.002)
Education	.326**	.322**
	(.022)	(.044)
Race (0 = white, 1 = nonwhite)	−.056	.075
	(.063)	(.148)
Homeownership	.500**	.251#
	(.057)	(.131)

(continued)

TABLE 1.2

The baseline explanatory model applied to two forms of local political participation—continued

	ALL	<$20K ONLY
Church attendance (higher values = less frequent)	−.137**	−.165**
	(.014)	(.035)
Time in community	.074**	.070#
	(.016)	(.038)
Gender (1 = male, 2 = female)	−.004	−.054
	(.039)	(.118)
Have kids over age 6	.274**	.240
	(.055)	(.178)
Constant	−0.493**	−0.604*
	(.134)	(.282)
N	12,903	1,766
Pseudo-R^2	.08	.05

Source: Data from 2000 Social Capital Benchmark Community survey

Note: The numbers presented are logistic regression coefficients (robust standard error).

**$p < .01$

*$p < .05$

#$p < .10$

Table 1.2(a) presents the results for one such form of participation—working on a local project. However, work on a community project is but one relevant form of local civic engagement. Individuals could be active in the community without reporting this particular form of participation. Hence, Table 1.2(b) replicates the analysis for a broader measure of civic engagement that distinguishes those who engaged in at least one of five forms of local political participation from those who participate in none of them. The five possible forms of participation are working on a community project; attending a political meeting or rally; signing a petition; participating in demonstrations, boycotts, or marches; and maintaining membership in a neighborhood group.[4]

Table 1.2 reveals that the standard model does a much poorer job of explaining these distinct local-level forms of political involvement than it did in accounting for voting in national elections. This is reflected in the low values for the model-fit statistics. In addition, some explanatory variables play a quite different role in predicting who engages in these local forms of participation compared with their familiar role in the literature on voting in national elections. In contrast with the higher voting rates that older individuals exhibit, we see a negative relationship between age and both measures of local political participation. This may reflect the greater inconvenience and greater energy required for these forms of participation compared with going to the polling booth once every four years. It may also be the result of older people being more likely to be the target of voter-mobilizing efforts (from groups such as the AARP) and younger people being more likely to be the target of mobilizing efforts by the kinds of groups orchestrating community projects and protests.

In addition, having school-age children plays an important role in explaining locally relevant forms of participation, although it was not a significant predictor of voting in national elections. When the form of political participation at issue is working on community projects, parenting is an important predictor regardless of income; when the broader index of five possible forms of local participation is at issue, having school-age children is a significant predictor for respondents overall but not for the poorest income group.

In light of these differences in how a standard society-centered model performs for explaining local participation (as opposed to voting in national elections), the analysis now turns to whether county governments' spending patterns on means-tested and universal social programs affect these distinct local forms of participation. The results in Table 1.3 provide limited evidence for policy-centered theory. When working on a community project is the specific form of participation considered, as in Table 1.3(a), participation is enhanced where spending on universal social programs (public health and hospitals) is higher; true to the notion that this is universal social program spending, this impact of heightened political involvement is apparent for respondents as a whole. However, for respondents in the lowest-income group, the coefficient, while properly signed, is not significant. The results for means-tested program involvement are even more puzzling. Participation on a community project is diminished where spending on means-tested programs is higher. But while there is significant evidence of this chilling effect of means-tested programs for respondents as a whole, the coefficient for the low-income subgroup that contains the targeted population for welfare and Medicaid is not significant.

TABLE 1.3

An expanded explanatory model of two forms of local political participation

(a) Worked on a community project in last 12 months

	ALL	<$20K ONLY
Age	−.012**	−.014**
	(.001)	(.003)
Education	.297**	.316**
	(.016)	(.039)
Race (0 = white, 1 = nonwhite)	−.011	.078
	(.068)	(.158)
Homeownership	.339**	.202
	(.050)	(.150)
Church attendance (higher values = less frequent)	−.208**	−.237**
	(.014)	(.034)
Time in community	.092**	.068
	(.017)	(.054)
Gender (1 = male, 2 = female)	.116*	.039
	(.033)	(.113)
Kids over age 6	.349**	.424#
	(.069)	(.222)
Welfare spending/poor person	−.004*	−.006
	(.002)	(.004)
Public health, hospitals spending/poor person	.003	.006
	(.003)	(.006)
Constant	−1.479**	−1.497**
	(.113)	(.316)
N	12,885	1,744
Pseudo-R^2	.08	.07
(b) Engaged in at least one of five forms of local political participation		
Age	−.008**	−.007*
	(.001)	(.002)
Education	.327**	.324**
	(.023)	(.044)

TABLE 1.3

An expanded explanatory model of two forms of local political participation—continued

	ALL	<$20K ONLY
Race (0 = white, 1 = nonwhite)	−.057	.072
	(.060)	(.144)
Homeownership	.493**	.234#
	(.058)	(.133)
Church attendance (higher values = less frequent)	−.138**	−.166**
	(.014)	(.035)
Time in community	.075**	.074#
	(.015)	(.039)
Gender (1 = male, 2 = female)	−.004	−.051
	(.039)	(.118)
Kids over age 6	.273**	.240
	(.056)	(.177)
Welfare spending/poor person	−.004#	−.005
	(.003)	(.005)
Public health, hospitals spending/poor person	.036	.005
	(.003)	(.004)
Constant	−.481**	−.606*
	(.143)	(.311)
N	12,903	1,748
Pseudo-R^2	.08	.05

Source: Data from 2000 Social Capital Benchmark Community survey and 1997 Census of Governments

Note: The numbers presented are logistic regression coefficients (robust standard error).

**$p < .01$

*$p < .05$

#$p < .10$

There is even less evidence for the twin hypotheses of policy-centered theory when the broader measure of civic engagement is at issue, as it is in Table 1.3(b). Higher levels of spending on public health and hospitals do not significantly enhance the participation of either residents as a whole or low-income individuals in particular, although both coefficients are properly signed. Again, there is more evidence that means-tested program spending dampens political engagement for the population as a whole than it does for the income group that is presumably the target of means-tested programs.

The small number of respondents in the lowest-income category may be part of the reason that the coefficients for that group are not significant in Table 1.3. But the emergence of demobilizing effects from means-tested programs for the overall population is puzzling. Those of higher income presumably have not had direct experience with the AFDC program (unless they did so much earlier in their life and then became success stories). So how can they be expected to have received the "your political voice doesn't matter" message that such programs presumably send?

There are a couple of possibilities. First, some nonpoor respondents may nevertheless have had personal experience with Medicaid via family members. If, for example, an individual has an elderly parent who needs nursing home care but does not have resources to cover it, that person may have had to help the parent "spend down" assets to become eligible for Medicaid and then observed the treatment that the parent received as a Medicaid-paid resident of a nursing home. Unfortunately, there is no way that individuals with such an experience can be distinguished from others in the data set.

In addition, an individual who has a friend on welfare could be indirectly affected by the welfare program. In particular, an individual who knows someone on welfare might vicariously experience the demeaning aspects of welfare. And in this pool of urban county respondents, a substantial number (40.8 percent) do say that they "have a personal friend who has been on welfare." Could this indirect, personal experience account for the broader, participation-dampening effects of welfare that have been observed so far?

To explore this, Tables 1.4 and 1.5 provide revised models of working on a community project and participation in one of the five forms of local civic engagement. The revised models isolate the likely "targets" of welfare program messages by selecting a group that consists of (1) those respondents in the lowest-income category and (2) those respondents, regardless of income, who said they have a personal friend who has been on welfare. This target group of "welfare-experiencing" respondents is compared with respondents who meet neither of these targeting conditions.

TABLE 1.4

Modeling participation on a community project, by welfare experience

	WELFARE EXPERIENCING	ALL OTHERS
Age	−.013**	−.009**
	(.002)	(.002)
Education	.339**	.275**
	(.019)	(.022)
Race (0 = white, 1 = nonwhite)	−.050	.024
	(.097)	(.076)
Homeownership	.362**	.337**
	(.079)	(.071)
Church attendance (higher values = less frequent)	−.233**	−.189**
	(.014)	(.025)
Time in community	.100**	.088**
	(.026)	(.020)
Gender (male = 1, female = 2)	.058	.163**
	(.051)	(.057)
Kids over age 6	.380**	.264**
	(.107)	(.093)
Welfare spending/poor person	−.007**	−.001
	(.002)	(.003)
Public health, hospitals spending/poor person	.004	.002
	(.003)	(.004)
Constant	−1.293**	−1.766**
	(.182)	(.214)
N	6,241	5,605
Pseudo-R^2	.10	.07

Source: Data from 2000 Social Capital Benchmark Community survey and 1997 Census of Governments

Note: The numbers presented are logistic regression coefficients (robust standard error).

**$p < .01$

*$p < .05$

#$p < .10$

TABLE 1.5

Modeling civic participation, by welfare experience

	WELFARE EXPERIENCING	ALL OTHERS
Age	−.011**	−.003
	(.001)	(.002)
Education	.380**	.302**
	(.031)	(.023)
Race (0 = white, 1 = nonwhite)	−.058	−.076
	(.083)	(.072)
Homeownership	.492**	.548**
	(.074)	(.094)
Church attendance (higher values = less frequent)	−.172**	−.116**
	(.020)	(.022)
Time in community	.070**	.080**
	(.024)	(.022)
Gender (male = 1, female = 2)	−.072	.015
	(.051)	(.062)
Kids over age 6	.442**	.080
	(.106)	(.072)
Welfare spending/poor person	−.007*	−.001
	(.003)	(.003)
Public health, hospitals spending/poor person	.003	.006*
	(.003)	(.003)
Constant	−.191	−.852**
	(.131)	(.229)
N	6,159	5,609
Pseudo-R^2	.10	.07

Source: Data from 2000 Social Capital Benchmark survey and 1997 Census of Governments
Note: The numbers presented are logistic regression coefficients (robust standard error).

**$p < .01$

*$p < .05$

#$p < .10$

The results are more supportive of policy-centered theory, yet suggest an important extension of that theory. First, when "experience" with the welfare program is extended to cover those with friends on welfare and those most likely to be on it themselves because of income limitations, the results reveal precisely the impact of means-tested spending that is predicted by policy-centered theory. For those experiencing welfare, the likelihood of involvement in a community project is diminished where a county government is more involved in means-tested social programs; there is no significant participation-dampening effect for other individuals (Table 1.4). When the broader measure of civic engagement is the dependent variable (Table 1.5), we again see that means-tested program involvement on the part of a county government diminishes the civic participation of people who have experience with those programs yet has no significant effect on others.

The hypothesis that county involvement with universal social programs enhances participation rates is not well supported by the results for a single form of participation—work on a community project. The coefficients for that form are properly signed but not significant. When the broader measure of civic engagement is at issue, however, we see that participation is enhanced where spending on universal social programs is higher, at least for those who do not experience welfare. But for those experiencing means-tested welfare, the universal health and hospital programs provided by county government do not enhance civic engagement (i.e., the coefficient for the public health and hospitals spending variables is signed in the direction of enhanced participation but is statistically insignificant).

That those experiencing welfare do not share in the participation-enhancing impact of the universal social programs in their area is of special interest, because county public health and hospital programs, although universal in character, are likely to be more important for the disadvantaged than for the better off who have more access to private alternatives. Furthermore, Schneider and Ingram's (1997) theorizing suggests that such universal social programs will only have mobilizing effects for a relatively powerless target group, such as welfare-dependent individuals. The results here are quite the opposite. They suggest that the chilling effects of means-tested programs trump the mobilizing effects of universal programs.

The evidence presented here is consistent with policy theorists' arguments about the impact of means-tested programs and with their overall argument that people who use government programs generalize from those program experiences to government overall. But that argument needs to be refined to include the apparently greater policy-learning importance of the means-tested program experience compared with the experience of universal programs.

Discussion

This analysis has applied hypotheses derived from the policy-centered tradition to the local level. The results of the analysis suggest several important implications for the policy-centered framework. First, the results show that the policy designs of means-tested and universal programs have contrasting consequences for *local* forms of civic engagement that have been found in studies of national-level participation. Existing research has primarily shown the disempowering effects of means-tested programs and the participation-enhancing effects of universal programs on voting in national elections or on social program claim making (Soss 2000; Soss and Keiser 2006; Mettler and Stonecash 2008).[5] However, this chapter reveals that contrasting impacts are also evident when locally oriented forms of participation are considered.

Moreover, the analysis suggests that these impacts on local civic engagement are tied to the levels of county government involvement in means-tested and universal programs. Even though programs such as Medicaid and welfare are federal or federal–state programs, administrative decentralization and matching requirements have pulled some county governments more deeply into Medicaid and welfare program involvement than others, as reflected here in their higher rates of spending in this means-tested category. To the extent that they are more involved, they are by definition implicated in creating the demeaning experiences and conveying the participation-dampening messages that means-tested programs send to recipients. Similarly, a great deal of county government spending on public health and hospitals comes from federal or state funding. But for the constituencies served by these universal programs, the federal or state funding behind the local hospital, clinic, or public health program may not be noticed. Instead, the universalistic program design behind this programmatic funding simply means experience with a government program that features accessibility to services without the hassles and demeaning features of means-tested programs. The results presented in this analysis are consistent with the notion that there are local participatory consequences for local government involvement in social programs, even if federal and state program design elements define the basic character of local government action in this sphere.

The chapter includes results that refine policy-centered theory. In particular, the results suggest that at the local level, means-tested programs have more potent interpretive effects than universal programs. This is suggested in two respects. First is the evidence that the chilling effects of means-tested programs trump the mobilizing effects of universal programs. For those experiencing means-tested programs, there is good evidence of diminished political participation but no significant evidence of mobilizing effects from their residence in counties with high levels of spending on universal programs.

However, there is a second sense in which means-tested programs are shown to have especially potent interpretive effects. The analysis supports a conclusion that means-tested programs send messages to a somewhat broader "target" population than policy-centered theory usually envisions. Current recipients or those whose income makes them eligible are not the only ones to experience the stigmatizing and disempowering aspects of means-tested programs. In addition, those who have a personal friend who has been on welfare also become quite aware of the demeaning and stigmatizing elements of these programs. The chilling effect of means testing on participation applies to this broader group of welfare-experiencing individuals. While it is beyond the capacity of this chapter to demonstrate all ways in which the target population for means-tested programs is broadened, the measure used here suggests that policy feedback effects can ripple through the friendship networks of recipients. Welfare programs' demeaning and discouraging messages are heard by those who know someone on welfare, presumably via the comments that welfare recipients make about the nature of their experiences with welfare programs. Thus, policy learning, at least with respect to means-tested programs, should not be viewed as happening to individuals in isolation; rather, it occurs in a social context where information is shared. As a result, the policy feedback effects of means-tested programs are amplified.

2

City Government and Neighborhoods

Intentional Empowerment and Reactionary Mobilization

Neighborhood-level political involvement is a less heavily studied form of participation than voting and, from some points of view, perhaps a narrower and less interesting form of political participation. However, a substantial case has been made for the importance of participation in neighborhood-based organizations, especially by those touting face-to-face involvement as a stepping stone for social capital formation (Putnam 2000) and inclusive, participative democracy (Berry, Portney, and Thomson 1993; Thomson 2001). Neighborhood-level politics is also important because of the less uplifting side of neighborhood organizations: they can be insular, enmeshed in factionalism and turf conflicts (Meyer and Hyde 2004), biased in their representation of diverse interests (Sullivan and Picarsic 2007), central to the not-in-my-backyard problem, and key obstacles to progressive action, such as the development of affordable housing (Goetz and Sidney 2008). Whatever the normative spin, neighborhood associations are clearly important players in urban political systems. Hence, citizen involvement in these organizations is far from trivial.

A focus on participation in neighborhood organizations therefore provides an important opportunity to apply policy-centered theory to a distinctively local form of political participation. Such a focus is particularly relevant because the urban politics literature already suggests that city governments' policies and programs with respect to neighborhoods can affect citizens' political involvement in neighborhood organizations. That is not the only explanation found in the existing literature for neighborhood organization involvement. As noted later, there is also a set of explanations drawn from standard models of how individual and contextual characteristics shape political participation, as well as attention to fundamental institutional arrangements for local governance. For purposes of investigating a policy-centered approach, however, the featured scholarship to date considers what city governments do to actively encourage participation in neighborhood-based organizations and how problematic action (or inaction) on the part of city governments may unintentionally mobilize neighborhood residents.

Furthermore, urban scholarship has generated at least a toehold for a policy-centered explanation of neighborhood-based political involvement. That scholarship suggests two ways in which city governments can foster citizen participation in neighborhood organizations: (1) empowerment and (2) creation of the occasion for reactionary mobilization. In brief, city governments can either *encourage* involvement at the neighborhood level by being responsive to neighborhoods as venues for interest aggregation and articulation—perhaps even delegating formal powers to neighborhood-based organizations—or *invoke* neighborhood-based political mobilization by being unresponsive to neighborhood inputs or ignoring conditions that neighborhood residents perceive to be important threats to their quality of life.

Empowerment

Recent urban scholarship in the empowerment genre has primarily featured local government's creation or delegation of governance roles to neighborhood-based organizations. This is featured in a long line of research, including Thomas's (1986) study of Cincinnati; Berry, Portney, and Thomson's (1993) study of five cities with high-level efforts to mobilize neighborhood involvement; Thomson's (2001) follow-up study of four of those five cities; Fung's (2004) examination of "empowered participation" in two areas in Chicago; and indirectly, Jun's (2007) study of the emergence of neighborhood councils in Los Angeles after charter revision called for their formation.

There are, however, several problems in using much of this line of work to substantiate a policy-centered model of neighborhood-level participation. The first is a matter of study design and causal inference. Studies in this genre tend to focus on one or a relatively small number of cities that are exceptional in their efforts to orchestrate neighborhood-level participation. Even where comparison cities are introduced, as in Berry, Portney, and Thomson's (1993) work, the design is driven by the initial selection of exceptional cases. Generalizability is therefore problematic for such an approach and extremely problematic for the single-city, exceptional case studies that are even more prominent in this genre.

The second problem with this line of work is that much of it tends to emphasize formal citywide arrangements that manifest neighborhood empowerment yet neglect other ways by which city governments might influence citizen participation at the neighborhood level. Fung's (2004) definition of empowered participation, for example, focuses on the need for neighborhood groups to have both external support from city governments (in the form of financing, expertise, etc.) and accountability to central authority so that they can be successful models of participatory democracy. But it does not explicitly include the idea that empowered participation requires a stream of decisions and actions on the part of a city government that shows residents their participatory efforts can yield desired responses from officials. Similarly, in their path-breaking study of cities deemed to have successful neighborhood organization systems, Berry, Portney, and Thomson (1993) emphasized the need for institutional arrangements that provide citizens with access to the system; information about issues affecting them; city resources, especially staffing, to facilitate the functioning of the organization; and formal powers that give neighborhood-level organizations official standing in discussions of citywide budget priorities, neighborhood allocations, and agenda setting. However, their study ignored the possibility that participation in indigenous or nascent neighborhood-based organizations might be encouraged by broad-ranging policy responsiveness to neighborhoods, even in the absence of elaborate structures of formally defined neighborhood governance such as those created in a few, notable cities. Indeed, perhaps for this reason Berry, Portney, and Thomson (1993, 97) found the "number of citizens actually involved in community participation activities is not greater in the core study cities than in the cities with which they were matched that have no citywide systems of participation."

This conclusion points to the third problem with existing scholarship on cities uniquely and formally organized to facilitate neighborhood-based participation. So far, there is scant evidence that these arrangements have generated more neighborhood-based participation than can be found in cities without such formal arrangements (Thomas 1986; Berry, Portney, and Thomson 1993; Fagatto and Fung 2006). Admittedly, this is in part because a number of the studies are not specifically looking for this outcome, even though the studies are grounded in broad rhetoric about the capacity for city governments to be instrumental in the formation of strong, face-to-face, participatory democracy. Some studies focus on organizational formation only (Yun 2007), but most focus on broad organizational success, with the extent of citizen participation in neighborhood associations treated as a relatively minor part of the meaning of organizational success. When low levels of participation are found, the result is typically treated as not damaging to the view that these structured arrangements should be seen as an important form of urban democracy. For example, Fung's (2004, 103–4) analysis of empowered participation in Chicago found participation in the beat meetings that are essential to community policing averaged a little more than twenty-one residents per police beat and that the parent turnout rate for local school council elections was typically no more than 16 percent. His conclusion that these levels of participation are nevertheless still high enough "for these bodies to function as problem-solving and planning groups" (105) shows why investigations of the "success" of officially empowered neighborhood-based groups do not provide quite the evidence needed to test the policy-centered theory's notion that government programs can facilitate political participation.

Reactionary Mobilization

In contrast to the empowerment version of how government policy can increase citizen participation stands an account that attributes high levels of formation of and involvement in neighborhood-based groups to city government failure to adequately respond to neighborhood needs, demands, or problems. From this perspective, high levels of political mobilization at the neighborhood level can emerge when there are perceived threats to the neighborhood, especially if the city government fails to adequately deal with those threats. The city government may even be the source of the threat, such as when city officials signal the intent to use eminent domain powers to displace landowners for a major development project or issue approvals for a land-use project viewed as an undesirable encroachment by those living next to where it will be sited.

A long line of work, typically in case study form, is consistent with this account of neighborhood organization activation in reaction to threats and policy nonresponsiveness. It includes work on the role of neighborhood organizations in reacting to racial and social change (Suttles 1968,

1972; Taub 1984). It includes studies of organizational formation, such as Logan and Rabrenovic's (1990) study of more than seventy neighborhood organizations in one area of New York State, which revealed that organizational formation was driven by proposed land-use changes that were opposed by the neighborhood. Likewise, Goetz and Sidney (1994) showed the ways in which neighborhood organizations in Minneapolis and St. Paul have become dominated by an "ideology of property"—that is, mobilized in reaction to affordable housing initiatives as a threat. And Sonenshein (1996) showed how objectionably high concentrations of liquor stores engendered neighborhood-based political participation in Los Angeles. Numerous other case studies provide similar evidence of the way in which perceived threats to neighborhoods, including government nonresponsiveness to certain neighborhoods, are the basis for mobilizing neighborhood residents for political action (Sonenshein 2004).

Acknowledgement of the two ways in which city governments can engender heightened neighborhood-level political activity fits well with Schneider and Ingram's (1997) theorizing about how the interaction of policy characteristics and target populations yields differential impacts on political participation. They proposed that favorable policy would have empowering effects for dependent populations—but not for advantaged populations; instead, negative or burdensome policies were hypothesized to generate mobilization and intensified participation among advantaged populations as they attempt to protect the advantages they already have. As applied to the policies at issue in this chapter, this means that neighborhood empowerment policies should be expected to have mobilizing impacts only on dependent populations, such as individuals with lower levels of income, education, or other resources crucial for political activation. For such individuals, generosity and responsiveness on the part of a city government constitute an assurance that their interests are officially important and that their political involvement will be met with the same kind of respect accorded to more advantaged populations. By contrast, Schneider and Ingram's theorizing suggests that more advantaged populations barely notice and largely take for granted whatever city governments might do by way of responsiveness to problems in their neighborhoods but that they quickly notice and quickly mobilize in a reactionary way if the responsiveness they have come to expect is missing.

Although it can fit with Schneider and Ingram's (1997) theorizing, the distinction between empowerment-based mobilization and reactionary mobilization contrasts with most of the empirical work in the policy-centered genre. That work (Soss 1999; Mettler 2002, 2007a; Mettler and Stonecash 2008) acknowledges that some government policies, programs, and actions send negative, hostile, or nonresponsive messages to recipients. But the expected impact of such policies and programs on recipients is typically demobilization rather than mobilization, without explicit theorizing about how impact might vary by target group. There are exceptions, stemming from empirical results at odds with the demobilizing hypothesis of policy-centered theory. For example, noting some of Soss's (1999) unexpected findings concerning public assistance claimants, Mettler (2007a) acknowledged that individuals who have negative experiences can be stimulated to political action. Although this limited acknowledgment to some extent incorporates the reactionary mobilization explanation into the orbit of policy-centered theory, the predominant thrust of policy-centered theory has been to simply view government programs that are harsh or hostile to recipients as having demobilizing impacts on those recipients.

Rival Explanations

Any assessment of the extent to which government action can foster participation in neighborhood associations must be tested against competing explanations of the causes of that form of political participation. The most commonly articulated competing explanations derive from consideration of characteristics that have generally been found to motivate or deter political participation in research on individuals. These demographic characteristics—most notably income, education, and race, as well as an assortment of others, such as length of residence—constitute a "standard socioeconomic model" (Berry, Portney, and Thomson 1993, 81) that, with some notable exceptions, is usually hypothesized to affect individuals' propensity to participate in neighborhood organizations. In standard models of political participation generally, greater participation is expected from individuals with higher levels of income and education; individuals with greater stakes in and familiarity with the community, as exemplified by length of residence; and so forth.

There is substantial empirical support in the literature for application of this standard model of participation to neighborhood organization involvement. For example, Fung (2004) reported that higher rates of mobility diminished participation in local school council elections, and Jun (2007) found Los Angeles neighborhoods with longer rates of residential tenure were able to successfully create neighborhood councils. Meanwhile, Berry, Portney, and Thomson (1993) reported that the level of involvement in neighborhood-based political activity is a function of socioeconomic status (combined income and education), both in cities with structured neighborhood participation arrangements and in those without.

One demographic characteristic has generated results for neighborhood organization involvement that are distinctive from the study of other forms of participation: race. Although the evidence is somewhat mixed, there is relatively compelling evidence that neighborhood-based political participation is higher among blacks than among whites. For example, Stoll (2001) found that in Los Angeles in 1993–94, blacks participated in more community-based voluntary organizations than did whites. Alex-Assensoh's (1998) study of Columbus, Ohio, showed that even in concentrated-poverty neighborhoods, black residents were more likely than whites to attend community meetings and that, with neighborhood poverty level held constant, blacks were more likely than whites to have worked to solve community problems. Fung (2004) found that in Chicago, parental involvement in local school council activities (notably elections) was higher in schools with higher proportions of black students. And Berry, Portney, and Thomson (1993) reported that among the poorest respondents in their five-city study, blacks were overrepresented in the highest levels of their community participation index—an index that includes citizen groups or neighborhood associations.

In addition to inclusion of demographic variables to control for these rival explanations, it is important to consider how institutional arrangements relating to neighborhoods might influence participation. There is by now a substantial literature on how reform government institutions such as at-large elections, nonpartisanship, and the council–manager form of government influence local politics. Generally, reform institutions have been found to diminish citizen participation in the form of voting. However, little attention has been paid to how these basic structures of local government influence participation in neighborhood associations, especially in the contemporary era of hybrid arrangements that mix elements of reform government with some elements of nonreformed government. The use of at-large versus ward (or district) elections is clearly the most relevant matter with respect to institutional impacts on citizen participation in neighborhood organizations. But the logic of ward elections suggests two competing possibilities. To the extent that neighborhood associations emerge to compensate for the lack of neighborhood-based interest aggregation in at-large systems, we might expect participation in neighborhood associations to be highest in cities with few or no council members elected by districts. On the other hand, neighborhood associations have the potential to be nurtured by and to function in cooperation with ward-based political party (or party-like) organizations in cities that have ward-based electoral arrangements. This possibility would mean higher rates of neighborhood association involvement in cities with district elections than in cities with at-large elections. In either case, it is important to control for the status of council election type when testing the policy-centered model of neighborhood mobilization.

Finally, existing scholarship suggests an important contextual explanation: participation is a function of city size. Oliver (2000) reported that, except for voting (which shows a distinctive pattern), rates of three distinctively local forms of political participation (contacting local officials, attending community board meetings, and attending meetings of voluntary organizations) decline with increasing city size, even when demographic differences are taken into account.

Keys to an Empirical Test

The challenge of testing the policy-centered model of neighborhood association involvement is that it requires several kinds of information that urban scholars virtually never have at their disposal. One kind is city-by-city survey results on resident involvement in neighborhood organizations for a range of cities. Another is information for those same cities on (1) the extent to which each city government engages in neighborhood-empowering actions, including both adoption of formal arrangements that give special powers to neighborhood-based organizations and responsive action with respect to the routine appeals of indigenous neighborhood organizations, and (2) the extent to which each city government is unresponsive to neighborhood inputs or to conditions that neighborhood residents perceive to be important threats. The problems of getting all this information for something akin to a representative sample of U.S. cities has largely constrained scholarship in this area to single-city case studies or limited comparison studies of a handful of cities.

This chapter attempts to move beyond these constraints in two ways. First, it uses data on neighborhood association involvement available in Putnam's (2000) Social Capital Benchmark Community (SCBC) survey data set. That survey involved large sample surveys conducted in 2000 in more than forty communities located in twenty-nine states. Second, the chapter uses data from content analyses, conducted by the author, of each SCBC city's daily newspaper for the entirety of 1999 to glean relevant information on government actions with respect to neighborhoods.

Although the SCBC survey is unique in its capacity to provide urban scholars with survey results from numerous jurisdictions, its "community" samples range from whole states (Montana), very large metropolitan areas (Silicon Valley), and other large regions to individual local government jurisdictions. State, regional, and large metropolitan area samples that did not generate a reasonable number of SCBC respondents from any specific city-level jurisdiction are excluded from this analysis, as were Kalamazoo, Michigan, and Lewiston, Maine, for which newspaper coverage in either LexisNexis or America's Newspapers (essential for the content analysis portion of the project) was not available. With these exclusions, there are twenty-nine communities for which there is either the original full sample of five hundred or more respondents from a single, city-sized jurisdiction or a substantial number of metropolitan core city respondents once assorted suburban or exurban respondents to the original full sample are deselected. The twenty-nine cities are not a random sample of U.S. cities. Hence, measures of statistical significance can only be used as heuristics rather than as true inferential statistics.

Despite these limitations, the availability of survey and content analysis data from twenty-nine cities is a substantial improvement in generalizability over single-city case studies or very small-*N* studies. This sample constitutes an especially significant improvement over small-*N* studies with a selection bias toward democracy-enhancing innovations. Furthermore, the study cities are diverse. They include five of the nation's nine largest cities, six cities in the range of 0.5 million to just under 1 million population, five cities with a population size between 250,000 and 499,999, seven cities with a population between 100,000 and 249,999, and six cities with a population less than 100,000. (See appendix A for a full list of the study cities.)

The key dependent variable for the study comes from the SCBC survey item asking respondents whether they participated in a neighborhood association in the past year (yes = 1, no = 0). The question is part of a battery of questions asking about participation in groups ranging from youth organizations to veterans, sports, and labor groups.

Explanatory variables representing the suite of individual characteristics from standard models of participation (e.g., race, education, income, and length of time in the community) are measured based on responses to relevant SCBC survey items. Total population in 2000 for each study city is drawn from U.S. Census Bureau data. Information on each city's electoral system (district versus at-large elections) was gleaned from a combination of city Web site searches and relevant newspaper article examinations for the most recent pre-2000 year in which a local election was held, supplemented where necessary by telephone calls to the office of the city clerk. A substantial majority of the study cities had either pure district systems (17 percent) or pure at-large systems (48 percent). However, seven cities (24 percent) had mixed systems, with at-large and district-elected members reasonably close to even in number. Hence, rather than the 0 = no and 1 = yes coding for district elections, cities with pure at-large systems were coded 0, those with mixed systems were coded 0.5 and those with pure district systems were coded 1.

The content analysis process that provided the featured independent variables was done in two stages. In the first stage, the author used the LexisNexis and America's Newspapers databases to cull all articles relevant to each city government's handling of neighborhoods and neighborhood issues in 1999. Stories on suburban city governments in the area and their activities relevant to neighborhoods in suburban jurisdictions were carefully excluded, as were articles including the word *neighborhood* that were not about neighborhood issues and city governments in the sense used here. In the second stage, the character of a city government's handling of or relationship with neighborhoods was coded as either positive (à la the empowerment thesis) or negative (à la the reactionary mobilization thesis).

Positive codes were given if a city government or city officials[1] were reported to be doing something favorable to the neighborhood—actions that could in principle empower neighborhood organizations or provide a positive stake in neighborhood collective action. Across the study cities, articles receiving a positive code show a huge variety of ways in which city government action might potentially empower neighborhood residents. They include stories of police officials trying to organize neighborhoods for block watch activities, zoning boards turning down proposed land-use changes explicitly because neighborhood associations have registered objections, city officials developing neighborhood parks or recreation centers that residents have been pushing for, and in a number of the cities, neighborhood organizations exercising powers of land-use review or neighborhood planning granted to them in a structured, citywide system of neighborhood-based participation.

Negative codes were given if a story indicated a threat to the neighborhood that a city government was ignoring, poor city service delivery performance for one or more neighborhoods, or a city government or city officials were reportedly doing something adverse to neighborhood interests and preferences. (See Appendix B for additional details on the content analysis methodology.) Articles receiving a negative code show a diversity of ways in which city governments might potentially mobilize residents who are reacting to nonresponsive, unhelpful local government. They include stories of city officials forging ahead with professional baseball park initiatives in the face of strong opposition from residents foreseeing noise, traffic congestion, and other externalities; residents complaining about inadequately tended-to problems of prostitution or drug use in their neighborhoods; city officials denying residents' demands for one-way traffic arrangements or other resident-favored solutions to traffic and parking issues; and residents complaining about chronic storm-sewer flooding.

Mixed, positive/negative coding, used sparingly, was given only if the story indicated (1) city government action that some neighborhood residents liked and other neighborhood residents disliked, (2) a city government had to step in to settle a matter of dispute in a divided neighborhood, or (3) government actions toward one or more neighborhoods had both positive and negative dimensions from neighborhood residents' point of view. Few stories received the mixed code—the average city only had six such articles during the year, while the average total number of neighborhood-affairs-related articles for a city was fifty-three.[2]

The counts of negatively and positively coded articles reflect that in each of the study cities, citizens are receiving both negative and positive messages about the city government's handling of and relationship with neighborhoods. Even in Birmingham and St. Paul, both among those that Berry, Portney, and Thomson (1993) identified as exemplars of neighborhood-based, participatory democracy, the content analysis revealed negative and positive articles about the city government's stance toward neighborhoods. We might therefore be tempted to combine these into a measure of the overall tenor of each city government's actions with respect to neighborhoods—perhaps by subtracting negative from positive articles. However, such a measure assumes that a negative message from a city government carries no more (and no less) weight than a positive message. Because the weight and the dynamics of positive messages and negative messages may not be the same, the analysis here includes measures of both positively and negatively coded messages. That is, separate variables for the counts of positively and negatively coded articles for each city, each adjusted for city population size, are included in the analysis.

Counts of the number of positive or negative articles for each city were standardized on the basis of population for two reasons. In principle, cities the size of Chicago have, because of their population, many more neighborhoods than cities the size of Charleston, West Virginia, and hence a more substantial base for generating stories about neighborhood activities. In addition, the daily newspapers serving large cities have many more pages available for local news reporting than do the daily newspapers serving smaller cities.

Results

Table 2.1 shows the results of testing for the impact of local governments' stance toward neighborhoods on neighborhood organization involvement, with controls both for individual-level characteristics typically expected to affect participation and for two contextual variables (presence of ward-based elections and city population size) representing other rival hypotheses. Consistent with expectations, participation in neighborhood organizations is significantly more likely among nonwhites, the better educated, those with higher incomes, older residents, those who attend church more often, and homeowners. Although gender and having school-age children may be important in some forms of civic engagement (see chapter 1), they are not significant predictors of involvement in neighborhood organizations. There is no evidence that either institutional arrangements for electing council members or city size matter. Residents of cities with ward-based elections for city council are not significantly more likely to participate in neighborhood organizations, and residents of larger cities are not less likely to participate.

Because Oliver's (2000) work on the importance of city size for citizen participation has had such an impact, a closer look at this factor at the

TABLE 2.1

City governments' stance toward neighborhoods and citizen participation in neighborhood associations

	ALL
Age	.015**
	(.009)
Income	.116**
	(.014)
Education	.111**
	(.015)
Race (0 = white, 1 = nonwhite)	.335**
	(.083)
Homeownership	.818**
	(.094)
Church attendance (higher values = less frequent)	−.085**
	(.020)
Time in community	-.008
	(.023)
Gender (1 = male, 2 = female)	.004
	(.051)
Have kids under age 17	.023
	(.052)
Ward-based elections	.263
	(.177)
City total population, 2000	.000
	(.000)
Positive articles (per thousand population)	−.985**
	(.329)
Negative articles (per thousand population)	-.010
	(.951)
Constant	−2.813**
	(.233)
N	8,317
Pseudo-R^2	.08

Source: Data from 2000 Social Capital Benchmark Community survey and author's original content analysis of relevant newspaper articles.

Note: The numbers presented are logistic regression coefficients (robust standard error) except where otherwise indicated.

$^{**}p < .01$

$^{*}p < .05$

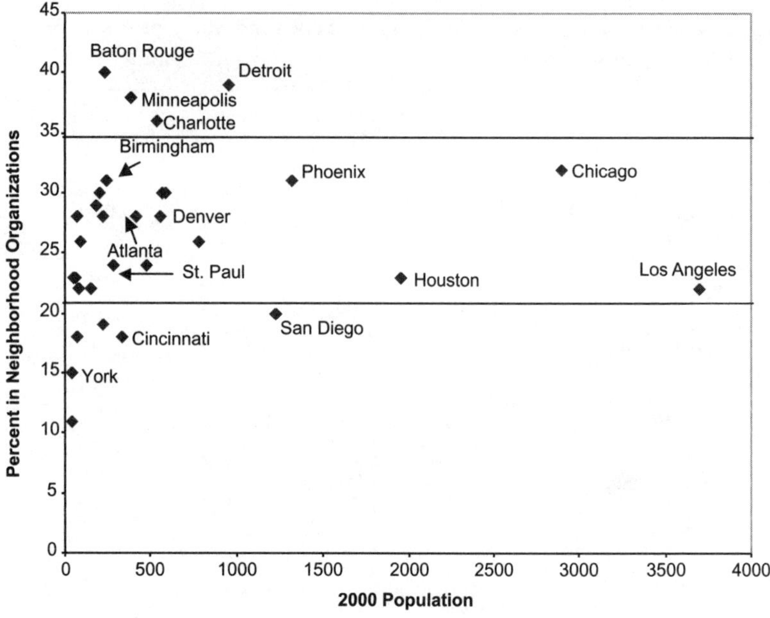

Figure 2.1. Neighborhood organization involvement by city size, SCBC core cities. Source: Data from 2000 Social Capital Benchmark Community survey and 2000 Census of Population.

aggregate, city level is in order. Figure 2.1, showing a scatterplot of the bivariate relationship between city size and rates of neighborhood association involvement, is presented as a follow-up to the results in Table 2.1. There is no hint in the scatterplot that the insignificant results for the population size variable are due to a curvilinear relationship between city size and magnitude of neighborhood organization involvement. The relatively small number of very large cities might seem to hinder a full picture of the size–participation relationship. However, in 2000 there were only nine cities in the United States with a city (not metropolitan area) population of one million or more. Five of those nine are represented here. All five are in the middling range with respect to citizen involvement in neighborhood organizations—not at the low end, as would be expected if city size dampens civic engagement. And for both the moderately sized and the smaller cities in Figure 2.1, there is no pattern of distinctively high or low levels of neighborhood organization participation.

Figure 2.1 also illustrates the importance of a broader sample of cities than the sample that has been the basis for most research on neighborhood association activity so far. One city that has a notable system of structured, citywide participation is Minneapolis (Fung and Fagatto 2006), which does show up in the cluster of highly participatory cities. However, Atlanta also has had (since 1974) a citywide participation structure of neighborhood planning units (NPUs) empowered to make recommendations on zoning, land use, and other matters and to participate in comprehensive planning (City of Atlanta 2010). The content analysis revealed that NPUs are still very active. Yet the level of neighborhood association involvement in Atlanta is unremarkable. Of the five cities in Berry, Portney, and Thomson's (1993) influential study of cities that are exemplars of neighborhood-based, participatory democracy, two are included here (Birmingham and St. Paul). Neither is in the cluster of highly participatory cities; instead, one anchors the top of the middling range of participation and the other is toward the bottom of the middling range. Clearly, if city governments can shape citizen participation at the neighborhood level, it must be via some mechanism beyond the formal, citywide structures featured in case study work on the subject.

Returning to the individual-level analysis in Table 2.1, for policy-centered theory, the featured variables are the measures of local governments' actions toward neighborhoods, drawn from content analysis coding of negative and positive articles about each study city's handling of its neighborhoods. The small and statistically insignificant coefficient for the negative articles variable provides little support for either the predominant view in policy-centered theory (i.e., more negative government action toward clients dampens participation) or the reactionary mobilization thesis. Given Schneider and Ingram's (1997) proposition that reactionary mobilization is primarily to be expected from the advantaged, Table 2.1's analysis was run separately for those with a relatively high income ($75,000 or more) and again for those with the highest income level ($100,000 or more) while removing income as a direct effect. The results (not shown) also failed to generate any evidence of reactionary mobilization.

However, the number of positive articles (per thousand population) about city governments' handling of neighborhoods is indeed an important predictor of involvement in neighborhood associations. But contrary to expectations, it is an *inverse* relationship. Net the effects of all other factors considered, individuals are more likely to participate in neighborhood organizations in cities where there is relatively little news of city government responsiveness to or empowerment of neighborhoods and are conversely less likely to participate in neighborhood organizations where a city government's stance toward neighborhoods is highly favorable.

This key result is glaringly inconsistent with much of policy-centered theory, which leads us to expect that high levels of favorable treatment to neighborhoods by city governments would *foster* participation in neighborhood organizations. Furthermore, the bottom line is not substantially different if we take account of the type of target population by focusing only on lower-income individuals who, according to Schneider and Ingram (1997), are the only ones likely to be mobilized by favorable policy. Such a subanalysis (results not shown) yields no significant evidence that the magnitude of city government responsiveness to neighborhoods heightens the neighborhood organization involvement of those in the lowest-income categories.

How might the unexpected results in Table 2.1 be understood? A key possibility is that what we are seeing is strong evidence for collective action theory. That is, if a city government is responding to concerns voiced by a small number of neighborhood "leaders" (e.g., directing resources to the solution of neighborhood problems or turning down proposed land-use developments that are hostile to existing neighborhood character), then for most residents collective benefits are to be had whether or not they are involved in the neighborhood association. As long as a handful of neighborhood leaders are willing to monitor the neighborhood and voice concerns to city officials and as long as those neighborhood leaders' concerns and preferences are reasonably consistent with those of their neighbors (Fung 2004, 106), the free-rider problem is solved. The more frequently the local newspaper provides stories of just such outcomes, the more reinforcement there is for free-rider behavior—hence the negative relationship between positive-toned articles and level of citizen participation. Local government responsiveness may therefore be empowering *neighborhood associations* (and the activists that keep them running) rather than empowering high levels of *resident participation* in neighborhood associations.[3]

This interpretation is consistent with small-*N* or single-city case study findings from cities that are making exceptional efforts to get citizens involved in neighborhood-level processes. For example, in their examination of the citywide participation program in Minneapolis, Fagatto and Fung (2006, 644–65) found limited participation of residents at the annual meetings that neighborhood associations held to discuss and ratify plans for how the neighborhood's share of public funds for improvement projects would be spent. Moreover, they found involvement in "actual planning and implementation processes are handled by a much smaller group of residents who are willing to commit the time and energy required to sustain the program." Noting the even more minimal involvement of all but a few residents, they wrote that Minneapolis' program "unintentionally creates 'offices' or 'positions' that limit participation in several ways—by drawing those with greater interests, [those with] more extensive capabilities, and those who are more comfortable participating under such circumstances." When interviewed, a number of residents indicated that they were intimidated from joining in a participation process "with a close-knit group of residents who have been engaged in local planning for years and speak an intimidating technical jargon."

The dynamic whereby some citizens have greater interests in and capabilities for participation than others and participate (or not) accordingly is presumably quite universal. The irony highlighted here is that in cities that provide a greater scope for meaningful neighborhood action, such a dynamic would be exacerbated. The technical knowledge and time demands of involvement, things that have the potential to discourage participation, are likely to be greater in places that have more substantial delegation of power to the neighborhood level. If those with the technical knowledge and time to serve as professional neighborhood activists or spokespersons do so, all the elements are in place for free-rider behavior to be maximized.

There is no way to directly test this interpretation of why local government responsiveness to neighborhoods dampens broad-based citizen participation in neighborhood associations. However, an indirect test is possible. The indirect test uses a question in the SCBC survey that asked each respondent, "How much can you trust people in your neighborhood?" (Possible responses were "a lot," "some," "only a little," and "not at all.") If government empowerment of neighborhood organizations diminishes the extent of neighborhood organization involvement by ordinary citizens because of free-rider dynamics, then that pattern should be most evident for individuals who are relatively trusting of their neighbors. By contrast, an important constraint on "free riding" on the efforts of neighborhood activists should be distrust of neighbors. For those who distrust people in their neighborhood, the prospect of letting a handful of activists from the neighborhood act on their behalf is presumably less appealing.

Table 2.2 shows strong evidence in support of the free-rider interpretation. Among those who trust their neighbors, city government empowerment of neighborhood organizations (measured via articles on positive responses to neighborhoods per thousand population) diminishes participation in neighborhood organizations—the same pattern that was observed for respondents overall. In stark contrast, among those who distrust their neighbors, the dampening effect of city government empowerment on individuals' involvement in neighborhood organizations disappears. The coefficient for positive articles is neither negatively signed nor statistically significant. Individuals who distrust their neighbors clearly are not disposed to assume that their interests will be served simply

TABLE 2.2

City governments' stance toward neighborhoods and citizen participation in neighborhood associations by level of trust in neighbors

	TRUST NEIGHBORS†	DISTRUST NEIGHBORS†
Age	.014**	.016**
	(.002)	(.004)
Income	.109**	.089*
	(.014)	(.040)
Education	.097**	.132**
	(.104)	(.046)
Race (0 = white, 1 = nonwhite)	.430**	.186
	(.086)	(.138)
Homeownership	.870**	.447**
	(.115)	(.146)
Church attendance (higher values = less frequent)	−.070**	−.150**
	(.024)	(.049)
Time in community	−.025	.032
	(.025)	(.049)

TABLE 2.2

City governments' stance toward neighborhoods and citizen participation in neighborhood associations by level of trust in neighbors—continued

	TRUST NEIGHBORS†	DISTRUST NEIGHBORS†
Gender (male = 1, female = 2)	.049	−.215
	(.050)	(.165)
Have kids under age 17	−.013	.213#
	(.046)	(.129)
Ward-based elections	.283	.179
	(.174)	(.274)
City total population, 2000	.000	−.000
	(.000)	(.000)
Positive articles (per thousand population)	−1.179**	.046
	(.381)	(.570)
Negative articles (per thousand population)	−.400	1.226
	(1.055)	(.803)
Constant	−2.740**	−2.564**
	(.260)	(.445)
N	6,464	1,661
Pseudo-R^2	.07	.09

Source: Data from 2000 Social Capital Benchmark Community survey and author's original content analysis of relevant newspaper articles.

Note: The numbers presented are logistic regression coefficients (robust standard error) except where otherwise indicated.

†Those who said they trust people in their neighborhood "a lot" or "some" are grouped into the trusting category; those who said they trust their neighbors "only a little" or "not at all" are grouped into the distrusting category.

**$p < .01$

*$p < .05$

#$p < .10$

because the government is responsive to their neighborhood organization and that hence their participation is not necessary. Although they do not show enhanced activation, the erasure of the participation-dampening effect that neighborhood empowerment has on more trusting residents is noteworthy, and it is consistent with the interpretation of government inadvertently exacerbating a free-rider problem.

A related interpretation of the initial findings in this chapter focuses on the possibility that by providing greater stakes to argue over, greater city government responsiveness to neighborhoods leads to more infighting, turf battles, and other unpleasantly divisive behaviors that deter the majority of residents from getting involved in neighborhood association activity. The content analysis process did uncover some evidence of such infighting, including one neighborhood that had two associations vying to claim the right to represent it. As noted previously, a mixed positive/negative code was given to this case, any story that reflected city government action that some neighborhood residents liked and other neighborhood residents disliked, or any story that indicated a city government had to step in to settle a matter of dispute in a divided neighborhood. Unfortunately, for the purpose at hand, the mixed code was also given if the story indicated government actions with both positive and negative dimensions, something that does not necessarily reflect a divided neighborhood. Although it is not therefore a perfect measure, the initial analysis was rerun with the addition of the variable mixed articles per thousand population. The results (not shown) are essentially the same for the control variables as in the original analysis, and the coefficient for the new divided neighborhood variable carries a negative sign—that is, cities in which there is more evidence of neighborhood-level infighting and divisiveness have lower levels of participation in neighborhood associations.

There is a modicum of evidence, then, to support two related interpretations of the finding that cities with greater levels of positive, empowerment-oriented action toward neighborhoods have lower levels of neighborhood association participation. A free-rider interpretation places the emphasis on the collective benefits that are typically at stake when cities respond to neighborhoods and the ways in which meaningful but demanding participatory processes reinforce the tendency for the vast majority to function as free riders while a tiny number of committed activists carry the ball. A divided neighborhood interpretation places the emphasis on the distaste many residents can be expected to have for the contention and acrimony that may be heightened when government responsiveness to neighborhood associations enhances the stakes. Both interpretations support the irony of the key initial finding: by being more "empowering" of neighborhood interests, city governments may inadvertently suppress broad-based participation in those neighborhoods.

Discussion

This project began with the goal of determining whether the policy-centered model of political participation, as developed in a strong line of empirical research on the impact of federal social programs on participation (Soss 1999; Mettler 2002; Mettler and Stonecash 2008), applies to city governments' programs or policy stances toward neighborhoods and the resultant levels of neighborhood association participation. The primary conclusion is that it does not. The policy-centered model hinges on governments' capacity to encourage participation, particularly among target populations that are usually low in power (Schneider and Ingram 1997), via program design elements that send empowering messages; the theory also stipulates that government policy can discourage participation, particularly among advantaged groups, via policy stances that are burdensome, negative, or threatening for advantaged groups. There are already hints in the literature that city governments' efforts to encourage widespread participation in neighborhood associations via structured, citywide arrangements for neighborhood involvement in governance have had surprisingly limited success in mobilizing large numbers of ordinary citizens (Thomas 1986; Berry, Portney, and Thomson 1993; Fagatto and Fung 2006). But even in cities without such structured arrangements, city governments might in principle have been expected to have the capacity to encourage neighborhood association involvement via ongoing actions and routine decisions that are responsive to neighborhood interests and concerns. Even more damaging to the policy-centered model is the finding here that this broader version of city governments' stance toward neighborhoods does not empower heightened participation either among residents generally or among traditionally low-power, dependent individuals in particular. Instead, it diminishes participation.

Is this because city governments' policy responses to neighborhoods are not as important as the major social programs featured in research on the policy-centered approach? Perhaps they do not send the kinds of empowering messages to neighborhood residents that the GI Bill sent to veterans or the Social Security retirement benefits program sends to the elderly. Or perhaps the stakes in the city government–neighborhood association connection are too trivial.

When property owners view development of a mammoth Rite Aid store in their neighborhood as a threat to both the use value and the exchange value of their property and city council members vote down the rezoning request specifically because of residents' concerns, the message of being an important part of the polity is surely as clear as it is when retirees are provided with monthly Social Security checks—possibly even more so, because Social Security benefits are widely viewed as something that the individual has earned through contributions. Or consider the message to residents of a blighted neighborhood when the mayor announces a multi-million-dollar redevelopment project for the area, including both private and public funding and including a promise that the content and character of the redevelopment plan will come from a participatory process, with area residents involved every step of the way. Even the most jaded residents cannot miss that this is an empowering message, with at least the possibility that participation would be worthwhile. These examples from Syracuse, New York, and Atlanta, Georgia, respectively, exemplify the numerous actions across the study cities involving substantial stakes for residents—actions that send messages that in principle could be viewed as encouraging participation. That cities engaging in relatively more of these actions engender lower levels of participation in neighborhood associations is a puzzle not likely to be solved by reference to the triviality of city governments' actions with respect to neighborhoods or a lack of participation-encouraging content to those stories.

Rather, what perhaps best distinguishes the positive actions of city governments in this analysis from deserving-messaged programs such as Social Security and the GI Bill is the collective nature of the benefits that are provided by a city government to neighborhood residents. Admittedly, Social Security recipients and those newly receiving GI Bill benefits can be thought of as members of a collective group of stakeholders. If it is needed, advocacy to sustain those benefits can be said to be in the collective interest of all such stakeholders, and the free-rider phenomenon might manifest there. But Social Security checks and GI Bill benefits are delivered *to individuals.* By contrast, most of the benefits that a city government provides for neighborhood residents are delivered *to neighborhoods.* The rules about Social Security and veterans' benefits are applied to individuals, the process of applying for such benefits is handled case by case, and people going through the process learn something about how government works and how they, as individuals, are viewed by government officials. By contrast, city governments' decisions to site parks in various city neighborhoods, refuse rezonings for land uses out of character with relevant neighborhoods in anticipation of residents' objections, or change the deployment of law enforcement resources in response to neighborhood-level needs and preferences are actions vis-à-vis spatial units representing the collective interests of residents. Because of this essential difference between key federal social programs that have been studied under the rubric of policy-centered interpretation and city government policies toward neighborhoods, we should perhaps not be surprised that city governments' efforts to empower neighborhoods have been swamped by the free-rider problem.

The results of this analysis create an ironic counterpoint to the substantial literature espousing various forms of city government-sponsored empowerment of neighborhood organizations, including collaborative partnerships (Kathi and Cooper 2005), empowered participation (Fung 2004), and "collaborative democratic design" (Sirianni 2007). The unexpected findings here do not, however, mean that neighborhood-responsive city government and city-sponsored arrangements for citizen participation at the neighborhood level are adverse to the well-being of residents or that city governments should be discouraged from neighborhood empowerment strategies. They simply mean that such strategies yield lower levels of participation than would be seen if residents had to fight for the ear of a city government; consequently, the implementation of empowerment is left in the hands of quite small groups of committed activists.

Providing that those activists represent their neighborhoods well, such an arrangement can yield considerable benefits for the free riders. The case study literature offers some criticisms on this front, suggesting that neighborhood empowerment strategies benefit white homeowners and are systematically biased against tenants, minorities, and the poor (Fagatto and Fung 2006; Goetz and Sidney 2008). This project finds that, net the effects of other explanatory variables, city governments' empowerment of neighborhoods encourages neighborhood organization involvement by nonwhites, suggesting that at least on the participation side there is, if anything, bias toward minority group interests. However, the research reported here does not really address the specific content of government responsiveness to neighborhoods and whether it systematically favors some neighborhood interests over others. What it does tell us is that the successful functioning of empowered neighborhoods is far from the broad-based, face-to-face democracy that some proponents may have envisioned. It emphasizes a conclusion that Berry, Portney, and Thomson (1993, 97) were forced to make about the cities that they chose as exemplars of participatory democracy:

> But face-to-face democracy can be intimidating. Even though these systems of citizen participation are centered in the neighborhood, where people may know many other participants, the give-and-take of small group politics remains an unattractive way to spend an evening for the vast majority of people.

And when a local government visibly provides neighborhood residents with the responsiveness they seek without requiring them to be personally involved, these results suggest that most residents simply free ride on the efforts of those few who are willing to be involved.

3

Community Policing

A Reform Policy for Police Responsiveness

Chapter 2 showed that local government responsiveness to neighborhoods in a broad sense can have unintended, demobilizing effects on citizen involvement with neighborhood associations. In that chapter, we saw how government responsiveness could stem from a variety of programs, policies, or actions, including the creation of neighborhood-level governance structures with powers to represent neighborhood interests, procedural requirements that give the neighborhood official input on land-use issues, or even a pattern of receptivity to neighborhood requests and complaints across an array of routine matters.

This chapter focuses on community policing—a particular program that, at least in theory, entails focused responsiveness to neighborhoods by one of the most salient agencies in city government. The program is of particular interest for the application of policy-centered theory because it sends powerful but somewhat mixed messages to differing subsets of the target population. In contrast with social welfare policy, which sends different messages to different target populations via their experience with different programs—some means tested and some not, all residents of an area with community policing in some sense experience the same program. However, as this chapter shows, they may not have *the same experience* with that program. Indeed, the "same" community policing program can send different messages to different kinds of residents.

Community policing, or what is sometimes called community-oriented policing services (COPS) is a multifaceted package of police reforms that swept the nation's municipal police forces in the 1990s. It is still an influential programmatic approach in many police departments. In its most quintessential form, community policing involves three elements: problem solving, citizen involvement, and decentralization (Skogan 2006).

The problem-solving element has to do with the importance that COPS attaches to proactive crime prevention, as contrasted with the dominant focus on law enforcement activity in traditional policing. The work of Wilson and Kelling (1982) on the theory of "broken windows" convinced early proponents of community policing that crime problems plaguing urban neighborhoods are shaped by problems such as vacant houses, graffiti, and vandalism that signify a breakdown of informal social control in the neighborhood. If left unresolved, such phenomena provide a visual signal that the neighborhood is not controlled by law-abiding forces, thereby encouraging criminal elements while allowing law-abiding residents to become immobilized by fear. Community policing therefore emphasizes an order-maintenance role for police—that is, police efforts to solve problems such as vacant houses, graffiti, litter, or unsupervised youth loitering on street corners. The assumption is that these order-maintenance actions are as important for crime prevention as is the deterrent effect of arresting individuals after crimes have been committed (Xu, Fiedler, and Flaming 2005).

The citizen involvement element of community policing points to the need for enhanced police–community relationships at the neighborhood level so that order-maintenance needs are appropriately identified and prioritized. Community policing is based on the philosophy that neighborhood residents are in a crucial position to be the "eyes and ears" of police departments—not only by reporting crime but also by providing information on neighborhood problems that can lead to crime. In addition, community policing emphasizes the need for problem-solving partnerships between citizens and police—partnerships that reestablish social order in the neighborhood. In this regard, community policing has been characterized as a vehicle for community building or social capital formation (Scott 2002).

The decentralization feature of community policing reinforces the first two elements by acknowledging the new role demands that problem solving and citizen involvement place on the street-level police officer within the police department. Only if street-level police officers have the incentives, training, and flexibility to follow through on community-oriented, crime prevention–focused activities can problem solving and partnerships with the community be realized.

An array of specific policing practices, tactics, and programmatic commitments have been introduced in the name of community policing. Early research on the subject documented some of this variety. Some cities, such as Las Vegas, had a decentralized, special unit that could send "teams of officers to police area commands throughout the city who have the latitude to engage in proactive activities to address specific community problems" (Weisel and Eck 1994, 59); other cities, such as Savannah, featured a more universal application, with nearly all police officers receiving formal training in community- and problem-oriented policing (60). The permanent (i.e., nonrotating) assignment of at least some patrol officers to neighborhood-sized "beats" has been a widely recognized component of community policing. The expectation is that such an assignment allows police officers to get to know neighborhood residents and business owners and maximizes the potential for interaction between residents and police. As a result, the community's priorities can be conveyed to police and residents can be encouraged to participate in problem-solving efforts, such as antitheft property marking campaigns or block watch activities. Some relatively old-time practices such as foot patrol, which brings police officers in closer contact with those they serve, have been reintroduced and have quickly become iconic examples of community policing (Zhao, Lovrich, and Thurman 1999, 75).

With respect to mechanisms for citizen involvement, neighborhood-level meetings bringing together neighborhood residents and police officials assigned to the neighborhood have been a common manifestation of community policing. For example, in Chicago, the monthly, neighborhood (i.e., police "beat") meetings of residents, police, and other city officials is, according to Skogan (2006, 11), the "most important mechanism for building and sustaining close relationships between police and the public." The police department puts a great deal of effort into publicizing the meetings and encouraging a good turnout. Other departments have obtained citizen input via the use of citizen surveys. But Skogan also makes clear that citizen involvement means more than this and that the form citizen involvement takes is quite varied across cities (57). Citizen involvement can include one or more of the following broad roles: learning about police via police educational programs for citizens; assisting police through ordinary reporting of crime and suspicious circumstances; "coproduction of safety" via participation in block watch, property marking, or other service delivery programs; and representation of the community via work on boards or committees that define and prioritize problems and solutions (57).

Community policing thus can be reflected in a variety of specific practices and tactics, and departments claiming to have implemented community policing may have somewhat different mixes of programmatic elements. Despite some debate about how a department's commitment to community policing should be measured (Maguire and Mastrofski 2000), it is clear that community policing in some form has become widespread in the United States. In their assessment of the extent to which community policing had been institutionalized by the second half of the 1990s, Zhao, Lovrich, and Thurman (1999, 80) identified twelve specific programs or practices that are "typical community policing practices," based on discussions in the research literature. These include (1) fixed (i.e., nonrotational) assignment of officers to neighborhood beats; (2) use of storefront stations, which provide a more accessible, neighborhood-level institutional presence; (3) use of special task units for solving problems in target areas; (4) deployment of officers on foot, bike, or horse patrol; (5) use of unpaid, civilian volunteers; (6) neighborhood block watch programs; (7) business watch programs; (8) victim contact programs; (9) use of community newsletters; (10) block meetings between the agency and the community participants; (11) crime education for the public; and (12) citizen surveys to keep police informed about local problems. In their panel study of 281 police departments nationwide, Zhao, Lovrich, and Thurman (1999) found the average number of these community policing elements implemented by surveyed departments increased from 8.9 in 1993 to 9.72 in 1996. Six of the elements (fixed neighborhood assignment of officers, special problem-solving units, foot/bike/horse patrol, neighborhood block watch, police–community block meetings, and crime education) were implemented by 90 percent or more of the departments. Zhao and colleagues attributed this widespread acceptance and adoption of community policing to the "strong endorsement of community policing by the Clinton administration" and the passage of the Violent Crime Control and Law Enforcement Act of 1994, which committed federal funding support for the hiring of one hundred thousand new police officers in departments willing to commit to using the new resources to advance community policing (He, Zhao, and Lovrich 2005, 295–96; Zhao, Lovrich, and Thurman 1999, 75).

There is, however, another perspective on community policing—one that points to two different *styles* that community policing can take. Although the mix of specific tactics that police departments use (foot patrol, storefront offices, citizen surveys, etc.) can add up to somewhat different versions of community policing, Terrill and Mastrofski (2004) argued that the truly watershed difference in versions of community policing has to do with the extent to which police use of coercion is given a central role. In what they call the partnership model, community policing emphasizes police working with the community to "solve long-term community problems . . . by working on the underlying causes of those problems using situational crime prevention . . . and other methods that focus attention on activities far removed from the actual application of the use of force." All tools of community policing are important here because of their potential to yield "preventive interventions" that should "make force unnecessary in many situations" (111). For example, if consultation with neighborhood residents and businesses shows that crime perpetrated by juveniles is a problem and that the neighborhood's view of problem solving emphasizes the development of constructive, alternative activities for juveniles, officers in the partnership model of community policing would work with both residents and other city agencies to develop summer basketball leagues and other recreational and job opportunities for youths.

By contrast, the version of community policing that is most directly related to Wilson and Kelling's (1982) broken-windows theory entails "aggressive order-maintenance practice." This version features police use of high-profile, coercive action against "public drunks, panhandlers, rowdy juveniles, prostitutes, and other street people" (Terrill and Mastrofski 2004, 112). In this version of community policing, partnering with neighborhood residents to identify programs to help prevent juvenile street crime would be less important than aggressive police intervention targeting rowdy street behavior by juveniles, even if the behavior does not violate the law—only neighborhood norms of order. In a comparative study of Indianapolis, Indiana, which adopted a broken-windows version of community policing in the 1990s, and St. Petersburg, Florida, which adopted a "community partnership" version, Terrill and Mastrofski (2004, 125) found the differing versions have implications for observed levels of police coercion. Direct observation of police–citizen encounters showed that in Indianapolis, the city with the broken-windows version of community policing, individuals stopped by police officers were about 20 percent more likely to be the subject of verbal coercion or physical restraint and 73 percent more likely to be subjected to physical coercion in the form of takedown maneuvers, strikes to the body, or other pain compliance techniques than were individuals in St. Petersburg.

Unfortunately, no aggregate data sources allow study, across a broader array of cities, of the consequences of this distinction in styles of community policing. More intensive case study work like that conducted in Indianapolis and St. Petersburg by Terrill and Mastrofski (2004) is required for that. Instead, this chapter begins with an assessment of whether the extent of a city's community policing commitment, measured via the presence of various program elements, has consequences for civic engagement. Combining information on community policing from the Bureau of Justice Statistics's (1999) Law Enforcement Management and Administrative Statistics (LEMAS) survey and from Putnam's (2000) Social Capital Benchmark Community (SCBC) survey that was used in chapter 2 makes it possible to test hypotheses about whether the scope of community policing either mobilizes or demobilizes individuals for relevant forms of civic engagement. The second part of the chapter is a case study tracing the history of Seattle's experience with community policing. The case study is motivated both by insights from Terrill and Mastrofski's (2004) argument about differing versions of community policing and by questions about the interaction of multiple, police-related programs. The case study helps with interpretation of several key findings from the quantitative analyses. In particular, the case study provides historical context and implementation details that reveal how and why community policing either fails to generate policy feedback effects or yields participation-dampening effects that are the opposite of social capital building.

Impacts of Community Policing: Policy-Centered Hypotheses

Like welfare, Social Security, and other social programs that are the focus of policy-centered research, community policing can be theorized to send messages to its target population about government officials' expectations and likely receptivity to them and hence to yield feedback effects that shape citizen participation. So what messages does a community policing program send to residents of a community? What forms of participation should be shaped by this policy feedback, and in what direction? A key theme of this chapter is acknowledgment that the message of community policing is likely to vary, based not only on what the police department is doing under the community policing rubric but also on *the character of the target population* (i.e., who in the community is on the receiving end of the message) and the nature of that target population's ongoing relationship with police. The following section begins with a theoretical overview focusing on the impacts that would be predicted from consideration of policy design elements alone. It is followed by a discussion of how expectations about a community policing program's impact are modified when we consider the interaction of program design and type of target population, as Schneider and Ingram (1997) suggested.

Hypothesized Impacts of Community Policing

Given its program design elements and the implicit messages entailed by those design elements, community policing is generally intended to *mobilize civic engagement.* Community policing is based on the theory that neighborhood-level social disorganization is the key cause of crime problems and government intervention can reverse the crime problem through problem-solving interventions designed in collaboration with neighborhood residents. For this to work, community policing involves features that maximize police accessibility and responsiveness to neighborhood residents. In theory, this should send encouraging messages that empower citizen engagement.

Several specific forms of citizen involvement should be enhanced under this model. To the extent that community policing is neighborhood based and frequently involves the use of neighborhood organizations as the forum for bringing police and neighborhood residents together, we might expect community policing to enhance residents' involvement in neighborhood organizations. More generally, community policing relies on meetings between police and various groups, in addition to neighborhood associations, that may be defined as stakeholders in the process of ameliorating social disorganization. Cities whose police department implements stronger forms of community policing may thus be hypothesized to positively influence the propensity of residents to *attend public meetings.* Finally, because community policing involves police efforts to encourage resident involvement in crime prevention projects of various sorts, we hypothesize that community policing would increase residents' propensity to *work on community projects.*

Although they should be the obvious focus from a policy feedback perspective, existing research on the impact of community policing has not emphasized these participatory outcomes, even though the success of community policing hinges on citizen participation. Instead, influenced by what Thacher (2004) called the "strong causal reasoning" that drives community policing reform, research often focuses on whether the implementation of community policing contributes to crime reduction—with results that are mixed (Kerley and Benson 2000, 49; MacDonald 2002; Zhao, Scheider, and Thurman 2002). The few, typically single-city case studies that focus on the impact of community policing on civic engagement tend to yield showings of negligible mobilization of citizens. If we focus on the most direct way in which community policing could be theorized to mobilize citizen participation (i.e., by at least encouraging participation in community policing meetings), case study evidence suggests disappointing results. For example, after noting the importance of neighborhood meetings with police in Chicago's version of community policing, Skogan (2004, 59) reported that in the late 1990s, "a good meeting by Chicago standards draws about 30 residents," or about 0.4 percent of the adult population of the neighborhood-based police assignment zone. Viewed from another perspective, Chicago's COPS program has generated somewhat more participation. Based on survey data, Skogan (2006, 119) reported that about 14 percent of all Chicagoans attended at least one such meeting annually; among those who attended, the average person went to between three and four such meetings. These participation results are nevertheless modest given that community safety is nearly always a high-priority issue for urban residents and given that the city of Chicago was an early and high-profile adopter of community policing.[1]

Although evaluations of the impact of community policing tend to ignore civic engagement, some research has focused on other phenomena in the complex chain of causal links that presumably lead from community policing inputs to crime reduction. One of these intervening phenomena is the citizenry's attitude toward police. Recent studies provide limited and mixed evidence that community policing enhances *trust in police* (Marschall and Shah 2007; Sharp and Johnson 2009). However, a summary of community policing studies done before 2000 shows that evaluations of individual cities' community policing programs were likely to show improvement in other attitudes toward police, such as satisfaction with their performance (Kerley and Benson 2000, 49). Similarly, Lyons (1999, 50) noted that, although evaluation studies were showing little or no impact on crime, fear of crime, or neighborhood disorder problems, such studies revealed "a positive impact on citizen attitudes toward the police." Hence, he suggested "that this reform, although mobilizing a rhetoric of democratic responsiveness to community concerns, is more accurately described as responsive to the needs of the police bureaucracy to manage public opinion" (50–51).

Despite this cynical view that community policing is motivated by the police department's need for better public relations, the possibility that community policing can shape residents' attitudes toward police is important from a policy feedback perspective. In policy-centered theory, program effects on individuals' views of government are, after all, a key mechanism for subsequent mobilization or demobilization. Trust may be the most important attitude toward government in this regard, as evidenced by a long line of scholarship on the connection between eroding trust and declining political participation in the United States. Hence, in addition to effects on neighborhood association involvement, attendance at group meetings, and work on community projects, the effects of community policing on individuals' trust in police are assessed in this chapter.

The final outcomes of community policing to be assessed here involve the *community-building* or *social capital–formation* role of community policing. Scholars of community policing are not equally comfortable with the notion that a police program can build community or enhance social capital (Correia 2000; Pino 2001), and empirical research examining such effects has yielded limited and mixed evidence that community policing has community-building effects (Duffee, Fluellen, and Renauer 1999; Kerley and Benson 2000; Scott 2002). But much of the rhetoric and logic behind the community policing reform program—most notably the idea of police developing problem-solving partnerships with residents to empower the reestablishment of informal order maintenance—points to a community-building role for this program. For this reason, this chapter also hypothesizes a community-building or social capital impact.

In sum, both rhetoric surrounding community policing and policy design elements of the program suggest that it should mobilize citizen involvement in neighborhood associations, attendance at public meetings, and involvement in community projects, as well as enhance trust in police and build social capital at the neighborhood level. The research on these hypothesized effects of community policing is limited in two respects. Community policing research has been dominated by a search for crime reduction impacts rather than a focus on civic engagement and social capital effects. The studies that do investigate the latter are primarily case studies that do not allow for comparison across numerous cities with differing commitments to community policing. All too frequently, the level of community policing is not measured in a way that is truly independent of the impact measures or even of a prior time period. A more systematic assessment of the impacts of community policing across multiple cities is therefore needed, even though the limited studies that exist have yielded scant evidence for the hypothesized results of community policing. That is the task of the initial analyses in this chapter.

Community Policing's Hypothesized Impacts Revisited: Who Is "the Community"? What Is the Target Population?

Considered in isolation, the policy design elements of community policing point to policy feedback effects such as enhanced trust in police, greater social capital, and residents mobilized for involvement in the specific forms of civic engagement outlined previously. However, for two reasons, policy-centered theory also requires that we clarify the "target" of this program. First, Schneider and Ingram's (1997) policy design framework emphasized that a given type of policy design has different effects depending on the type of target population. To the extent that community policing is a positive, benefit-providing program, their formulation suggested that it should be expected to have the trust-enhancing, social capital–building, and civic engagement–empowering impacts outlined previously when a dependent population is the target. In the context of community policing, a dependent target population evokes residents of impoverished neighborhoods beset by substantial crime and order-maintenance problems. By contrast, Schneider and Ingram's theorizing suggests community policing has little effect on already-advantaged groups, such as the residents of better-off neighborhoods where serious crime is low and informal mechanisms for order maintenance are already present.

In the context of community policing, is there the equivalent of Schneider and Ingram's (1997) category of "deviant" target populations? Answering this deals with the second reason our hypotheses about program impact take into account the various targets of this program. Getting specific about the "community" in community policing and who constitutes a quite different kind of target leads us to acknowledge that this program is likely to send different messages to different elements, even within the same neighborhood. In particular, relatively powerless or marginalized elements of the community, such as street prostitutes, unemployed young males, and racial minority group members, may hear the message of community policing as a message of a partnership to which they are not invited—perhaps even a call to arms against them in cities taking a broken-windows approach to community policing. In short, there is a deviant target population that is relevant here. Because of the order-maintenance emphasis of community policing, it is not necessarily limited to actual criminals but also includes a variety of marginalized elements of the community. Rather than allocating benefits, community policing allocates burdens to this target population and sends them disempowering messages. In Schneider and Ingram's framework, no policy feedback consequences would be observed for this target population except for the maintenance of already-low levels of civic engagement.[2]

A number of analysts have emphasized that community policing sends "competing messages" (Lyons 1999, 2) to different residents of the community. Recalling that the New York City Police Department was a "poster child for community policing" at the time of a horrendous beating of Haitian immigrant Abner Louima by its officers, Lyons argues that the officers' action in the name of the department's version of community policing (which emphasized zero tolerance of behaviors that challenge the community's sense of order) sent a "fear inducing message" not only to Louima but also to "other similarly power-poor members of New York communities . . . [that] you are not part of the community we are partnering with when we tell our stories about community policing" (2–3).

Similarly, Skogan's (1994, 178–79) assessment of the initial years of community policing in Houston depicted a place where a number of community policing activities were conducted in a way that "favored the interests of racially dominant groups and established interests in the community." Existing community organizations were relied on to get the word out about activities at the community substation, to decide who would participate in police ride-alongs and to attend meetings with the district commander. As a result, the community policing program in Houston "worked well" for those active in some community organizations, "but less affluent area residents did not hear about the programs and did not participate in them." Worse still, the community organizing team held its organizing meetings "in parts of the target area dominated by white residents owning single-family homes. The largely black residents of large rental buildings in the area were quickly identified as the source of problems in the community and became the targets of their activities." Not surprisingly, the positive effects of community policing in both target areas of Houston "were confined to whites and home owners" (179).

Scott's (2002) Indianapolis study also provided evidence that this sort of nonrepresentative participation in the community policing partnership has corrosive impacts on the very outcomes that community policing is supposed to enhance. He identified neighborhoods with majority black populations that also had neighborhood association leaders reporting a lot of difficulty in obtaining participation by black residents. This measure of nonrepresentative participation was a strong predictor of diminished levels of social capital. He concluded, "Lower levels of social capital may be produced by the conflict and distrust that exist within neighborhoods characterized by this form of limited participation" (160).

Given this pattern of case study results, as well as the retuning of hypothesized impacts that occurs when type of target population is considered, this chapter's initial analyses of the overall impacts of community policing are reassessed with an eye to target group differences. Some target groups that might be given a message of marginalization by community policing (e.g., teenage males and street prostitutes) cannot be examined with the survey data at hand. At a minimum, however, racial differences in the impact of community policing are assessed. The case study of Seattle that follows provides additional detail showing how the impacts of community policing vary based on its differing target populations.

Data Sources and Measurement Issues

The dependent variables for this analysis are drawn from Putnam's (2000) SCBC survey data set. Fortunately, that survey contains individual items measuring each of the relevant forms of civic engagement: participation in a neighborhood association in the past year (1 = yes, 0 = no), work on a community project in the past year (1 = yes, 0 = no), and frequency of attendance at a public meeting discussing school or town affairs (1 through highest recoded to 1 = yes, 0 = did not attend). The survey also contains a usable question about trust in police—"How much can you trust the police in your local community?" (1 = a lot, 2 = some, 3 = only a little, 4 = not at all). Finally, two questions that can serve as measures of neighborhood-level social capital are available from the survey. One is a question asking how often the respondent talks with or visits immediate neighbors (from 1 = never to 7 = just about every day).[3] Because of its relevance as an attitudinal measure of community social capital, the measure of trust in neighbors—paralleling the trust measure for police—is also used.

Measuring the extent to which community policing is practiced in each of the communities from which SCBC survey respondents are drawn[4] is a more challenging task, because community policing is based on principles of proactive problem solving, citizen involvement, and decentralization and because an array of specific practices or program elements have been introduced under the banner of this reform idea (Maguire and Mastrofski 2000). This paper takes an approach like that of Zhao, Lovrich, and Thurman (1999, 80), who identified specific activities or practices typical of community policing in 1999 based on discussions in the research literature. The featured explanatory variables here are two indices of the extent to which each city's police department practiced community policing in 1999, the year before the administration of the SCBC surveys in each community. The indices, based on data from the 1999 LEMAS survey are as follows.

The first index (CommPol policies) is a count of positive responses on a ten-item battery of policies asked about in the special section of the LEMAS survey devoted to community policing. These are questions on whether or not the police department (1) trained citizens in community policing; (2) gave patrol officers responsibility for specific geographic areas or beats; (3) assigned detectives to cases based on geographic areas or beats; (4) actively encouraged patrol officers to engage in problem-solving projects on their beats; (5) included collaborative problem-solving projects in the evaluation criteria of patrol officers; (6) formed problem-solving partnerships with community groups, municipal agencies, or others through specialized contracts or written agreements; (7) had any neighborhood-level substations (fixed or mobile); (8) used foot or bike patrol for routine patrol operations; (9) used surveys of the citizenry; and (10) provided community policing training for at least some in-service sworn officers.

The second index (CommPol meetings) is a count of the number of types of community groups with whom police officers had regular meetings. The groups asked about include advocacy groups, business groups, domestic violence prevention groups, local public agencies, neighborhood associations, religious groups, school groups, senior citizen groups, tenants' associations, and youth service organizations. The 1999 LEMAS data set shows the majority of municipal police departments had regular meetings with school groups (71.6 percent), neighborhood associations (58.9 percent), and business groups (52.5 percent) and meetings with senior citizen groups and domestic violence prevention groups are also quite common (49 percent and 46 percent, respectively). However, police departments are noticeably less likely to have regular meetings with advocacy groups (37 percent) or tenants' associations (27 percent).

For all municipal police departments reporting in the LEMAS survey in 1999, there is substantial variation on each of the indices of community policing practice. Table 3.1 reveals this variation. It also shows that police departments in somewhat larger cities score higher on both indices and exhibit less variation on them. Police departments in the study cities used here, most of which have a population of at least one hundred thousand, are similar (at least with respect to community policing practices) to all police departments in cities with a population of at least one hundred thousand.

TABLE 3.1

Two measures of community policing: means (and standard deviations) for municipal police departments

	MUNICIPAL POLICE DEPARTMENTS		
	ALL	>100K POPULATION CITY	STUDY CITIES
Index of			
CommPol policies	4.5	7.5	7.8
	(2.7)	(1.9)	(1.7)
CommPol meetings	4.8	8.1	8.9
	(3.3)	(2.4)	(2.0)
N	3,246	211	27

Source: Data from 1999 Law Enforcement Management and Administration Survey.

Results: Modeling the Impacts of Community Policing

Impacts on Civic Engagement

The initial analysis focuses on the extent to which community policing affects the mobilization of residents overall for three relevant forms of civic engagement: (1) participate in a neighborhood association, (2) work on a community project, and (3) attend a public meeting. Table 3.2 shows the results of modeling each form of civic engagement using the two measures of community policing, as well as the familiar suite of individual-level attributes and contextual controls used in the previous chapter.

In addition to those controls, we should consider the possibility that cities using community policing are more broadly committed to decentralized government and citizen empowerment. If so, any observed link between community policing and civic engagement may be spurious—that is, resulting from the other neighborhood-responsiveness programs of the city rather than from COPS per se. This suggests that a control for generalized neighborhood responsiveness should be included. He, Zhao, and Lovrich's (2005) three-wave panel study of 281 municipalities' community policing programs in 1993, 1996, and 2000 suggests that this concern about a spurious relationship may not be warranted. Their measures of broader city commitment to community mobilization are not significantly linked with community policing in multivariate analysis. That result suggests that a broader city policy orientation toward encouraging of citizen involvement is not a lurking third variable that explains both use of community policing and civic engagement outcomes. Just to be sure, however, the analyses presented later include a control for citizen empowerment: the measure of positive articles about city governments and neighborhoods introduced in chapter 2.

The results in Table 3.2 suggest (1) neighborhood association involvement is a distinctly different phenomenon from the other two forms of civic engagement and (2) the impact of community policing is limited and primarily evident with respect to neighborhood association involvement but, most important, (3) community policing has, if anything, a *dampening* effect on neighborhood association involvement—the opposite of what the program in theory should yield.

As expected and consistent with the results in chapter 2, participation in neighborhood associations is higher among older, better-educated, and higher-income people; homeowners; frequent church attendees; and blacks. Gender, having children at home, and length of time in the community are

TABLE 3.2

Community policing and other explanations of three forms of civic engagement

	NEIGHBORHOOD ASSOCIATION	COMMUNITY PROJECT	PUBLIC MEETING
Individual attributes			
Age	.014 (.002)**	−.008 (.001)**	−.004 (.002)*
Education	.117 (.017)**	.267 (.022)**	.224 (.015)**
Income	.116 (.017)**	.109 (.015)**	.118 (.013)**
Homeownership	.817 (.107)**	.119 (.069)#	.234 (.060)**
Church attendance (higher values = less frequent)	−.081 (.023)**	−.188 (.020)**	−.145 (.020)**
Time in community	−.007 (.022)	.103 (.023)**	.072 (.020)**
Gender	.015 (.049)	.182 (.048)**	.025 (.060)
Have kids under age 17	.045 (.059)	.091 (.054)#	.999 (.053)**
Race (1 = white, 2 = black)	.483 (.087)**	.093 (.062)	.342 (.085)**
Contextual controls			
Positive articles (per thousand population)	−.952 (.362)**	−.280 (.264)	.244 (.313)
Ward-based elections	.176 (.191)	−.216 (.087)*	−.109 (.092)
City total population, 2000	.000 (.000)	−.000 (.000)	−.000 (.000)
Community policing context			
CommPol meetings	−.060 (.027)*	−.030 (.017)#	.009 (.018)
CommPol policies	.021 (.039)	.034 (.018)	.006 (.021)
Constant	−2.982 (.348)**	−1.467 (.211)*	−2.231 (.251)**
N	7,068	7,067	7,072
Pseudo-R^2	.08	.08	.10

Source: Data from 1999 Law Enforcement Management and Administration Survey, 2000 Social Capital Benchmark Community survey, and author's original content analysis of relevant newspaper articles.

Note: The numbers presented are ordered logistic regression coefficients (clustered robust standard error) except where otherwise indicated.

**$p < .01$

*$p < .05$

#$p < .10$

not significant predictors. Some of these individual attributes play the same role in explaining the other two forms of participation. However, there are differences consistent with the conclusion that neighborhood association involvement is distinct from these other forms of participation. For example, younger people and individuals with school-age children are more likely to have worked on a community project and to have attended a public meeting. Parental involvement in school-related activity appears to be heavily manifested in these latter two forms of civic engagement, not surprising given that the questionnaire item for the latter referred to public meetings "discussing school or town affairs"—thus cuing respondents toward school-related activity in a way that other questions did not.

Other elements of the results in Table 3.2 suggest that neighborhood association involvement differs from work on community projects or attendance at public meetings in another way—the latter two may entail participation that is broader based than the neighborhood. Resident involvement with community projects is more prevalent in cities that are *less* reliant on ward-based representation. Stated another way, where ward-based elections channel interest aggregation to the neighborhood level, citizens are less likely to be mobilized for community project involvement. Finally, the control for overall city government responsiveness to neighborhoods (positive articles per thousand population) is significant and negative when neighborhood association involvement is at issue, as it was in chapter 2. However, this control variable is not a significant predictor of working on a community project or attending public meetings—again suggesting that the not-necessarily-neighborhood-specific character of these latter two forms of participation make them distinctively different from neighborhood association involvement.

Differences in the three forms of civic engagement are important to keep in mind in considering the featured variables in Table 3.2: those involving community policing. The results yield scant evidence that community policing has an impact on residents' civic engagement, and that impact is primarily confined to neighborhood association involvement (though there are borderline significant results with respect to working on community projects). Furthermore, impact is seen with only one of the measures of community policing practice: the index of types of groups with which police hold regular meetings. The emergence of significant results for the community policing meetings index, even with a control for overall responsiveness, should allay concerns that the observed relationships between this aspect of community policing and participation outcomes is an artifact of overall responsiveness of the city to neighborhoods. But perhaps the most important result is the *sign* of the significant and near-significant coefficients for community policing meetings. The higher the city's score on police holding community outreach meetings with various types of groups, the *less* likely residents are to participate in neighborhood associations or to work on community projects. Like the broader neighborhood responsiveness orientation examined in chapter 2, community policing activity actually appears to diminish civic engagement.

There are several possible interpretations of this result. As with overall responsiveness to neighborhoods that was examined in chapter 2, it is possible that community policing engenders free riding with respect to neighborhood association involvement. That is, community policing may empower neighborhood associations (and the small number of activists who are the stalwarts of these organizations) more than neighborhood residents. Hence, the more extensive the efforts that police make to work with these community groups, the less likely it may be that ordinary citizens become involved with neighborhood associations, which appear to be taking care of the problem for them.

Free riding is not the only possible interpretation. Higher scores on the meetings index mean that the police department is meeting with many types of groups, not just neighborhood associations, and some of these groups may not be neighborhood based. To the extent that community policing emphasizes police meetings with advocacy groups, business groups, or other groups, this policing reform could shift residents' attention and mobilization from neighborhood associations.

Yet another possibility is that community policing meetings, which enhance the salience of crime issues, create fear among residents who might otherwise have been less conscious of crime issues. Rather than enhancing participation in neighborhood associations, this heightened fear of crime could deter civic engagement—an ironic result indeed. Finally, there is the possibility that community policing efforts at outreach are greater in places where civic engagement has long been a problem. Although the measures of community policing used in this analysis are from 1999 and the measures of civic engagement are from 2000, it is still possible that places with low levels of participation in community life attracted stronger community policing efforts by police departments. If so, we would observe the results found here if community policing failed to reverse the problem of low civic engagement in places that adopted the reform for those reasons.

With the data available, it is not possible to determine which of these interpretations are valid. From the standpoint of policy-centered theory, however, settling that matter is not important. All of the interpretations point to the failure of community policing to yield enhanced civic engagement, even though the program's design elements seemingly invite it. And although Schneider and Ingram's framework might lead us to expect a more mobilizing impact on dependent populations than on advantaged or deviant populations, the demobilizing impact observed here is not predicted by their framework.

Trust in Police and Neighborhood Social Capital

In addition to civic engagement, community policing has been hypothesized to influence trust in police. Recalling that responses to the question about trust in police are coded such that higher values mean less trust, Table 3.3 (column A) reveals unsurprising results for the demographic and contextual controls. Trust in police is lower in larger cities. Older, better-educated, and higher-income people; homeowners; those attending church more frequently; and women have higher levels of trust in police. But most notable of the individual attributes is race. Black respondents have much lower levels of trust in police than do white respondents, even when the other indicators of life circumstances are taken into account. But the featured variables are those involving community policing. In contrast with research suggesting community policing has improved residents' satisfaction with police performance or other attitudes about police (Lyons 1999; Kerley and Benson 2000), these results provide no evidence that community policing can enhance *trust* in police. If anything, coefficients for both measures of community policing are signed in a direction suggesting greater *distrust* of police, though neither is significant.

Results with respect to social capital building are also disappointing for proponents of community policing (see Table 3.3, columns B and C). When we consider whether more extensive community policing practice enhances residents' trust in their neighbors, coefficients for both the extensiveness of police–community meetings and the index of community policing policies are again signed in the direction of diminished trust and are in any case insignificant. Nor is social capital as measured via frequency of visiting or talking with immediate neighbors enhanced by community policing.

TABLE 3.3

Community policing and other explanations of trust in the police and neighborhood social capital

	(A) TRUST POLICE	(B) TRUST NEIGHBORS	(C) VISIT NEIGHBORS
Individual attributes			
Age	−.018 (.002)**	−.026 (.002)**	.014 (.002)**
Education	−.059 (.014)**	−.174 (.018)**	.001 (.014)
Income	−.045 (.014)**	−.148 (.016)**	.007 (.015)
Homeownership	−.014 (.071)	−.653 (.064)**	.318 (.056)**
Church attendance (higher values = less frequent)	.134 (.018)**	.072 (.021)**	−.058 (.016)**
Time in community	.012 (.021)	−.084 (.019)**	.059 (.022)**
Gender	−.156 (.056)**	−.096 (.041)*	−.121 (.045)**
Have kids under age 17	−.089 (.042)*	−.072 (.051)	.231 (.065)**
Race (1 = white, 2 = black)	1.489 (.079)**	1.133 (.080)**	−.311 (.062)**
Contextual controls			
Positive articles (per thousand population)	.451 (.305)	.366 (.279)	.120 (.168)
Ward-based elections	.122 (.118)	.213 (.131)	.098 (.054)
City total population, 2000	.000 (.000)*	.000 (.000)**	−.000 (.000)
Community policing context			
CommPol meetings	.009 (.021)	.015 (.019)	.016 (.010)
CommPol policies	.023 (.027)	.019 (.025)	−.028 (.015)#
Cut 1	1.211 (.400)	−1.367 (.379)	−1.911 (.206)
Cut 2	3.199 (.408)	.881 (.389)	−1.568 (.195)
Cut 3	4.487 (.413)	2.397 (.385)	−1.190 (.186)
Cut 4	—	—	−.652 (.183)
Cut 5	—	—	.215 (.180)
Cut 6	—	—	1.635 (.171)

TABLE 3.3

Community policing and other explanations of trust in the police and neighborhood social capital—continued

	(A) TRUST POLICE	(B) TRUST NEIGHBORS	(C) VISIT NEIGHBORS
N	6,965	6,907	7,045
Pseudo-R^2	.07	.13	.02

Source: Data from 1999 Law Enforcement Management and Administration Survey, 2000 Social Capital Benchmark Community survey, and author's original content analysis of relevant newspaper articles.

Note: The numbers presented are ordered logistic regression coefficients (clustered robust standard error) except where otherwise indicated.

**$p < .01$

*$p < .05$

#$p < .10$

Acknowledging the Racial Divide in Responses to Police

So far, the analysis has focused on respondents overall, with race included as one among many individual attributes. However, it is impossible not to notice the extraordinarily large impact that race has on trust in police. This echoes a long line of research showing strong racial differences in reactions to police more generally (Weitzer and Tuch 1999, 2002; Brown and Benedict 2002; MacDonald and Stokes 2006; Sharp and Johnson 2009). There is therefore a strong possibility that the impacts of community policing are quite different for black and white residents. Hence, it may be revealing to model these impacts of community policing separately for white and black respondents.

Table 3.4 presents truncated results when the models presented in Table 3.2 are rerun separately for black and white respondents. The individual-level and contextual controls that are not the primary focus of the analysis are left out of the tables for ease of presentation, though the results presented for the community policing variables are from models that included all individual attributes, contextual controls, and policy context shown in Table 3.2.

TABLE 3.4

Black–white differences in the impact of community policing on three forms of civic engagement: truncated results

	WHITE RESPONDENTS	BLACK RESPONDENTS
Participate in a neighborhood association		
CommPol meetings	−.070 (.031)*	−.033 (.041)
CommPol policies	.030 (.044)	−.013 (.047)
N	5,455	1,613
Pseudo-R^2	.08	.09
Work on a community project		
CommPol meetings	−.022 (.020)	−.054 (.019)**
CommPol policies	.021 (.025)	−.003 (.019)
N	5,455	1,612
Pseudo-R^2	.09	.08
Attend a public meeting		
CommPol meetings	.022 (.022)	−.027 (.037)
CommPol policies	.005 (.022)	.008 (.033)
N	5,459	1,613
Pseudo-R^2	.11	.09

Source: Data from 1999 Law Enforcement Management and Administration Survey, 2000 Social Capital Benchmark Community survey, and author's original content analysis of relevant newspaper articles.

Note: The table presents only the coefficients for the community policing variables, suppressing the coefficients for the individual attributes and contextual controls that were included in each model.

The numbers presented are ordered logistic regression coefficients (clustered robust standard error) except where otherwise indicated.

**$p < .01$

*$p < .05$

#$p < .10$

None of the measures of community policing significantly affect the propensity of either whites or blacks to attend public meetings. Beyond this shared null result, however, some racial differences are evident in Table 3.4. For whites, the extensiveness of community policing meetings is the one manifestation of the program that significantly influences involvement in neighborhood groups; however, the coefficient is negative, showing that this aspect of community policing activity diminishes civic engagement. By contrast, black involvement in neighborhood groups is not significantly affected by community policing. Meanwhile, whites' propensity to work on community projects is unaffected by community policing, but for blacks this form of civic engagement is negatively affected by the extensiveness of community policing meetings. It is not entirely clear why community policing affects different forms of civic engagement for black and white respondents. However, in Table 3.2, neighborhood association activity is particularly pervasive for black residents of these study cities. The importance of neighborhood association involvement for black residents may be such that they are resistant to any deterrent effects that community policing has on this form of civic engagement. On the other hand, we should not make too much of these racial differences in community policing impact. The results as a whole show community policing has a dampening effect on one or another form of civic engagement for both black and white respondents.

Table 3.5 shows one potentially important black–white difference in the impact of community policing: its impact on trust in police.

TABLE 3.5

Black–white differences in the impact of community policing on trust in the police: truncated results

	WHITE RESPONDENTS	BLACK RESPONDENTS
CommPol meetings	.023 (.027)	−.029 (.017)#
CommPol policies	.028 (.031)	−.005 (.024)
N	5,374	1,591
Pseudo-R^2	.03	.02

Source: Data from 1999 Law Enforcement Management and Administration Survey, 2000 Social Capital Benchmark Community survey, and author's original content analysis of relevant newspaper articles.

Note: The table presents only the coefficients for the community policing variables, suppressing the coefficients for the individual attributes and contextual controls that were included in each model.

The numbers presented are ordered logistic regression coefficients (clustered robust standard error) except where otherwise indicated.

**$p < .01$

*$p < .05$

#$p < .10$

Community policing appears to enhance trust in police among blacks but not among whites—a result that at least approaches conventional levels of statistical significance. As with the other results reported so far, this impact stems from more extensive community policing meetings, not from the community policing policies index. Why might more extensive police outreach to an array of groups build blacks' trust in police? The results are consistent with the finding in existing case studies (to be developed in the later analysis) that black residents react with hostility to community policing in places where police are biased and unrepresentative in the selection of community groups with whom they partner under the community policing banner. In places where community policing involves meetings with a broader array of community groups, police are sending a message of more inclusive partnering, thereby minimizing the appearance of narrow and biased partnership and presumably earning higher trust among black residents. The lack of impact on white residents also makes sense, given that the issue of bias in police selection of community groups with which to work has not been as problematic as it has for blacks and trust in police has not been as low.

Despite this intriguing finding regarding trust in police, there is scant evidence of racially differentiated impacts of community policing on community building (data analysis results not shown). Neither the coefficients for the impact of community policing on trust in neighbors nor the coefficients for the impact on frequency of visiting with neighbors are statistically significant for either blacks or whites.

Summation

Across a range of hypothesized impacts and for both respondents as a whole and racial subgroups of respondents, community policing has (with one possible exception) at best no impact and at worst counterproductive impacts. The propensity to attend public meetings is unaffected by the city's commitment to community policing. In cities with more extensive community policing meetings, participation in neighborhood associations is less likely, especially among whites, and working on a community project is less likely, especially among blacks. Social capital in the form of trust in neighbors and more frequent visiting with neighbors is not significantly affected by the scope of the city's community policing efforts. Community policing does not enhance whites' trust in police. The only hint of a result consistent with the hopes of proponents of community policing is the sign of the coefficient, suggesting, for blacks, community policing that involves outreach to an array of groups enhances trust in police. However, this coefficient is not significant at conventional levels.

There is thus no strong evidence that more substantial versions of community policing mobilize urban residents; if anything, there is evidence of demobilization. How might we understand these results? To address this question, the next section turns to case study evidence that can provide both subtle details about community policing implementation and community response to it and relevant historical and contextual information that may be important in understanding the community's reaction to this policing reform program.

Reasons for Community Policing's Negligible and Counterproductive Impacts: A Case Study Exploration

Seattle is an interesting case to consider in regard to community policing. By 1999, Seattle was one of the cities to be included in the SCBC survey that would appear to have institutionalized community policing at a fairly high level. Seattle's police department scores a little higher than the average study city on the index of community policing policies and half a standard deviation higher than the average study city on the index of community policing meetings. Yet the city does not have a particularly impressive showing in terms of the civic engagement outcomes assessed previously, especially given the city's demographics. Instead, in 2000, Seattle residents were only a couple of percentage points more likely than residents of the other study cities to belong to a neighborhood association or attend a public meeting and about seven percentage points more likely to work on a community project (see Table 3.6). These minimally higher rates of civic engagement in Seattle are especially curious given that Seattle scores so highly on education level (among study cities, only St. Paul and Boulder rank higher on this) and a highly educated populace should help to drive up civic engagement rates. Once education and a few other demographics (age, income, and homeownership) are taken into account, whether a respondent is from Seattle or not has no influence on these civic engagement outcomes, despite the city's apparent commitment to community policing.

TABLE 3.6

Community policing outcomes: A comparison of Seattle with the other study cities

	OTHER STUDY CITIES (%)	SEATTLE (%)
Participate in a neighborhood association	27.4	29.7
Work on a community project	36.4	43.2
Attend a public meeting	40.6	42.0

Data from 2000 Social Capital Benchmark Community survey.

When the racial differential in the impact of community policing is considered, the results for Seattle are even more disappointing and curious from the perspective of the community policing ideal. In Seattle, only 14 percent of black respondents trust police "a lot," compared with 51 percent of white respondents. This 37 percentage point differential in whites' versus blacks' trust of police is even larger than the 32 percentage point differential observed among respondents of the other study cities. Similarly, while the differential in black versus white participation (in terms of "work on a community project") is negligible generally, it is more noticeable in Seattle than in the other study cities.

Seattle thus becomes a good case for exploring the disappointing results of community policing. Seattle does represent a special case in one regard: Most accounts of community policing reform in major cities in the 1990s suggest community policing was initiated and promoted by high-level police managers, who were responding to their own perceptions of public discontent with police (Lyons 1999, 50). In Seattle, the pressure for community policing came from the community, and this reform idea had to overcome strong opposition from the city's police chief at the time. In one sense, this makes the relatively disappointing impacts of community policing in Seattle even more curious. As Lyons argues, police-initiated community policing may be "more responsive to the social control and legitimation needs of the police bureaucracy than to the concerns of the communities the police serve" (50). Conversely, community policing reform that grows from the grass roots should be expected to be a more authentic version of the community empowerment aspects of community policing. Yet there is no evidence of such empowerment in the form of boosted levels of civic engagement in Seattle.

Fortunately, several in-depth case studies of policing in Seattle for relevant periods (Lyons 1999; Reed 1999; Miller 2001), as well as other scholarly analyses that more briefly document aspects of policing in Seattle (Beckett and Herbert 2008), are available for secondary analysis. These, coupled with supplemental case information drawn from newspaper coverage of 1994–99 events in Seattle, allow detailed assessment of how features of Seattle's community policing effort yielded a set of mixed programmatic messages to different constituencies in the community. The Seattle case thus reveals something about community policing in practice that may help contextualize the results of the overall quantitative analysis.

Community Policing Era No. 1: Implementing Distorted or Bastardized Community Policing

Community policing was formally put into place in Seattle in 1990 (Reed, 1999, 56–58) in response to pressures from the South Seattle Crime Prevention Council (SSCPC). In his case study, Reed concludes that in the 1985–93 period, what emerged from this collaboration was "a bastardized version of the philosophy of true community policing" (30)—a conclusion mirrored by critiques in Lyons's (1999) case study. The depiction of Seattle's approach as "bastardized" community policing is based on several characteristics of the program in this first era of Seattle's uptake of the program.

One characteristic is the police department initially partnered with a single community organization—the SSCPC—an "elitist group" whose meetings were "by invitation only" and not widely publicized (Reed 1999). Two neighborhoods with reputations for gun violence and street crime were to be the target of community policing, but there was limited effort to develop problem-solving partnerships with a spectrum of residents of these areas. Instead, the police department chose to work only with a group that was

> subtly involved in legitimating the status quo in the south end. . . . Several of the SSCPC leaders owned the local real estate agency, local newspaper, and private businesses in the low-income/high-crime area enclaves. With the influx of diverse populations, these small business owners and residents felt that their way of life was

> threatened, and the status quo was being upset by the behavior of street criminals and "riffraff." (60)

Lyons (1999, 136–37) noted that originally the number of black or Asian members of the SSCPC was limited; with the departure of one black and one Asian member about two months after the group's partnership with the police department was formalized, the organization had only an 18 percent minority representation though it covered an area of Seattle that had a 60 percent minority population. "No recognized leader of any African American community in Southeast Seattle joined the SSCPC" because, according to a prominent black minister in the city, crime prevention councils like the SSCPC were perceived by the black community as serving "more to justify police actions and act more as agents of the city than agents of the community" (137).

There were at least two other South Seattle groups at the time with strong interests in crime issues (Lyons 1999, 79–80). One of these other groups—Neighbors Against Drugs—had a membership that included a multiracial mix of homeowners and a history of successful, broad-based mobilization of this constituency. In reaction to perceptions that police were not being adequately responsive to neighborhood concerns about crack houses and that police leadership was too unwilling to "let the community get involved and reluctant to have officers walk beats" (87), the group had been regularly organizing rallies and was behind a petition drive to remove the police chief (85). But neither Neighbors Against Drugs nor the other South Seattle group felt welcome in the chamber of commerce–oriented SSCPC and so did not join with it when the police department chose to define the "community" in community policing as the SSCPC.

A second feature that made community policing less than the ideal in this first era was limitation in the scope of the effort. The small, specialized six-member teams of community policing officers in the two designated areas of the city bore the full weight of doing community policing work for the department. They were the only police officers who were expected to attend neighborhood meetings and engage in order-maintenance activities. There appeared to be no police leadership commitment to reorient the police department more comprehensively to a community policing approach, and the patrol officers not included in one of the specialty community policing teams viewed the work of those teams as "social work, not police work" (Reed 1999, 31). Reed argues that even in the target areas, the crime prevention emphasis that theoretically characterizes community policing was eclipsed by a crime control emphasis (32). That is, rather than efforts directed at resolving crime-fostering community problems, the police department worked hand in hand with the SSCPC to identify existing crime hot spots or problems and target tactical resources to fight those crime problems.

Community Policing Era No. 2: The Drive for a Truer Version of Community Policing

In 1994, Norm Stamper became the new police chief in Seattle. His appointment was significant, given his previous experience with community policing in San Diego and his evident commitment to the program. Within one month of becoming Seattle's police chief, Stamper had opened a crime prevention center "as a point of contact between police and community," and four months later a second such facility was scheduled to open. More importantly, the new chief brought in a civilian expert on community policing with whom he had worked in San Diego. Nancy McPherson was to head up a new Community Policing Bureau in the department, and she was charged with "changing the culture of the department" and training Seattle police officers to work with communities ("Community Policing Taking Hold in Seattle" 1994). Importantly, her job definition called for her to provide this training across the entire force of one thousand nine hundred officers, rather than to a handful of specialized community policing officers (Raley 1994).

Efforts to broaden and deepen Seattle's version of community policing were also evident in Stamper's appointment of a seventeen-member Community Policing Action Council. Neighborhoods and organizations from across the city were represented on the council, which was slated to meet monthly ("City Crimefighters" 1995). The theme of broadening and deepening community policing in Seattle was also evident in the interview that McPherson gave to the media shortly after her appointment as the civilian director of the Community Policing Bureau. McPherson emphasized,

> Traditional policing has focused on officers responding to calls and often dealing with the same people and the same problems without the time or resources to eliminate or at least modify those problems. One of the principal aims of the new system will be

> to provide uniformed police patrol officers . . . more discretionary time to work with private citizens to identify problems and to develop 'proactive and preventive' means of suppressing crime in their neighborhoods. (Dunsire 1995)

In pursuit of this more comprehensive model of community policing, Stamper began to move designated police officers from the small, specialized community policing teams run by a specialized supervisor back into regular patrol units reporting to a regular commander. The move, criticized by some council members who were accustomed to having a specialized community policing officer working in their area (Shukovsky and Jamieson 1996), was presented by the police department as a way of transitioning to a system in which all officers would be expected to engage in proactive, community policing–style police work. The specialized community policing officers assigned to public housing buildings and high schools were, however, to remain in place (Brown 1996).

Before long, however, Stamper had to at least temporarily move specialized community policing officers into regular squads, not as a transition to department-wide community policing but for crime call response roles. The demand for police officers to deal with regular crime calls in the summer months of 1998 was so heavy and the department's capacity to recruit and field new patrol officers was so limited that Stamper was forced to make this temporary personnel shift while insisting that the department's commitment to community policing had not changed (Santana 1998). Although these remaining community policing officers were returned to their specialized duties in the fall as promised, the event exposed the department's chronic shortage of officers—a shortage with obvious implications for the department's capacity to carry out labor-intensive, proactive problem solving and community-partnered order-maintenance activities while still handling emergency calls.

Ignoring the Pressures for Police Reform apart from Community Policing

Messages about the police–community relationship and about police officials' willingness to be receptive to citizens' input on police issues are embodied in the design and practice of Seattle's community policing program as it evolved over time. The case history already suggests many low-income and minority members of the Seattle community likely received a different and less empowering message from Seattle's community policing program than the one received by middle-class whites, especially in the initial era of community policing; it also suggests some constraints on implementation of a full-blown community policing program—constraints that could be expected to limit the empowerment impacts of community policing in Seattle more generally.

Having acknowledged the community policing promise of a more responsive version of policing was not articulated in a vacuum, it is important to consider yet another contemporaneous historical development that would have made the message of community policing ring hollow, especially to minority residents and possibly some other groups in Seattle. The message sent by the department's adoption of community policing came when the community, and especially Seattle's minority community, was pressing for a different kind of reform—civilian control of, or at least more civilian involvement in, the disposition of complaints about police misconduct. Hostility to this idea from the police department surely tempered any notion of a police–community partnership.

Seattle's system for handling allegations of police misconduct was the topic of a study conducted for the department by MM Bell in 1989—one of several studies that the department commissioned under Stamper's predecessor. The study documented that the department's structure and process for handling misconduct complaints was far from transparent to citizens and that other agencies and community organizations viewed that structure and process as closed to citizens, lacking in objectivity, and unduly secretive (Lyons 1999, 120). Not surprisingly, the MM Bell study uncovered considerable citizen interest in having more community involvement in handling misconduct complaints. However, the Seattle Police Department was opposed to external review of misconduct, and even though complaints about excessive use of force had increased in the late 1980s by 150 percent, the MM Bell study did not recommend the adoption of external review but rather concluded that the department's internal investigations unit could deal with the matter by doing a better job of actively seeking citizen input on complaints (121–23).

Concerns about police accountability in this specific sense of dealing with inappropriate use of force and other types of police misconduct were particularly evident among some leaders of the minority community in Seattle's south end and central district. A nonprofit organization, Mothers Against Police Harassment (MAPH) was formed in the central district in 1990 to "educate and coordinate parents and community organizations interested in addressing excessive police force" (Lyons 1999, 139–40). MAPH "received a cool reception from the SSCPC" (139)—the community organization that initially was the focus of the community policing partnership—and because of MAPH's concerns, the nonprofit was hostile to community policing in the 1985–93 period (Reed 1999, 88). For MAPH, partnering with the police department for neighborhood-based problem solving would simply mean a loss of control, leaving unresolved the problem of lack of police accountability for undue harassment of black youth.

The Seattle Police Department's intransigence on the issue of internal investigations of misconduct was thus an important part of the subtext of the department's message about community empowerment in the initial era of Seattle's experience with community policing. The issue was still unresolved in 1994 as Stamper prepared to take the reins as the city's police chief, marking a new era in community policing. Just before he was sworn in, a Police–Community Relations Task Force weighed in on the issue of internal investigations of police misconduct. The task force had been created at the insistence of one city councilwoman, whose vote in favor of the controversial Drug Traffic Loitering Ordinance in 1992 (discussed later) was contingent on the city having such a task force report. In its report, the majority of the task force, consisting of individuals representing civil liberties, minority, and gay rights groups, called for "increased civilian involvement in internal [police] investigations" (Goldsmith 1994).

In the first year of Stamper's tenure, pressures for a civilian review board diminished and the number of citizen complaints lodged against the police department declined noticeably. The local media attributed these favorable developments to the appointment of former King County Superior Court Judge Terrence Carroll as a special auditor of internal investigations ("Complaints against Cops Show Encouraging Drop" 1995). Nevertheless, there were still voices from the minority community articulating dissatisfaction with what they saw as unduly aggressive behavior by police, particularly in their handling of youth. A former president of the Central District Neighborhood Council, for example, explained that young people she knows well were still telling her about being "thrown up against patrol cars and searched." From her point of view, the new chief had "not made a priority of changing the 'broadbrush' approach police use to deal with young black males" (Whitely 1995).

Simultaneous Implementation of Other Controversial Police Programs

As difficult as it may be for community policing to change residents' attitudes toward police or residents' involvement in neighborhood activities relating to the coproduction of order maintenance and public safety, the task would surely be further complicated if controversial police programs were introduced while community policing was trying to gain a foothold. Yet this is precisely what happened in Seattle. Throughout the two phases of the city's experience with community policing, the police department was also involved in other high-profile programs or policy changes. For many lower-income and black residents, the character of these other programmatic changes was such that a community policing message of partnership and responsiveness would be undercut. Stated another way, these additional programs could reinforce a perception that the message of community policing is positive, constructive, and supportive for some residents but quite the reverse for others. Case study evidence about community politics surrounding these parallel programs suggests they did yield this bifurcated response from residents.

Operation Weed and Seed in Seattle

When Seattle's newly formalized community policing program was less than two years old, the mayor proposed a Weed and Seed program for Seattle (Reed 1999, 61). Weed and Seed is a U.S. Department of Justice program first initiated in 1991. Funding is provided to selected city governments to "stabilize the conditions in high-crime communities and to promote community restoration" (Dunworth and Mills 1999, 3). Like so many federal programs before it, Weed and Seed calls for enhanced coordination and planning. It also includes a call for community policing in the sense of proactive, community–police problem solving. But the most distinctive and high-profile aspect of the program is the conceptualization of a two-stage process of "weeding" followed by "seeding." Weeding involves "concentrated and enhanced law enforcement efforts to identify, arrest, and prosecute violent offenders, drug traffickers, and other criminals operating in the target areas. . . . The object is to remove criminals from the target areas." Only after weeding is successful does this program call for seeding efforts, involving investments in human services and neighborhood revitalization projects intended to deter crime (3).

In Seattle, the Weed and Seed program was "originally opposed by some residents and community-based organizations that objected to the federal proposal and [to the] proposed 'weeding' tactics of the Seattle Police Department on the grounds of perceived civil liberties and civil rights violations"; in particular, black residents of the central portion of south central Seattle were, "insulted and angry" about the program, "which they say would be a tool for police to harass Black teens" (Reed 1999, 62).

Drug Traffic Loitering and Order-Maintenance Ordinances

While Seattle's Community Policing program was slogging through its second year and just before the introduction of the Weed and Seed program, Seattle was experiencing controversy over its two-year-old Drug Traffic Loitering Ordinance. The ordinance empowered police to arrest individuals on suspicion of being gang members—a development that raised concerns in the black community about potential police harassment of young black males. Miller (2001, 84) noted that "the original hearings on the Ordinance, as well as renewal hearings, were highly contentious." Despite the controversy, the ordinance was renewed—a decision that was sure to send the message to the black community that Seattle's version of community policing would be coercive and driven by the police department's needs more than the community's concerns.

In the summer of 1997, even as Stamper tried to manage the conflict between his commitment to a comprehensive community policing approach and the lack of enough police officers to do community policing while handling a flood of crime calls, the city of Seattle enacted one of a family of so-called civility laws that the city has pursued as tools for order maintenance. Under the Parks Exclusion Ordinance, individuals can be banned from city parks for criminal behavior or even for breaking a park rule (Byrnes 1998). As Beckett and Herbert (2008, 110–11) noted, such parks exclusion laws are one of several weapons that Seattle and other cities have provided to police departments pursuing the broken windows version of community policing—a version that Terrill and Mastrofski (2004) associated with coercive police action. Parks exclusion laws give the authorities "an even broader and more flexible means of regulating public spaces and removing those deemed 'disorderly'" (Beckett and Herbert 2008, 110). Not surprisingly, the Parks Exclusion

Ordinance has added to the controversy over police activity in Seattle. The American Civil Liberties Union (ACLU) questioned the constitutionality of the ordinance because it meted out punishment without due process. And in a report released in the spring of 1998, the ACLU noted that 44 percent of the exclusion notices issued in the first five months of the ordinance involved racial minorities, whereas the city at the time had a minority population of only about 20 percent. At the same time, the SSCPC lauded the ordinance for helping to reclaim a neighborhood park for use by law-abiding residents (Byrnes 1998).

Seattle has also joined other cities in using trespass ordinances in novel ways that allow more aggressive order maintenance. In particular, policies of "trespass admonishment" allow police to arrest individuals for criminal trespass when they enter certain public spaces such as parks, libraries, schools, public housing complexes, or public transportation sites, provided that the individuals have been warned in advance either by posted regulations or by a specific admonishment notice (Beckett and Herbert 2008, 113). Trespass admonishment can be used to ban individuals from public spaces even if they have not engaged in criminal acts, and police issuing such civil trespass admonishments do not have to provide an official record of the reason (114–15).

In Seattle, revamping of trespass law and policy in this direction began in the late 1980s (Angelos 1988). By 1994, when then-new Police Chief Stamper was pushing hard to expand community policing, controversy was erupting over both the city's use of trespass admonishment in the tourist-trendy Pike Place Market area and the city's more specific ordinance prohibiting people from sitting or lying on sidewalks in commercial districts from 7:00 a.m. to 9:00 p.m. A coalition of homeless advocates staged a sit-in at Pike Place Market to protest the alleged use of trespass admonishments to drive out the homeless. The racial dimension to the controversy was evident because of the 81 trespass admonishment cards issued in the preceding year, only 30 percent had gone to whites while 70 percent had been issued to black, Hispanic, or Native American individuals ("Sit-In at Market Will Focus on Sidewalk Law" 1994).

Discussion

Community policing is one of a number of urban programs that ostensibly has the intended effect of mobilizing citizens for civic engagement. If the program were to have such an effect, it would not be an unintended policy feedback result that is ancillary to the main purpose of the program, as is the case with the social programs that launched policy-centered theory. Rather, just as with the broader neighborhood empowerment programs that are the focus of chapter 2, increased civic engagement is a key purpose of the program, at least as a middle-range outcome on the way to expected crime reduction impacts.

However, there is scant evidence that community policing has the intended effect on civic engagement. In addition, little evidence shows it helps build social capital in the sense of trust in neighbors or indeed trust in police.

There are many possible reasons for the failure of community policing to generate the intended policy feedback effects—reasons that are explored in more depth in chapter 6. For the moment, it is enough to note several key considerations. First, the free-riding problems that are apparent for city governments' efforts at general neighborhood empowerment may also be at work for this specific program of neighborhood responsiveness.

Second, there are special complications involved in this programmatic attempt to mobilize civic engagement for the purposes of achieving enhanced neighborhood order and security. Citizens are being asked to get involved not only in the neighborhood but also with both the police and their neighbors and in activities (e.g., block watching and the reporting of social order problems in the neighborhood) that can be sensitive or even explosive. It is likely that activating the citizenry for this form of civic engagement requires high levels of social capital and trust in police, and despite the hopes of some proponents of community policing, this chapter has shown that community policing itself appears to be incapable of enhancing either of these.

Third, case study evidence suggests the way in which community policing programs are implemented may make it even less likely that the program can have a broadly mobilizing effect on the desired forms of civic engagement. Selective police department partnerships with some community organizations may send a message to other segments of the community that they are not part of the "community" in community policing. The simultaneous implementation of other policing innovations with program design elements suggestive of aggressive, top-down policing tactics can erode the message community policing is meant to send. Implementation of community policing while community pressures for other kinds of police reform are being resisted may also shape the meaning that residents draw from community policing. In short, both the elements surrounding the implementation of community policing and the program's policy design are part of the "social and political construction of program beneficiaries" (Mettler 1998). Taken together, they appear to yield at best no feedback effects and at worst counterproductive feedback effects in the forms of diminished civic engagement.

4

City Government, Economic Development Incentives, and Business Influence

For critics of what is often called *corporate welfare,* there can surely be no more offensive comparison than that between the Temporary Assistance for Needy Families (TANF) welfare program in the United States and the subsidy-focused, "supply side" (Eisinger 1988) version of development policy that has characterized state and local government treatment of businesses for years. Welfare as addressed in TANF is not only means tested, and therefore targeted to those who on income grounds are demonstrably in need of it, but also encrusted with a host of performance and accountability requirements meant to separate the deserving from the undeserving poor. In addition, the 1996 welfare reform legislation that created TANF set overall limits on how long individuals can remain on welfare. Recipients are in this way expected to deliver on the implicit promise that welfare will be the mechanism to lift them out of poverty, and within a fairly short time frame. By contrast, local governments and their state agency partners are by now in at least their fourth decade of providing a host of subsidies to businesses, either to lure them into the community or to stave off the threat of departure of those already in the community. These financial incentives include loans and loan guarantees, land giveaways or write-downs, and tax increment financing districts, which finance development projects by diverting future tax monies accruing to the project area from all uses except for paying off project-related bonds. Perhaps the poster child for what is often seen as the locally provided version of corporate welfare is tax abatement, which provides that for a specified period (frequently ten years) a certain percentage (typically at least 50 percent) of the property tax that a company should pay on real estate improvements is forgone.

Until recently, most local governments tended to provide tax abatements and other subsidies in a universal rather than a targeted fashion.

That is, rather than being choosy about which companies should receive such subsidies and which are not desirable enough to warrant them—on grounds of the number or quality of jobs created, the fit between the type of enterprise and the community's economic development aspirations, and so forth—virtually all companies angling for an abatement as part of their site selection process are granted one. As recently as 2003, Sands, Reese, and Kahn (2006) found nearly half of the local governments in the state of Michigan had never denied a tax abatement that had been requested. In addition to being far from carefully targeted to only "worthy" companies, tax abatements have been surprisingly free of performance accountability conditions. If promised jobs did not ensue, subsidies to tax-abated companies nevertheless continued in many cities because there were no mechanisms in place to cancel them. Still other communities found themselves taken advantage of when companies that were given tax abatements to invest in the community subsequently left, sometimes just as the end of the tax abatement period loomed and sometimes because another community was offering a better deal.

In the past two decades, however, many city governments and states have changed their business subsidy policies to try to better target them to companies poised to make worthwhile and durable investments in the community and to hold companies receiving subsidies accountable for their promised performance. This chapter describes these policies in greater detail and provides information from several sources on the prevalence of such policies.

More importantly, the chapter tests two versions of policy-centered theory as it applies to cities' economic development activities. One parallels policy-centered theorists' work on welfare by testing whether a more universal use of business subsidies has a different impact on the political engagement of businesses than does a version of business subsidies that adds accountability controls. The other, arguably less demanding version of policy-centered theory tested in this chapter replicates the work of Sullivan and Green (1999) by examining whether cities can adopt policies in a way that shows their autonomy from business influence.

With respect to the first, cities whose economic development subsidy policies include targeting and accountability controls differ from cities that provide business incentives to all comers, without qualifications or conditions—much in the same way that the nation's welfare program, especially in its form since the passage of the Personal Responsibility and Work Opportunity Reconciliation Act of 1996, differs from entitlement programs such as Social Security retirement benefits. Because policy-centered theorists have found political empowerment effects from universal programs and demobilization effects from means-tested programs, the simplest hypothesis would be the expectation that cities using universal development incentives empower businesses whereas cities giving incentives encrusted with accountability controls (or refusing to give development incentives) dampen the political involvement and power of business.

However, Schneider and Ingram (1997) suggested that the impact of public policy depends not just on the character of the policy but also on the interaction between type of policy and type of target population. In their schema, open-ended and generous programs such as universal development incentives are not expected to affect the political engagement of an advantaged group such as local business owners or developers. Members of such a target group are already "positively oriented toward policy and politics" and already powerful players in local politics via their interest group and electoral activity (141); they take government provision of generous benefits to them for granted. However, when business subsidy policy is such that subsidies are grudgingly given and encrusted with accountability controls, advantaged groups would be expected to mobilize in reaction to this threat to their entitlement.

Indeed, the process of adding accountability controls to a city's business subsidy policy may well have occurred in a process featuring a shift in public perception of businesses "from deserving to greedy or privileged," thereby moving business out of the advantaged category and into the "contender" category of social construction (Schneider and Ingram 1997, 116). As with an advantaged target population, Schneider and Ingram theorize that when a contender group is the target population for negative or threatening policies like the business subsidy reforms at issue in this chapter, increased political mobilization is to be expected (117). According to these authors, the only difference between the contenders and the advantaged in this scenario is likely to be the form of political mobilization (141–43). Those in the advantaged group are expected to escalate their involvement in visible and conventional forms of political mobilization, including electoral mobilization; contenders are expected to mobilize politically in ways that are less visible, such as heightened use of "influential connections and campaign contributions" (143).

Research on urban politics is largely society centered rather than policy centered, however. To the extent that variation in business influence in cities is even acknowledged, urban scholarship tends to be oriented toward examining how business influence affects government policy, rather than the other way around. When the *impacts* of local development policy are studied, the focus is typically on the economic growth impacts rather than the possible impacts on political influence or community involvement that are the stuff of policy-centered theory. Substantial empirical evidence is therefore required for convincing support for this application of policy-centered theory.

However, a pair of research studies tests a somewhat different version of policy-centered theory as applied to this topic. Drawing from work that helped inspire policy-centered theory, most notably Skocpol's (1985) state-centered framework, Sullivan and Green (1999) and Sullivan (2002) argued that the essence of the theory is the notion that the state has the capacity to devise and implement policies that are relatively autonomous from business influence. For Sullivan and Green, state-centered theory in the urban context is represented by scholarship depicting local government as an activist initiator of economic development policies that may be far from the preferred policies of business elites. From this point of view, testing policy-centered theory in the urban economic development realm does not require evidence of the *impacts* of subsidy controls on businesses; rather, it requires evidence that business influence does not unduly constrain city governments from adoption of such stringently accountable subsidy policy.

This chapter begins with a description of the emergence of local government controls on economic development incentives for businesses and provides information on the extent to which they have become prevalent in the United States. Then, taking up the version of policy-centered theory that Sullivan and Green (1999) drew from Skocpol's (1985) work, the chapter examines whether adoption of these targeted and accountable subsidy policies is constrained by the scope of business influence in communities. Other things being equal, if the addition of controls to development incentives is possible only in places where business already has relatively little influence, this version of policy-centered theory is not supported; conversely, if the addition of controls to development incentives occurs regardless of business influence, possibly even in the face of strong business involvement in local politics, then evidence supports Sullivan and Green's version of policy-centered theory. Finally, the chapter tests the version of policy-centered theory that most closely parallels the work of contemporary policy-centered theorists on means-tested versus universal social policies by examining whether the adoption of controls on development incentives affects business influence and business participation in community affairs.

Emergence of Targeted and Accountable Incentives

Written in 1997, LeRoy's *No More Candy Store* chronicles an emergent backlash against the problems of local governments' freewheeling provision of economic development incentives to businesses and the first glimmerings of efforts to tame these business subsidies. One sign of this was the activity of both state and local government professional associations, which began to consider the issue in the mid-1990s. For example, the National Council for Urban Economic Development convened a task force to review the issue, and the National Governors Association debated the issue in the early 1990s and released a set of policy recommendations. These included a statement of the responsibility of businesses to deliver on the promised benefits for which a subsidy was given and the obligation of governments to have mechanisms in place to recover subsidy monies from recipient businesses that do not deliver on their side of the deal.

More importantly, both states and cities began to adopt policies designed to prevent the misuse of business subsidies. St. Paul, Minnesota, was one of the pioneers, adopting an ordinance in 1989 that relies on company disclosure at the application stage to empower the city to better target companies that should be awarded incentives. Companies requesting financial incentives from the city are required to provide information not only on the number of jobs to be created by the company's proposed investment but also on the number of jobs that might be displaced, the wage and skill levels of affected jobs, the characteristics of affected employees, and the company's track record of creating promised jobs (LeRoy 1997, 18).

The St. Paul ordinance also required a public hearing on the job impact statement, direct submission of that statement to a variety of labor stakeholder groups (e.g., local labor unions and potentially displaced worker groups) and other affected or interested community associations, and company assistance to any displaced workers, including job retraining and health-care benefit coverage for one year (LeRoy 1997, 20). In the 1990s, Hammond and Gary, Indiana, passed tax abatement reform ordinances with comprehensive disclosure elements. The Gary ordinance, for example, requires not only information on a subsidy applicant's company financial situation but also job-quality information for the proposed project, estimates of the percentage of new jobs that would go to Gary residents, and information on all public subsidies received by the company in the state of Indiana for the previous decade and job results associated with those incentives (18–19).

These policies, at least in principle, transform government-supplied business incentives from a relatively universal entitlement to a more targeted benefit that is given to businesses deemed "worthy" because their location or expansion plans would provide the type and magnitude of benefits *to the community* that warrant the cost of their provision. However, such targeting is effective only if the promised benefits of the business location or expansion plan are realized. This is problematic, given the history of local governments being taken advantage of by companies that create fewer or lower-paying jobs than estimated or companies that stay in the community for a limited time, only to move when the local subsidy is due to expire or when a competing jurisdiction offers a heftier subsidy. Consequently, the movement that brought policies designed to better target local business subsidies has also brought policies designed to hold businesses accountable for the subsidies they have received. Cities have begun to award business subsidies with performance agreements that lay out the conditions for continued receipt of the subsidy. Such conditions typically include the number of jobs to be created and the wage levels of such jobs, and they sometimes include the share of jobs to be provided to local residents (Sullivan and Green 1999). By the late 1990s, local government practitioners were being urged to make business subsidies contingent on performance and to clearly specify expected performance so that business subsidies could function as development incentives rather than "developer give-aways" (Oden and Mueller 1999).

But what happens if businesses receiving tax abatements or other local subsidies fail to meet the stipulated conditions in the performance agreement? At a minimum, a subsidy policy featuring accountability presumably includes provisions for reducing or canceling the subsidy in these circumstances. It is sometimes argued that because of the "legal nature of the contract or award," a city government issuing a business subsidy such as a tax abatement "will always have termination as its legal recourse" if the subsidized company fails to comply with the conditions of the award

(Dalehite, Mikesell, and Zorn 2005, 169). This assumes that the city uses the aforementioned performance agreements in awarding subsidies—an assumption that is by no means warranted. Even when local officials have performance agreements in place, it may be difficult for local officials to rescind a business subsidy, even for a business that is failing to meet the conditions of that subsidy. In a 1999–2000 survey of government officials in 14 cities, Weber reported that city officials found it extraordinarily difficult to "penalize nonperforming firms that stay" in the community. The potential litigation costs are high, and canceling a subsidy to a struggling company is viewed by city officials as undermining the city's efforts to help businesses succeed in the community (2002, 50).

The nuclear weapon of accountability is the clawback provision, through which local governments can take legal action to recapture subsidy monies from businesses that have failed to live up to the conditions of their performance agreement. Clawback policies can be written to empower city governments to seek to recapture a portion rather than the entirety of the subsidy monies expended if the subsidized company accomplishes part of what it agreed to do but falls short (Good Jobs First 2010, 1). An early, high-profile, and much-cited example of what amounted to a clawback effort was the city of Chicago's 1985 lawsuit against Playskool and its parent company Hasbro after Playskool used a $1 million Industrial Revenue Bond issued by Chicago to buy equipment and then moved the equipment to Rhode Island as part of a company reorganization. In an out-of-court settlement, the company agreed to provide enhanced financial assistance to the seven hundred unionized workers in Chicago affected by the loss of Playskool (LeRoy 1997, 6).

More recent examples of cities going beyond cancellations and using clawback provisions to reclaim subsidy monies that they had dispensed are relatively rare. However, San Antonio's post-2000 experience clearly illustrates the dynamics under which clawbacks get utilized. Early in the decade, three companies that had enjoyed the financial benefits of tax abatements from San Antonio (Sony Electronics, American Airlines, and Amnitek) shut down operations in the city shortly after their tax abatement periods expired. Because there were no clawback provisions in San Antonio's written agreements when those companies received abatements, the city could take no action to recover the funds. In the light of this harsh lesson, San Antonio city officials became more aggressive about recovering funds from subsidized companies with disappointing performance records. In 2004, San Antonio's city council not only voted to rescind the tax abatement agreement that it had with Alcoa, which had shut down its plant and laid off 175 employees, but also got the company to agree to pay the city nearly $730,000 for abatements already received. In 2007, San Antonio's city council dealt similarly with Oberthur Gaming Technologies (later bought out by Scientific Games), which planned to close its San Antonio plant and lay off more than 300 workers. The city council voted to rescind the company's abatement and to attempt to claw back $823,000 in already-abated taxes (Lorek 2007).

How prevalent are the various subsidy reforms or development incentive controls discussed here? Drawing on several sources of information, it appears (1) there has indeed been a sea change in the direction of more requirements and controls imposed on businesses as a condition of receiving these incentives but (2) some cities and states have gone substantially farther than others and (3) some requirements are more prevalent than others.

Table 4.1 presents data bearing on this matter from two surveys of economic development practices in city and county governments conducted by the International City/County Management Association (ICMA), as well as data from the 1994 ICMA survey as reported by Sullivan and Green (1999). The surveys, sent to the chief administrative officers of all municipalities with a population of more than ten thousand and all counties with a population of at least fifty thousand and with an elected or appointed single executive, typically have response rates of at least 30 percent, although the rate for 2004 was only about 20 percent. For consistency with Sullivan and Green's results, Table 4.1 excludes jurisdictions that did not offer incentives. However, the decision on whether to offer incentives is an important element of development policy. Nearly 33 percent of jurisdictions surveyed in 1999 and 28 percent of those surveyed in 2004 did not offer incentives. Later in the chapter, a measurement of development incentive policy that takes this into account is introduced. For the moment, the focus is on the uptake of controls on incentives that are given.

The results in Table 4.1 show a substantial surge in the regular use of performance agreements as a condition for providing business incentives, although more than one-third of the communities offering such incentives still did not always require them in 2004. The use of cost-benefit analysis before offering business incentives has become even more prevalent. That, along with the substantial increase (from 1994 to 1999) in the percentage of communities that have formal, written criteria laying out eligibility for

TABLE 4.1

Prevalence of municipal controls on business incentives

	2004 (%)	1999 (%)	1994 (%)
Responding cities providing incentives that			
Always require a performance agreement as a condition for providing business incentives	61	59	28
Require a cost-benefit analysis before giving incentives	75	77	56
Have formal, written criteria for eligibility	n.a.	65	38
Measure the effectiveness of business incentives	84	81*	n.a

Source: Data from International City Management Association's 1999 and 2004 Economic Development surveys and Sullivan and Green (1999).

*Rather than first asking whether the city measures the effectiveness of business incentives and then asking how, in 1999 the survey asked which of several measures of effectiveness of business incentives was used. The response for the most commonly used effectiveness measure in 1999—number of jobs created—is used here.

incentives is evidence of improvement in local governments' capacity to target incentives to businesses that meet certain standards. And by 2004, the majority of responding cities claimed to be checking on the effectiveness of the business incentives that they provide.

Some research finds even greater prevalence of subsidy controls. Sullivan's (2002) survey in 1998 of economic development officials in U.S. cities that have a population of 2,500 or greater yielded the findings that 75 percent of local governments require signed performance agreements from subsidized companies and 71 percent have formal, written criteria for eligibility. More than half (54 percent) of respondents to that survey's question about clawbacks indicated that clawback clauses were included in performance agreements. Along with the ICMA survey data, such evidence suggests local governments have been moving for some time into the business of better targeting development incentives and making companies more accountable for them.

On the other hand, these figures do not adequately emphasize the extent to which business subsidies for economic development are still awarded universally in some areas, perhaps especially Rust Belt areas that are desperate for economic development. For example, Sands, Reese, and Kahn's (2006) study of tax abatement practices in the state of Michigan as of 2003 suggested that, at least in that state, few local governments had transitioned to a more targeted, accountability-based method of granting these subsidies to businesses. Based on evidence from state records of tax abatements given to companies in the two decades ending in 2001, as well as a 2003 survey of chief executives of townships, cities, and villages in Michigan, they found that in nearly half of the localities surveyed, requested tax abatements have never been denied and that in nearly a third of the communities conditions were never placed on abatements. In addition, 30 percent of the communities had no policies governing the granting of abatements, and another 40 percent had only informal, unwritten ones. Furthermore, the majority of these Michigan communities (55 percent) never do a cost-benefit assessment of abatements or other meaningful assessment of the effects of the abatements they have given. Given these results, it is hard to imagine widespread uptake of clawbacks by localities in this state. As Sands, Reese, and Kahn (2006, 50) noted,

> For most communities, even if conditions are placed on the abatement . . . there are no mechanisms in place to assess the extent of job creation after the fact. Given this, it would be almost impossible to institute any claw-backs or impose other penalties if the conditions were not met. And it is entirely possible that firms know going in that it is likely they will not be held accountable for any lack of performance on abatement conditions.

A limitation of the ICMA survey data is that it does not provide definitive information about the kinds of standards companies are being asked to meet as a condition of receiving subsidies. But follow-up questions in the survey about measuring the effectiveness of business incentives suggest that for the vast majority of communities, the sheer number of jobs created is the gold standard of performance. But are they good jobs? Information from a different source shows that relatively few city governments provide incentives only to those companies that provide "good" jobs, as defined by wage rates and health benefits. In 2003, Good Jobs First, a think tank and activist organization devoted to accountable economic development and smart growth policies, compiled a list of states, cities, and counties that have such wage- and health benefit–related job-quality standards as part of their subsidy programs. Only forty-six cities and counties made the list. Although some jurisdictions were surely overlooked in the list making, an examination of the requirements of those that *are* listed underscores that local governments are not choosy in targeting for high-quality jobs. Some jurisdictions that made the list demanded only a specific wage floor (with no reference to health benefits) and frequently a wage floor that was less than 30 percent above the roughly $6.50 per hour minimum wage level that characterizes most states. Cleveland, Ohio, for example, required that companies pay at least $9.20 per hour; Winston-Salem, North Carolina, required that companies pay at least $8.00 per hour to be eligible for their Target Area Business Assistance Program and $9.00 per hour to be eligible for their general economic development assistance; Dane County, Wisconsin, pegged the required wage to 100 percent of the federal poverty level for a full-time worker supporting a family of four (or $8.70 per hour in that year), and Columbus, Ohio, stipulated that jobs pay 150 percent of the federal minimum wage. Most communities on the list, however, either required that jobs created have health benefits or provided a two-tier wage floor requirement—a lower one if health benefits were provided and a higher one if they were not. Here, too, the requirements are typically not extraordinarily demanding. Rochester, New York, for example, required that companies receiving city incentives of $50,000 or more pay hourly wages of $8.88 with health benefits or $9.92 without (Purinton 2003).

The ICMA surveys do not include questions about city and county policies with respect to either cancellations of subsidies for nonperformance or clawbacks of subsidies already paid out, although Sullivan's (2002) survey suggested that a little more than half of local governments used clawback language in their performance agreements by 1998. This is consistent with Weber's (2002, 50) assertion that "cities and states *have* become more aggressive about holding firms to their promises." But most examples from her survey involve cancellations rather than actual clawbacks. Most notably, Indianapolis canceled tax abatements to five companies in a single year (1996). The only example given of an actual clawback involved a voluntary repayment by a Kansas City, Missouri, company that did not meet its performance promises (Weber 2002, 50). Good Jobs First has not compiled a list of local governments that have such policies, although it estimated that the number of cities using clawbacks is a matter of "dozens" and its listing of state governments that have clawback provisions in their programs for state financial assistance to businesses includes only twenty states (Good Jobs First 2010). Other research also suggests the adoption of clawback provisions is still relatively limited. Dalehite, Mikesell, and Zorn (2005) found that in only fourteen of the thirty-five states that have stand-alone tax abatement programs is there a state policy provision to specifically require or enable local governments to use clawbacks.

Adoption of the various subsidy controls outlined here is clearly far from universal. But the sea change that has led to waves of adoption of these controls has yielded great variation in cities' economic development subsidy policies. Some cities have moved aggressively to adopt numerous controls, with a resulting development subsidy policy that parallels means-tested welfare. Other cities are still using what amounts to universal corporate welfare—providing tax abatements to virtually any company that requests them, with few or no questions being asked about job creation or other performance criteria and no means of canceling the subsidy for nonperformance.

What impact do these policy design differences have on the businesses that are the targets for these programs? Variation in cities' development subsidy policy provides an opportunity to test this policy-centered theory–style question. It also provides the opportunity to test a related question about what initially influences the adoption of these policies. The remainder of the chapter deals first with the question about adoption of a subsidy control policy, followed by a final section of the paper that tests the core question for policy-centered theory: Does the restrictiveness of a city's business development subsidy policy influence the civic engagement and political power of business?

Analyzing Cities' Adoption of Business Subsidy Reforms

Although policy-centered theory as developed and explored in this volume is primarily about the impacts or consequences of public policy on political participation, there is a branch of policy-centered theory that focuses on policy development. Like policy-centered theory more generally, this line of work stands in stark contrast to society-centered explanations. The latter emphasize the ways in which various interests or social forces outside of government determine the shape of government policy. In reaction to the prevalence of society-centered explanations, scholars, most notably Skocpol, developed "state centered" explanations of policy that focus on the degree to which governments have the capacity to pursue and implement policy with relative autonomy from such interests (Skocpol 1985; Evans, Rueschemeyer, and Skocpol 1985).

In their study of city governments' adoption of development subsidy controls, Sullivan and Green (1999) acknowledged scholarship on urban politics has been dominated by a society-centered approach that depicts the city as driven by a "growth machine" and the local state as inevitably subservient to business interests (Logan and Molotch 1987). Contemporary analyses continue to reflect the view that, at least in the development policy realm, business influence is both inevitable and strong. For example, Bartik (2005, 146) asserted, "Local economic development decisions have been dominated by local business interests, including Chambers of Commerce, newspapers, banks, and real estate developers." To some extent, these claims have been tempered by Stone's (1980, 1989) influential regime theory. That theory depicts the local state as having interests that may differ from those of the business elite. But regime theory still acknowledges the need for city government collaboration with the business elite to obtain the resources to accomplish goals—an acknowledgement that leaves theorizing about cities' development policies still largely in the society-centered camp.

There is little room in this body of influential research for notions of development policy being relatively autonomous from business influence. Nevertheless, Sullivan and Green (1999) investigated cities' adoption of development subsidy controls using a Skocpol-style, state-centered approach and data from the ICMA's 1994 survey of economic development policies in cities and counties; Sullivan's (2002) study replicated part of the Sullivan and Green (1999) study using an original survey done by Sullivan in 1998. These two studies, which are updated and replicated in this chapter with some adaptations and refinements, found some support for a Skocpol-style interpretation of city government adoption of subsidy controls. In particular, governments' capacity was found to be important in that subsidy controls were more likely to be implemented by larger cities and by cities with more economic development staff—both considered to be measures of governments' capacity to pursue their own development policy agendas. These findings appear even with controls for the competing, society-centered explanation that stringent controls on development subsidies are possible only when local governments are not constrained by laggard local economies and fiscal stress—both of which presumably create public pressure to attract business investment with no-strings-attached subsidies.

However, Sullivan and Green's (1999, 275–76) finding that local governments are less likely to adopt subsidy controls when business influence is high should be viewed as evidence *contradictory* to Skocpol's state-centered theory, although Sullivan and Green do not interpret it that way. The best test of state-centered theory should focus on the extent to which cities' economic development policy is relatively autonomous (i.e., not unduly influenced by) private business. But if cities that set requirements as conditions of subsidy award tend to be cities in which business influence is weak and if places in which business influence is strong do not have such requirements, we would have to conclude that local governments do not tend to pursue policy with relative autonomy from business influence. There would be at least weak support for state-centered theory if strong business influence makes no difference to local governments' adoption of performance agreements, and there would be even stronger support for state-centered theory if local governments are more likely to adopt subsidy controls when business influence is strong. The last scenario reflects state-centered logic in that government would presumably be taking action to protect the community's interests in precisely those situations in which it is most called for—that is, when business is influential enough to have the potential to push uncontrolled subsidies too far if government does not protect itself.

The findings of the most relevant studies to date are therefore mixed with respect to the application of Skocpol's state-centered theory to local governments' development subsidy policy. To update these findings, this section replicates the Sullivan and Green (1999) study with some refinements. The first refinement is use of data from two time points (as well as replication within a single-year data set). Data from the 1999 ICMA survey are used to measure the various explanatory concepts used in the Sullivan and Green study.[1] To get leverage on the question of causal direction, the measures of development subsidy policy that are the dependent variables for the analysis are drawn from a later ICMA survey, one done in 2004. The cost of doing so, however, is the loss of a substantial number of cases. A jurisdiction could only be included if it had completed surveys for both years—a requirement that yields an especially large loss of cases given the low response rate for the 2004 survey. There is an additional loss of cases due to missing data on one or more survey items.

The second refinement is use of both the Sullivan and Green measure of business influence and an alternative measure of business influence. The item used by Sullivan and Green to measure business influence in the 1994 survey was fortunately available again in the 1999 survey. Government officials were asked not only which groups or institutions participated in developing the jurisdiction's economic development strategy but also which of them was the *top* participant. If one of the five categories of possible private sector participants (chamber of commerce, private business, utility, private economic development foundation, and public–private partnership) was named as the top participant, business influence in matters of economic development is considered to be high in the community; if none were named, business influence is considered to be low. Of the roughly two hundred cities for which there is both a 1999 and a 2004 completed survey and for which the question is relevant (because business incentives were given), private business influence is high in fewer than thirty cases, or about 14 percent of the time. This is virtually the same as Sullivan and Green's finding of business influence in 15 percent of the cases in 1994.

Clearly theirs is a very stringent measure of business influence, possibly so stringent that cities in which private sector entities are influential (without necessarily being the top participant) are erroneously deemed to have low influence. Hence, an alternative measure, introduced in a second wave of the replication, is a count of how many of the five private sector entities were indicated as participating in developing economic development strategy. In stark contrast with the Sullivan and Green measure of business influence, a substantial majority (65 percent) of local governments reported at least one private sector entity's involvement in development strategizing and 27 percent reported three or more private entities were involved. Given the substantial evidence of business influence in the case study literature of urban politics, this measure may well be more realistic than the one showing a small minority of cities have such influence.

The third refinement is use of a dependent variable that does not treat subsidy controls in isolation from the related issue of whether or not the city offers development subsidies. On the ICMA surveys, respondents were first asked whether or not the city provides business incentives for economic development. The follow-up questions about possible subsidy controls were only for those that provide business incentives. The Sullivan and Green (1999) analysis, which examined only the adoption of subsidy controls, ignored that the two phenomena are logically linked. Local governments decide whether to offer incentives and, if so, which of several controls to place on them. The availability of controls that can be placed on subsidies may even make it more palatable for local governments to provide subsidies—an argument that was supported in Sullivan's (2002) later research. The key point here is that the result of these two kinds of decisions is a spectrum of development incentive policy, ranging from the most generous at one end (incentives provided with no subsidy controls, scored 0) to the most stringent at the other end (no incentives provided), with intermediate categories for cities providing incentives with one, two, or three of the following types of subsidy controls: a cost-benefit analysis before giving incentives, a performance agreement in all cases, and the measurement of the effectiveness of business incentives. The last is used to substitute for the written statement of eligibility that Sullivan and Green used, because that item is not available on the 2004 survey. Of the jurisdictions responding to both the 2004 and the 1999 surveys and having no missing data on these items, 28 percent did not give incentives, 32 percent gave incentives but used all three controls, 22 percent gave incentives but with two of the three controls in place, 11 percent gave incentives but used one of the controls, and only 7 percent gave incentives free of any of the controls.

Table 4.2 shows the results of the replication. Model 1 uses the highly restrictive measure of business influence paralleling the one that Sullivan and Green (1999) found to be inversely associated with uptake of subsidy controls in that year. Model 2 uses the alternative measure just described.

Both models replicate Sullivan and Green's results with respect to the importance of fiscal stress, even though an alternative measure of fiscal stress is used here. Cities desperate for business investment because of their high property tax rates are significantly less likely to put controls on development incentives, let alone refuse to give them; in model 1, economic distress functions in the same fashion. However, there is virtually no evidence here for state-centered theory. Contrary to Sullivan and Green's (1999) state-centered hypotheses, neither city population size nor economic development staffing predicts the stringency of local governments' development incentive policy. Furthermore, the results show that

TABLE 4.2

Accounting for local governments' 2004 development incentive policy

EXPLANATORY VARIABLES	MODEL 1	MODEL 2
Constant	3.127	3.243
Economic and fiscal stress related		
Unemployment rate, 1999	−.074*	−.049
Property tax rate, 1999	−.009*	−.006*
Have local sales tax, 1999 (1 = no, 2 = yes)	-.060	−.046
State-centered theory related		
City population, 1999	.006	.011
Percentage of city staff devoted to economic development, 1999	.002	.007
Business influence high (0 = no, 1 = yes), 1999	−.139	—
Business influence alternate measure, 1999	—	−.148*
N	146	155
R^2	.08	.09

Source: Data from International City Management Association's 1999 and 2004 Economic Development surveys.

Note: The numbers presented are linear regression coefficients.

**$p < .01$

*$p < .05$

when the extent of business influence is measured with the demanding indicator used by Sullivan and Green, that factor has no statistically significant impact. When business influence is measured by the number of private sector entities participating in setting development strategy (model 2), business influence is a significant predictor of policy, *but in the direction suggesting private sector interests constrain cities from taking up more stringent incentive policies.* This is decidedly not consistent with a state-centered view of city policy in the economic development realm.

These replications of Sullivan and Green's study are, however, potentially skewed by the loss of cases that occurs when a later-year survey is used to measure the dependent variable. To cross-check the results, a follow-up replication was done, measuring both the explanatory variables and the dependent variables with information from a single year (as Sullivan and Green did) but a more recent year—1999.[2] Doing this expands the cases for analysis to well more than four hundred local governments. The results, presented in Table 4.3, provide even more dramatic evidence against policy-centered theory. Neither city population size nor economic development staffing is significantly linked to local governments' development incentive policy in 1999. Indeed, the only significant predictor is business influence, again in a direction showing that private sector involvement constrains cities from taking up more stringent incentive policies.

Policy-centered theory clearly has been influenced by the work of Skocpol and other writers emphasizing the potential autonomy of state interests from society-centered influences and the importance of governments'

TABLE 4.3

Accounting for local governments' 1999 development incentive policy

EXPLANATORY VARIABLES	COEFFICIENTS
Constant	2.623**
Economic and fiscal stress related	
Unemployment rate	.006
Property tax rate	.003
Have local sales tax (1 = no, 2 = yes)	.119
State-centered theory related	
City population	.015
Percentage of city staff devoted to economic development	.002
Business influence	−.165**
N	437
R^2	.04

Source: Data from International City Management Association's 1999 Economic Development survey.

Note: The numbers presented are linear regression coefficients.

$^{**}p < .01$

institutional capacity for policy development. However, in contrast with the conclusions of Sullivan and Green (1999; Sullivan 2002), that interpretation does not appear to be supported when the topic at issue is a city's development policy. Instead, there is plenty of evidence for what society-centered urban scholarship has long claimed—the influence of business on city policymaking.

Moving to application of a full-blown, policy-centered perspective requires that we ask a different question: Does the character of a city's business subsidy policy shape the influence of business in the community? The next section turns to this key question.

Applying Policy-Centered Theory to Development Subsidy Reforms: The Impact of Policy on Business

This section presents an analysis of cities' policies for subsidizing business development that is framed by the core thesis of contemporary policy-centered theory. Rather than focusing on the factors that shape the adoption of policy, that core question has to do with the impacts or consequences of government policy for the target audience—most notably impacts or consequences that have to do with the empowerment or mobilization of the target audience. To apply this policy-centered framework to local governments' subsidy policies, it is first necessary to be clear about (1) the relevant targets of city governments' subsidy policies, (2) the types of behaviors or actions by those recipients that are of interest, and (3) the nature of the theorized connection between government policy and target group actions or behaviors.

With respect to the first of these matters, the targets, in the narrowest sense of the term, of local government policy regarding business subsidies are the individual companies that receive them. From a broader perspective, all businesses in the community can be conceived of as part of the group affected by development incentive programs. To the extent that local government provides tax abatements, loans, land write-downs, or other subsidies, all businesses in the community might be viewed as potential recipients, especially in communities that use such programs for business retention, as well as business attraction. And as the next chapter shows, to the extent that local government clamps down on the generosity of its incentives by more careful targeting, more demanding performance requirements, and the threat or actual use of cancellations or clawbacks, a programmatic message about local governments' stance vis-à-vis businesses is being sent. That message is heard by actual and prospective recipients of local subsidies and even by the local business community more generally.

Acknowledging this broader target group for business subsidy policy is consistent with a strong theme in both the literature on economic development and the everyday discourse of business owners about the importance of what is usually called the local "business climate." The concept of business climate refers to local government actions vis-à-vis specific businesses as signaling either an open-ended receptivity to business location and expansion or a demanding selectivity that is unfriendly to many businesses. This chapter examines evidence based on this broader view of who constitutes the relevant target group that might be affected by local governments' development incentives policy; the next chapter presents evidence from interviews with individual business owners who have directly experienced the tax abatement process in one case study community.

What behaviors or actions are relevant for a policy-centered analysis of the impact of development incentives policy on businesses? Unlike policy-centered research on individuals who are receiving either means-tested or universal social program benefits, the relevant behaviors or actions here are not so much voting and other forms of participation relevant to the study of mass political behavior. Rather, the relevant behaviors here are the distinctive forms of elite-level business involvement (e.g., participation in economic development policymaking) that translate into the business influence that has already been considered political *input* in the first part of this chapter.

In addition to affecting the level of businesses' policy participation or political influence, local incentives policy might also be expected to influence the level of businesses' *corporate citizenship*. This rich term is relatively rarely used by scholars of urban politics, who tend to see the actions of businesses as self-interested rather than community spirited and tend to focus more on the political involvements of the business sector rather than the broader contributions of businesses to the community. However, case study work by both Nevarez (2000) and Reese and Rosenfeld (2002) suggests business volunteerism in the form of direct contributions to the city's broader economic development mission and even "philanthropic support of surprisingly progressive interests" (Reese and Rosenfeld 2002, 652) can be important roles for businesses, perhaps especially in small and medium-sized communities. In their case study work on nine communities, Reese and Rosenfeld found several cases showing business involvement can entail "a greater level of business volunteerism and support for all aspects of the community. This extends from art to education, includes more emphasis on quality of life issues, and in some cases reduces the use of public funds for economic development" (658). Corporate citizenship is thus a potentially important form of civic engagement.

In this chapter, evidence about overall business activities in the community, in both the policy involvement sense and the corporate citizenship sense, is drawn from the ICMA surveys of economic development. Evidence about the impact of development incentive policy on individual business owners who are recipients of tax abatements is presented in the next chapter's case study, which includes interviews of such business owners conducted by the author in the winter of 2008 and information gleaned from local newspaper reports.

Finally, with respect to the third issue mentioned at the outset of this section, it is important to consider how we should theorize the connection between cities' business subsidy policy and businesses' policy involvement and corporate citizenship. Adopting a direct parallel with work on the impact of means-tested versus universal social programs, we would be led to hypothesize that a tougher, more control-encrusted, and generally less generous development incentive policy should dampen the influence and corporate citizenship of the business sector, whereas more open-ended and generous provision of incentives would enhance policy influence and corporate citizenship. This is an important starting point. However, it neglects another possibility that would suggest just the opposite. That is, relatively stingy development policy may mobilize the private sector, as businesses and other private sector entities push for a reversal of the stingier, more accountable policy that they dislike. In chapter 2, a reactionary mobilization thesis of this kind was examined with respect to the neighborhood organization involvement of urban residents. Because the target group for this policy (businesses) would in their schema be considered advantaged, or at least a contender group for high power and status, Schneider and Ingram (1997) also suggested that negative, undesirable policy yields mobilization. Therefore, we proceed with the hypothesis that empowerment of local businesses might result *either from especially generous development subsidy policy or from especially stingy subsidy policy.*

Sine Qua Non of Community Involvement: Being There

Before turning to an assessment of the impact of business subsidy policy on the political and civic involvement of businesses, an important preliminary consideration must be tended to. Local governments' development incentive policies cannot logically be expected to shape the political participation or the corporate citizenship of recipient companies (let alone other businesses in the community) if such incentives are ineffective in getting companies to come to the community or to remain there as they expand. What is known about this issue?

There is an enormous literature on the subject. Surprisingly few studies examine evidence deal by deal, company by company. However, some research has surveyed broad samples of business executives to obtain information about their siting decisions and the role of tax abatement availability in those decisions. That approach has been plagued by both the problem of finding the relevant individuals in a business establishment who were involved in making specific location decisions of interest and the critique reported in Fisher et al. that "executives may have a direct interest in saying that incentives are important even if they were not." Most importantly, the results of this style of research are mixed. Some studies suggest the availability of incentives is important in company location decisions, and others suggest such subsidies are not important. This diversity in results may stem partly from different studies inquiring about different types of subsidies or economic development programs (Fisher et al. 1997, 117). Furthermore, these studies tend not to take into account differences in program elements, such as the municipal controls on tax abatement that are at issue here, let alone more subtle elements of development program administration that may affect how business prospects perceive themselves to be treated.

Apart from the research based on surveys of executives, research on the topic of actually getting and keeping businesses tends to look at communities' aggregate levels of incentives given and then see whether that is linked with job growth or business investment growth in the community. The huge literature on this question is mixed. In their assessment of that literature, Peters and Fisher (2004) described several waves of studies, with the first wave (ending in the late 1980s) yielding a consensus that tax incentives have either no impact or a minor impact at best. In the 1990s, a second wave of research yielded the contrasting conclusion that tax incentives and other development subsidies have positive impacts on investment and employment growth in the majority of cases, although the results are sometimes ambiguous. Scholars argued that this shift in the consensus bottom line about development incentives was due to the uptake of better statistical modeling methods and possibly to bigger differences in the size of the incentive packages offered by communities. However, both the holdout critics of the studies in the 1990s and the results of later studies focusing on specific types of incentives other than tax abatement push Peters and Fisher (2004, 32) to conclude that "in fact, there are very good reasons—theoretical, empirical, and practical—to believe that economic development incentives have little or no impact on firm location and investment decisions."

If extant research yielded greater consensus that development subsidies are ineffective in attracting and retaining business, it would be an important threat to the logic of the policy-centered hypotheses. However, there is clearly lack of agreement about this. Furthermore, existing research on the matter does not examine whether the stringency of a city's development subsidy policy, defined in terms of the adoption of the various controls considered in this chapter, has a bearing on the capacity of these subsidies to recruit businesses. This provides room for us to proceed with an analysis of the consequences of tax abatement policy stringency on business involvement in a city's development policy and on corporate citizenship.

Impacts on Business Involvement in Policymaking and Corporate Citizenship

Three analyses of the relationship between the stringency of a city's development subsidy policy (the independent variable) and the private sector's involvement in development policy (the dependent variable) were examined—one measuring the independent variable in 1999 and the dependent variable in 2004, one measuring both variables in 1999, and one measuring both variables in 2004. Because all three yielded the same pattern of results, only those for the most recent year, 2004, are presented. Table 4.4(a), which shows the impact of subsidy policy on business involvement in economic development policymaking, reveals a nonlinear relationship. But the pattern is exactly opposite what was hypothesized. Rather than private sector involvement in policymaking being maximized where subsidy policy is either especially generous or

TABLE 4.4

Impact of 2004 development incentive policy on business involvement in economic development policymaking and corporate citizenship
(a) Economic development policymaking

	DEVELOPMENT INCENTIVE POLICY STRINGENCY				
	NUMBER OF CONTROLS				NO INCENTIVES
	ZERO	ONE	TWO	THREE	
A. Business Involvement, 2004					
At least one private participant (%)	62	87	86	90	75
	Pearson chi-square value = 58.726, sig. = .000				
Mean number private participants	1.60	2.37	2.46	2.61	1.66

(b) Corporate citizenship

	DEVELOPMENT INCENTIVE POLICY STRINGENCY				
	NUMBER OF CONTROLS				NO INCENTIVES
	ZERO	ONE	TWO	THREE	
B. Corporate Citizenship, 2004					
Private companies underwrite marketing efforts (%)	42	74	69	72	61
	Pearson chi-square value = 25.114, sig. = .068				
Mean number of underwriting roles	.48	1.05	0.99	1.08	.83
(Number of cities)	(40)	(62)	(123)	(182)	(155)

Source: Data from International City Management Association's 2004 Economic Development survey.

especially stingy, private sector policy involvement is instead *minimized* either where a jurisdiction's development policy is restrictive to the point of offering no incentives (one end of the spectrum) or where its policy is at the most generous end of the spectrum—that is, giving incentives with none or only one of the commonly used restrictions. Where a jurisdiction's policy is in the middle range, combining the generosity of incentives available with the toughness of controls on those incentives, private sector involvement is maximized. This suggests unusually high levels of private sector participation require both the presence of a benefit that transforms the business community into a stakeholder and the addition of objectionable restrictions on the policy that motivate influence attempts.

The same pattern is evident in the 2004 data when the impact of subsidy policy on corporate citizenship is examined, as shown in Table 4.4(b). Corporate citizenship is measured using a 2004 ICMA survey question about the roles private companies play in underwriting the marketing efforts of local governments. The answer categories allow for as many as four possible roles to be indicated, including charitable in-kind contributions, charitable cash donations, joint marketing partnerships, and an "other" category.Corporate citizenship in the form of underwriting activity is maximized where incentives are available but subject to controls and minimized either where no incentives are given or where incentives are given with virtually no strings attached. The results for corporate citizenship, however, are not as robust as those for business involvement in policymaking.[3]

The patterns in Table 4.4 are opposite those initially hypothesized. On further reflection, however, they are nevertheless consistent with policy-centered theory's contention that government programs can either mobilize or demobilize political involvement, depending on the characteristics of the policy. The problem with the initial hypotheses guiding this analysis is that they characterized policy in one-dimensional terms (or in the Schneider and Ingram–inspired hypothesis, in one dimension contingent on type of target group). What is of the most interest in Table 4.4 is that mobilizing effects appear to result from the interaction of two characteristics of policy: the provision of subsidies and the addition of accountability requirements that can be viewed as a threat to the business sector's ensured access to those subsidies.

But do these results hold up in a multivariate analysis that controls for rival explanations? And what rival explanations are relevant? When considering the participation of ordinary citizens in community politics, as was the case in chapters 1–3, the rival explanations are obvious. They come from powerful theories of political participation that demand we take into account factors such as individuals' level of education, income, and race, as well as institutional arrangements such as reform government structures that have been shown to affect the participation levels of individuals. Here, where the focus is on the business sector rather than citizens and on specific forms of possible business involvement in economic development rather than broader forms of political participation, there is no strong theoretical grounding for choosing relevant control variables.

However, research on the relationship between the private sector and the public sector in local politics, and especially in economic development politics, suggests at least one important control—city size. Reese and Rosenfeld (2002, 647), for example, questioned whether the importance of private sector resources that is theorized on the basis of large cities' experience is as relevant in smaller cities. Although their concern is to understand what types of development policy are adopted rather than the impacts of that policy, Reese and Rosenfeld's relevant point for this analysis is that the politics of economic development are different in smaller and larger cities. Hence, a control for city size is in order.

In light of this, Table 4.5 replicates the analysis presented in Table 4.4 but separates cities above and below a population of one hundred thousand. There is indeed a difference in the two kinds of cities with respect to the impact of policy on private involvement in development policymaking. Table 4.5 shows that the curvilinear pattern observed in Table 4.4 is strikingly apparent for smaller cities; for larger cities, the pattern is much less clear, although the small number of cases makes assessment of the pattern for large cities difficult. When corporate citizenship is the outcome of interest, again, the pattern is evident for smaller cities but there is no clear pattern for larger cities.

Discussion

Although policy-centered theory was developed primarily with an eye toward the impact of social programs on individual recipients, this chapter shows some evidence that the theory is applicable to the programs that city governments adopt to attract and retain businesses. Just as welfare, Social Security, and other social programs have consequences for the civic engagement or demobilization of individual recipients (depending on the message sent by specific program design elements), so do cities' development policy choices have consequences for the empowerment and civic

TABLE 4.5

Impact of 2004 development incentive policy on business involvement in economic development policymaking and corporate citizenship, controlling for city size

(a) Business involvement 2004: percent with at least one private participant in economic development policymaking

	DEVELOPMENT INCENTIVE POLICY STRINGENCY				
	NUMBER OF CONTROLS				NO INCENTIVES
	ZERO	ONE	TWO	THREE	
Among smaller cities	60	86	84	89	75
	Pearson chi-square value = 45.836, sig. = .001				
(Number of cities)	(35)	(57)	(94)	(141)	(141)
Among larger cities	80	100	93	93	86
	Pearson chi-square value = 17.991, sig. = .588				
(Number of cities)	(5)	(5)	(29)	(41)	(14)

(b) Corporate citizenship 2004: percent with at least one form of private sector underwriting of city government's marketing efforts

	DEVELOPMENT INCENTIVE POLICY STRINGENCY				
	NUMBER OF CONTROLS				NO INCENTIVES
	ZERO	ONE	TWO	THREE	
Among smaller cities	37	77	71	69	75
	Pearson chi-square value = 29.896 sig. = .019				
(Number of cities)	(35)	(57)	(94)	(141)	(141)
Among larger cities	80	40	62	83	86
	Pearson chi-square value = 17.341 sig. = .137				
(Number of cities)	(5)	(5)	(29)	(41)	(14)

Source: Data from International City Management Association's 2004 Economic Development survey.

engagement of businesses in the community. There is some evidence that, at least in smaller cities, city governments' choices about whether to provide business subsidies and how many controls to place on such subsidies influence the level of corporate citizenship. There is even stronger evidence, again mostly for smaller cities, that the character of development subsidy policy shapes private sector involvement in development policymaking. As Reese and Rosenfeld (2002) surmised, in large cities, the private sector is highly involved in development policy regardless of the character of subsidy policy. In smaller cities, private sector actors are more likely than not to be at the table when government is engaged in economic development policymaking, no matter what the character of subsidy policy. But when such smaller cities enter the hardball realm of adding teeth to their business subsidy policy, the private sector shows levels of engagement in policymaking that rival those of the largest cities.

Urban scholars are unaccustomed to a finding that policy shapes business mobilization. The society-centered views that predominate in most theories of urban development typically put business interests in the role of powerful forces shaping policy, not "clients" or "program recipients" being influenced by policy. Consistent with this society-centered view, an early section of this chapter reveals that the involvement in policymaking of private sector entities such as chambers of commerce, individual private businesses, and private utilities strongly constrains local governments from aggressively pursuing strong eligibility standards for subsidies, performance agreements, and other elements of a more stringent development subsidy policy. However, the chapter also shows that, once adopted, the stringency of subsidy policy has implications for subsequent private sector engagement in policy development. In precisely the reversal that a policy-centered framework represents vis-à-vis society-centered explanations, we see public policy can shape business influence, in addition to being shaped by that influence.

Policy-centered theory has not paid much attention to the mixed messages that public policy can send. Yet the findings in this chapter underscore the importance of such mixed messages. Mobilization of business—that is, private sector involvement in policymaking—is maximized neither where businesses have to fight for the availability of business subsidies nor where city governments have chosen to provide subsidies in a nearly universal, no-questions-asked fashion. Rather, business empowerment is maximized where public policy combines availability of subsidies with accountability controls. Such policy sends the mixed message that the business sector is valued in the community but that no individual business is necessarily deserving of or entitled to such a subsidy. Like means-tested social welfare programs, the adoption of accountability controls puts the business community in the position of having to prove worthiness for a benefit. The positive message of subsidy availability is thereby shaded with all negative messages associated with the term *corporate welfare* and with the movement to reform corporate welfare with accountability controls.

5

The Impact of Development Incentive Policy Reform

A Case Study

Does the character of city governments' business subsidy policy shape political action and community involvement by local business executives? The preceding chapter presented some evidence that it does. Data from nationwide city surveys suggests an inverted U-shaped relationship between the extent to which a city adopts reforms or controls on business subsidies and the business leaders' political and community activation. Although the pattern appears to apply to smaller rather than larger cities, there is enticing evidence that the local businesses sector is most mobilized when city government offers incentives but has moved beyond little or no requirements associated with those incentives to the adoption of more substantial municipal subsidy controls.

However, analysis of cross-sectional surveys cannot provide information about change processes. In addition, the surveys used in the preceding chapter are of local public officials reporting on city policies and the actions of local businesses in the aggregate. Although suggestive, such evidence requires that we make inferences about the impact of subsidy policy on the behavior of businesses without direct evidence of the reactions of recipients of business subsidies to their experience with their city's subsidy policy. Finally, the large-*N* quantitative analyses in the preceding chapter are not well suited to uncovering information about the processes by which public policies affect recipient behavior. Work in the policy-centered tradition suggests public policy can have feedback effects via several quite different processes, including providing material stakes for mobilization (or threats to material stakes), defining both membership and status in the community, shaping the way in which individuals understand their rights and responsibilities in the community, delineating group divisions, and shaping the ongoing salience of an issue (Mettler and Soss 2004). But which, if any, of these processes are behind the patterns found in the preceding chapter? In particular, do local business owners, plant managers, and other local business leaders react to the addition of accountability controls on tax abatements primarily in terms of the dollars-and-cents implications for their company—that is, does the adoption of municipal controls simply change the material stakes? Or do such business leaders also react to adoption of these accountability controls in a way that shows that subsidy policy reform sends messages about worth and status in the community? If the symbolic, message-sending side of policy is relevant for these business leaders, then it would constitute evidence that policy-centered theory applies to elite, advantaged recipients in some of the same ways it has been shown to apply to the mass behavior of welfare recipients and other less-advantaged policy targets. If it is not relevant, then a policy-centered interpretation of business subsidy policy is warranted—but only in the less interesting sense. We would be talking about little more than the well-established notion, dating to the work of precursors of policy-centered theory (Lowi 1964; Wilson 1973, 1980), that the character of policy shapes the activation of organized interests.

To tackle these kinds of questions and to provide information about the dynamics of the relationship between policy change and behavior of policy recipients, this chapter presents a case study of one city's experience with several waves of reform of tax abatement policy over more than a decade. The city—Lawrence, Kansas—is a convenient one, given the author's location. However, the community is a good choice for several other reasons. First, as noted previously, the pattern of connection between city subsidy policy and business activity that is of interest appears to be a phenomenon of smaller cities. Presumably, the dynamics of economic development deal making for larger cities are quite different. Hence, teasing out the processes behind the pattern identified in the preceding chapter requires a focus on a smaller city. At a population of roughly ninety thousand in the 2005–7 period (U.S. Bureau of the Census 2008), Lawrence is an ideal case, small enough to fit into the smaller-city category but large enough to be a metropolitan statistical area core city. Second, this small metropolitan statistical area is dominated by the city of Lawrence such that governmental policy and business behavior dynamics are not complicated by multiple, large, competing suburban jurisdictions. Finally, and most importantly, the city of Lawrence has gone from informal handling of tax abatements with no municipal controls to adoption of a formal policy for tax abatements that includes several important accountability controls. There were several stages along the way as various issues with tax abatements were discussed, yielding policy reforms that episodically added municipal controls to an increasingly formalized and strict policy. Tracing this history allows direct examination of the processes of policy development, business reaction, and policy feedback effects.

This chapter presents this case study narrative and associated interpretations of policy feedback effects. As with all case studies, information is gleaned from a variety of sources, including local newspaper articles, local government documents, and the author's interviews with business owners or plant managers at many of the companies that were granted tax abatements within the past decade and in some cases earlier tax abatements as well. All of the author's interviews were conducted in confidentiality, and the names of interviewees are withheld by mutual agreement.

Phase 1: The City Gets Serious over Tax Abatement Reform

The city of Lawrence is home to the University of Kansas (KU), as well as Haskell Indian Nations University, and it is the county seat of Douglas County. Its economic base is a mix reflecting both a university and local government presence and a long-standing tradition of small to medium-sized manufacturing and distribution enterprises. The city's top five employers (by number of employees) include KU, Lawrence city government, public schools, and the local hospital, as well as an information services company for business, government, and professional testing. The next largest employers in the city are a Hallmark Cards manufacturing plant, the company producing the local newspaper and broadband services, a garage door manufacturer, a Kmart distribution center, an alcohol and drug abuse counseling center, and a plastics manufacturer (Chamber of Commerce of Lawrence, Kansas 2010).

The city has grown steadily and substantially since the 1950s, with new housing developments reaching ever farther into previously undeveloped portions of Douglas County. Real estate and land development interests have been influential throughout the city's postwar history, though they have occasionally been seriously challenged by environmentalists, spokespeople for managed growth, and opponents of particular residential developments or highway projects with development implications.

Lawrence city government incorporates all elements of classic reform government institutions. The five-person city council, referred to as a city commission, is elected at large in nonpartisan elections. One city commissioner serves as a titular "mayor," but the office is largely symbolic, carrying little in the way of governing powers. The executive function of the city is in the hands of a professional city manager who serves at the pleasure of the city commission. In contrast with the frequent turnover that is characteristic of city managers generally, city managers in Lawrence tend to have relatively long tenures. This has allowed the development of a highly professionalized city administration, including two assistant city managers and long-term, well-credentialed agency heads for police, fire, public works, and the like.

Planning and development is to some extent a joint function of the city and the county governments. A city–county planning commission with five city appointees and five county appointees develops recommendations on various land-use matters—recommendations that cannot be enacted unless approved by the city commission, the board of county commissioners, or both. One assistant city manager specializes in community development, including infrastructure planning, code enforcement, housing, and community development. Economic development in the sense of business attraction and business retention activity is partially delegated to the Lawrence Chamber of Commerce's Lawrence–Douglas County Economic Development group, though the public sector incentives available for business attraction and retention are a matter for city commission policymaking.

As explained by Kirk McClure, a professor of architecture and urban planning at KU and a member of the city's review committee for public incentives (personal message to author, May 29, 2008), before 1991, Lawrence did not have an elaborate municipal policy concerning the use of tax abatements or other incentives for economic development. Instead, the city was granting tax abatements case by case, using broad powers granted by state enabling legislation that allowed tax abatements either to be given to companies that were also being financed through industrial revenue bonds (IRBs) or to be given to companies separate from any IRB consideration. The state's enabling legislation consisted of passage of a constitutional amendment in 1986 to permit either cities or counties to give "tax relief to businesses that expand or build new facilities in Kansas." With little in the way of policy specifics to go on, the city of Lawrence granted tax abatements to five companies between 1986 and 1989, including three local companies undergoing capital expansions ranging from $350,000 to $5 million, as well as a newcomer to the Lawrence scene—Standard Liquor Corporation of Wichita, which wanted to build a $2.2 million distribution facility in the community (Hoyt 1989).

In this early period, one member of the city commission, Mike Rundle, was consistently criticizing the city's tax abatement decisions and pushing for a formalized and improved policy on abatements. In particular, Rundle critiqued the city for granting abatements without the necessary information to demonstrate that the abatement was needed by the company or to demonstrate that the benefits to the community exceeded the costs. Most of his criticisms, and especially his call for some proof that a company needed tax abatement to be enticed to the community, initially fell on deaf ears. As Bob Schumm, a fellow city commissioner, argued, "There are so many factors. A company might locate here without getting a tax abatement. Who's to say if they would or they wouldn't. We might not give them one; then they might say they wouldn't locate here, and we'd find ourselves chasing after them saying we'd go ahead and do it" (Taylor 1989a).

By late 1989, however, at least two factors combined to create pressure for change in the way that Lawrence was using its tax abatement powers. First, the state legislature was slated to take up a bill to deal with perceived abuses in the tax abatement system statewide. The bill, introduced by a western Kansas legislator who was also the chairman of the state's Republican Party, had elements that echoed Rundle's call for more information about companies' need for abatements and continuing audits of companies receiving abatements. Second, the state's newly revamped system for property tax classification and reassessment was perceived by state legislators as creating "mounting taxpayer anxiety over taxes" (Hoyt 1989); local officials were feeling this pressure as well. In Lawrence, at least two of the city commissioners who were otherwise unconvinced by Rundle's critique of tax abatements nevertheless said they believed that the city's tax abatement policy needed to be good enough to withstand the political fallout that would ensue when the new property tax system produced big tax increases for some property owners. Schumm, for example, stated, "The more that a particular person doesn't pay [property taxes], everyone else in the community has to pick up that particular share. There's an equity issue, especially since the law changed very dramatically" (Taylor 1989b).

But even as these elements opened a window of opportunity for reform of tax abatement policy, another phenomenon was taking root—one that would strongly shape businesses' reactions to proposed changes in tax abatement. That phenomenon involved the introduction of a style of discourse local business owners found to be unduly harsh, inappropriate, and antibusiness in tone and a number of business owners took personally. Evidence of this reaction on the part of businesses can be found in the comments of long-term business owners who were interviewed by the author in 2008.

One such business owner claimed, "It's obvious, and it's a well-known fact, that Lawrence is anti-business"—something that he depicted as a long-standing trait. He went on to say that businesspeople, chamber members, and the like from across Lawrence "know business owners from elsewhere who are interested in coming to Lawrence and then when they find out how anti-business the city is they don't want to come because of the bullshit of the city commission and city hall" (Interview E 2008).

In 1989 and 1990, when the city was in the opening stages of what would be a lengthy, multistaged saga of tax abatement policy change, business owners may well have reacted personally to critical comments that either were directed to other businesses (whose circumstances were quite different from their own) or were not about any particular business but rather about general principles or businesses in the abstract. Examples of each of these illustrate the introduction into the community discourse of language that business owners would easily have seen as antibusiness.

In the process of making the argument that the city should require a business to show tax abatement was necessary for a proposed relocation or business expansion, Rundle was quoted in the local newspaper as stating,

> Businesses who ask for abatement want to reduce their property tax liabilities and increase their profits. . . . There's nothing wrong with that because, theoretically, we are going to benefit from the addition of jobs and the improvement of our tax base. . . . [However,] if our abatement allows for excessive profits to be made, then we're giving an unfair advantage to one business over another. (Taylor 1989b)

Although he was making an argument in principle about how tax abatements theoretically could be problematic rather than pointing the finger at any business in particular, the phrases "excessive profits" and "unfair advantage" are prime examples of language that could, and apparently did, set business owners' teeth on edge.

During this early period of policy debate, the comments of a state senator representing Lawrence provide an example of actual finger-pointing at two businesses—finger-pointing that would raise hackles in the business community. In discussing the bill on tax abatement reform that the state legislature was scheduled to take up, Wint Winter, a Kansas state senator, stated that the abatements given by Lawrence to Standard Liquor Corporation and to a local company, Allen Press, "went against the 'intent of the Legislature' when lawmakers put the constitutional amendment up for a vote" in 1986. Specifically, Winter claimed, "Standard Liquor and Allen Press got cities within Kansas into a bidding war over the company's location by asking for tax abatements on expansion projects," whereas the state legislature had, according to Winter, intended that tax abatements be used in the competition with other states for industry and jobs (Hoyt 1989). Given that Allen Press is a company with a long history in the community and a company that prides itself on being a good corporate citizen, such criticism would have been a shot across the bow both to that company specifically and to the Lawrence business community more generally.

In short, the earliest phase of business incentive policy change in Lawrence was triggered by the interjection of external forces and events that gave urgency to an internal critique that had been largely carried by a lone wolf critic on the city council. As the call for policy change unfolded, however, the language of criticism was taken personally by the business community. Not surprisingly, business-friendly members of the city commission began to respond with harsh language of their own. This became apparent when two faculty members from KU weighed in at a spring 1990 city commission meeting with critical comments about the city's handling of tax abatements—comments sparked by the city commission's decision to approve a partial tax abatement on equipment for the Garage Door Group to go along with the approval they had given the previous year for an abatement on the land and the facility used by the company. A professor from KU's School of Business pointedly questioned city commissioners about their failure to adequately analyze abatement requests, and Professor Tim Miller, a member of the Department of Religious Studies at KU and a local activist, registered an "objection to having my money used to subsidize profit-oriented corporations and to having decisions about the distribution of that money made by a private pressure group whose meetings are closed to the public," an apparent reference to the Lawrence Chamber of Commerce, which advises companies about applying for tax abatements. In response, Commissioner David Penny angrily noted that the criticism was coming from professors at the university, which he described as having been "abated for a hundred years . . . at 100 percent"; he went on to state, "I don't think it's correct for people who are working for employers who have 100 percent abatement in our community to come down and complain" (Taylor 1990a).

This sort of angry sniping across increasingly rigid lines emerged relatively early in the policy debate. Another characteristic of Lawrence's policy debate, evidenced in this example and throughout the city's long process of policy change, was that the hostile rhetoric about policy sometimes occurred during consideration of a particular tax abatement request and frequently occurred with high-level officials of the requesting business present. In the example just mentioned, the hostile interchange occurred at a meeting at which an amendment to an existing tax abatement was being considered for a company that had just the previous year been successfully brought in as the first to locate in the city's new East Hills Business Park. One local business executive explained why this sort of sniping over tax abatements in the presence of business applicants is so problematic from the point of view of the local business community. Referring to a similar situation that had recently occurred, he commented that the "company got dragged through the mud because of a political fight that was going on down at city hall between grassroots actions and the commission and they [the company] became the victim." He went on to say,

> And that happens in economic development and abatements all the time. . . . A lot of times these issues get risen up to a level of discussion, whether it be at the PIRC [the city's tax abatement advisory committee] or the commission level, where they're really arguing policy, and the applicant happens to be in the room as the gunfire is moving between the two sides. And that's bad, that's really bad. (Interview B 2008)

Tax abatement critics' 1989 push for reform was given additional impetus in 1990 by probusiness individuals who wanted a settled policy to prevent such toxic policy discussions from erupting every time a specific applicant for tax abatement was before the city commission. The new president of the community's chamber of commerce, Gary Toebben, indicated in a December letter to Rundle that the chamber was researching a new abatement policy that it could recommend to city government, with one of the goals being "to recommend a policy that removes the 'trial-like' atmosphere applicants endure when seeking abatements from the city in exchange for locating or expanding their industries in Lawrence." Toebben's letter stated,

> We need a process that does not put potential new business neighbors on "trial" before the city commission. . . . This statement may sound harsh, but that is how recent applicants have felt. In a public setting, we question the applicant's profitability and send a mixed message as to whether we are looking to recruit solvent companies that have a good chance of success or newer companies that need the abatement to survive. We discuss wages and benefits and make judgments as to whether the jobs provided are "good." (Taylor 1990b)

Those critical of tax abatement, most notably Rundle, had expanded their list of criticisms and on occasion aired them at city commission sessions when individual abatement applications were up for discussion. In June, for example, Davol received commission approval (on a four-to-one vote) for the second phase of its major plant expansion. In addition to criticisms about the need for a cost-benefit analysis before abatements are granted, Rundle and Miller criticized Davol's beginning wage levels for general laborers (four to eight dollars per hour), with Miller calling the four-dollar-per-hour wage an "insult" to the community's labor force (Taylor 1990c). In October at a city commission study session, Rundle spoke of his preferences for tax abatement policy reform that would include a requirement that tax-abated companies sign a performance contract stipulating the specific benefits they would generate in exchange for the abatement and be subject to annual reviews to ensure the benefits were generated (Taylor 1990d).

In November, the unsettled abatement policy situation resulted in a failed business attraction case that spurred Toebben's letter from the chamber of commerce. Famous Brands' request for a ten-year, 50 percent tax abatement for its proposed wholesale liquor warehouse and distribution center was before the city commission, which turned it down when Schumm joined Rundle in voting against it, generating a two-to-two tie (and hence nonapproval), with one commissioner absent. Instead, city commissioners voted to issue Famous Brands a five-year, 25 percent abatement—half of what companies had typically been granted by the city—even though the company had provided "substantial financial information" to the city government and had agreed to "enter into a contractual arrangement with the city to ensure its performance." In their arguments against the larger abatement, Rundle and Schumm stated that the company's proposal did not merit the higher abatement. Stated Schumm: "I don't believe it's of the value of a high-tech company . . . where you have a tremendous amount of capital improvement as well as tremendously high-paying jobs and support jobs" (Taylor 1990e).

Not surprisingly, Famous Brands chose not to locate in Lawrence. In a lengthy, open letter to the city that was published in the local newspaper, executives from Famous Brands made clear how the city's action affected them:

> We were discriminated against and will therefore not be coming to Lawrence. We will expand our facilities in Topeka where we can get more fair and favorable treatment. . . . We were so confident of getting fair treatment in Lawrence we made an unqualified announcement last June that we were building a new facility in Lawrence. In time it was falsely stated by someone we were going to come to Lawrence whether or not we got the tax abatement granted others. We clearly stated before the commission voted that this was not the case, but this false premise was apparently used as an excuse for one vote against us. The "crowning blows" came at the commission meeting when we were denied the same treatment accorded others and then offered substantially less. ("Text of Letter from Famous Brands" 1990)

These comments clearly indicate that the company was both embarrassed (given their early public statements about building in Lawrence) and aggrieved by a decision-making process in the community that they perceived to be unfair. We could easily critique these business leaders for an entitlement mentality, but if it is an entitlement mentality it was fostered by precedents set by the city in its previous abatement decisions. One city commissioner interviewed for this case study explained that the real problem is not a sense of entitlement so much as the problem of nonpredictability of city action.

> The business community doesn't necessarily want everything. They just want to know what it [the standard for getting a development incentive] is, when it's going to happen, and make it predictable about what the delivery is going to be. Unfortunately, the political process, as you well know, is not very good at doing that . . . for businesspeople, they take it personally, which I think is unfortunate. (Interview A 2008)

Over the next year and a half, Lawrence city government, with input from a chamber of commerce task force, the joint city–county Economic Development Advisory Council, and various experts at KU, adopted a revised tax abatement policy. That revised policy included many elements currently in practice, as well as some elements Rundle and other critics had been pressing for.

The first and major piece was adopted in September 1991 when city commissioners approved a new tax abatement policy that explicitly targeted businesses that are environmentally sound, are small to medium sized, offer wages and benefits that *on average meet or exceed the average in the community* (based on a state government wage survey), and have an investment proposal in taxable property or payroll that would have a *significant cost-benefit impact* on local government. In addition, it was focused on businesses for which the abatement can "reasonably be expected to make a difference in determining whether the new business . . . would locate in the city" (City of Lawrence, Kansas 1991). The policy document laid out a list of costs and benefits to be considered and the requirement that applicants submit the information necessary for such an analysis.

The new policy also contained an antipirating statement stipulating the city's intent to avoid participation in bidding wars between cities within the state and a stipulation that no exemption be granted if it would create an unfair advantage for one business in the city over another that competes for the same consumer market. It laid out guideline amounts of abatements to be granted, with a 50 percent abatement for ten years being the standard for investments of less than $30 million and consideration of larger percentage abatements allowed for investments of at least $30 million.

An administrative review committee was designated as the body that would review requests for tax abatements, analyze the relevant information, and make recommendations to the city commission. Membership on the committee would consist of the titular mayor (or a city commissioner designated by the mayor), the city manager, the county administrator, a school district representation, a professional financial analyst, and the chair of the joint city–county Economic Development Advisory Council, with the city's finance director and the county appraiser serving ex officio. A public hearing would be required before tax abatement could be granted. Finally, the policy established the requirement that each company receiving a tax exemption complete an annual report to ensure ownership and use of the tax-abated property and other qualifying criteria were being satisfied.

News coverage makes clear that the development of this revised abatement policy, the initial draft of which was put together by the chamber of commerce's task force, was in direct response to the strident debates in the preceding year, culminating in the Famous Brands episode. As the chair of the Economic Development Advisory Council noted, the new policy "doesn't allow the process to become so politically raucous that it's embarrassing for the community" (Mellinger 1991).

This new policy document went some distance toward responding to Rundle's criticisms that the city had not been obtaining adequate information from tax abatement applicants to help determine whether the abatement was needed, adequately analyzing the costs and benefits of the proposed investment for the community, or following up with annual reviews. The requirement that cost-benefit analyses be performed before the granting of an abatement was firmed up further four months later when city commissioners adopted data requirements and a statistical model for the cost-benefit analyses devised by the university's Institute for Policy & Social Research, along with the suggested benchmark of $1.25 in benefits for every $1.00 in costs as a minimum threshold for warranting tax abatement (King 1992a).

The new policy did not resolve the concerns of critics who wanted tax breaks to be given only if there was clear evidence that the company would not be able to locate or expand in the community without the abatement. Furthermore, the requirement that tax-abated companies pay at or above average local wage levels would soon be shown to be too low of a bar for an activist segment of the community. And as ensuing years would show, the full meaning and implications of being choosier about the kinds of businesses that should be given tax breaks was not yet clear. But for the first time in its history, the city had legislatively adopted a relatively comprehensive, formal policy for handing out tax abatements, the primary weapon in its armory of development incentives. The policy included only one of the municipal controls on subsidies examined in the previous chapter: the requirement that a proposed subsidy pass the test of a formal cost-benefit analysis. But that municipal control carried with it informational and assessment implications that would before long open the door for additional municipal controls.

Phase 2: The Calm before the Storm

Roughly one year after the city adopted its first formal policy on tax abatements and instituted a clearer process for applicants to follow, local officials were enjoying a noticeable decline in conflict over development incentives and local leaders were attributing the relative peacefulness to the new policy. Every one of the five applicants for a property tax abatement in the first year after the policy reform easily qualified for and was granted a 50 percent, ten-year tax abatement, an outcome that the director of the university's Institute for Policy & Social Research claimed was the result of the city's new policy, including its cost-benefit model. This, he noted, "imposes a discipline into the decision-making process of the commissioners," as well as discouraging companies with nonviable investment proposals from applying. Acknowledging that city staff "hand out the policy to people and then never hear from them again," City Manager Mike Wildgen agreed that the applicants "that come to us now are pretty strong." On a somewhat less positive note, the economic development director for the city's chamber of commerce noted that the new policy with its cost-benefit analysis requirement had chased away some businesses that would have met the cost-benefit standard but who did not want the public scrutiny that was involved. According to this chamber official, because "even closely held businesses are asked to divulge information about their financial operations that they normally would consider private," it was possible to imagine a company that would do well in such a cost-benefit analysis nevertheless avoiding a tax abatement request because it "didn't want to go through the in-depth review by the city" (Mellinger 1992).

Despite this cautionary note, the city's development incentives policy activity moved along relatively smoothly for the next five years. During this period, the business establishment and local government appeared to be on the same page about the community's decision to be choosier about the kinds of companies that should get tax abatements. This was particularly evident in the equanimity with which community leaders handled the news in 1993 that two major companies—Russell Stover Candies and Wal-Mart—bypassed Lawrence as a possible location for new manufacturing, distribution, or both types of centers in favor of locating in other Kansas communities. Referring to Russell Stover's decision to locate in Abilene, where the company got a 100 percent property tax abatement, the economic development director for the Lawrence Chamber of Commerce simply noted that under Lawrence's new policy some development projects can qualify for tax abatement of more than 50 percent but "the Russell Stover project wouldn't have been one of them. There were a lot of part-time jobs involved and most of them are minimum wage jobs. . . . It's not really what the Lawrence City Commission has said they were looking for" (Toplikar 1993a).

Chamber officials were more disappointed when Wal-Mart chose the neighboring community of Ottawa for its distribution center because the jobs involved were expected to pay $8.17–$9.39 per hour. But it was clear that Wal-Mart's decision to bypass Lawrence stemmed not from any problem with city policy but from the current existence of a Kmart distribution center in Lawrence; Wal-Mart apparently did not want to locate in a place that had a distribution center for its principal competitor (Toplikar 1993b).

Despite the lack of strong conflict over development incentives in this period, there were signs that disagreement and the perceived need for more development incentive policy change percolated below the surface. For one thing, at least two city commissioners were signaling that they wanted to take up consideration of whether there should be limitations on the granting of repeated tax abatements to the same company (King 1992b). In addition, in contrast with the equanimity about the Wal-Mart and Russell Stover cases on the part of the chamber of commerce and other local officials, the local newspaper used those instances to editorialize critically about the status of the city's economic development efforts. The editorial included critiques that the "attitude projected by recent [city] commissions has been anything but friendly and cooperative" to prospective businesses and claimed that the city's reputation among people selecting real estate and sites for major companies was that "Lawrence is an extremely difficult city in which to build"; the editorial also aired a complaint that city officials and those involved with updating the city's comprehensive master plan "for some reason or other . . . look down their noses at minimum wage jobs or blue collar jobs and at companies that employ more than 200 people" ("Job Search" 1993). In addition to these hints at continuing disagreement and unresolved issues, the process of updating the city's comprehensive plan provided the occasion for both the chamber and interested city officials to revisit the city's business attraction and retention activities, with leaders on both sides signaling that they were "looking for 'a range of possibilities' for bringing new, 'good-paying' jobs to Lawrence, both through expansion of current businesses and attraction of new ones" (Fagan 1993b).

Still other cracks in the surface calm emerged in conjunction with city commission decision making over a pair of tax abatements awarded in late 1993 and late 1994. On a divided result of three votes to two votes, the city commission agreed in the fall of 1993 to a $1.5 million IRB and a ten-year, 50 percent tax abatement for Carrousel Printwear—a screen printing company already in the community that was planning a major expansion. This was done even though the official cost-benefit analysis conducted as part of the review of the proposal yielded results showing only $1.03 in benefits for every $1.00 in costs, far less than the $1.25 cost-benefit ratio that had been discussed as a benchmark when the city's cost-benefit model was adopted. In voting against the proposal, Commissioner Jo Anderson pointed to the $1.03 ratio for the project, saying, "This really bothers me a lot." The other nay-voting commissioner was concerned about the possibility that tax abatement to a screen printing company could give it an unfair advantage over other screen printing businesses in the community. That claim was denied by the president of Carrousel, who argued that the company's emphasis was out-of-town business contracts (Fagan 1993b).

In November 1994, Anderson was happy to join the other commissioners in unanimously approving a ten-year, 50 percent tax abatement for an expansion project by the Garage Door Group, a company already located in the city's business park. However, the meeting again featured critiques from the public present at the meeting, most notably objections from two professors with KU's School of Business who argued that the abatements were both unnecessary (because the business expansion allegedly would have occurred without them) and unfair (in that the forgone tax burden was shifted to others). In response, the vice president and chief operating officer of the Garage Door Group argued that the addition of 150 new employees to the community should vastly outweigh the estimated $800,000 in foregone property taxes; after the meeting, he went on to state, "Last year, we put $3.6 million worth of salaries and wages into this community. . . . I offer no apologies" (Fagan 1994a). Thus, the pattern of individual businesses getting caught in debates over tax abatement, either within the commission or between city commissioners and activists in the community, was still being evidenced even in this period. The Garage Door Group executive's pointed response is evidence of a continuing pattern in Lawrence, a pattern in which businesses are given subsidies but the critical rhetoric associated with the application process puts business executives on the defensive and stokes the business community's claim that the city is not business friendly.

This period saw the emergence of a new venue in which this pattern could play out. The city's new tax abatement policy called for annual reports on all companies receiving abatements, reports that were ultimately up for review by the city commission. In the summer of 1994, those reports showed Packer Plastics, a large manufacturing company that had received a major tax abatement, had cut 66 jobs in the 1992–94 period. Noting this, Anderson raised questions about the city continuing its abatement for Packer Plastics. The possibility that the cutback might be due to a downturn in the economy was not a compelling excuse to her. As she noted, "I don't think the city should be in the business of protecting businesses and keep them from suffering from market forces. . . . That's business. . . . If it's not making money for us, then let's not do it" (Fagan 1994b).

In response, the chairman of Packer Plastics told a newspaper reporter that abatements should not be judged on jobs only and that in any case the company had 200 more employees than it estimated it would have by that date when it applied for its previous tax abatement. He also explained that its latest abatement, which had helped finance new equipment, made it possible for the company to keep the 474 workers that were left after the loss of one of its key contracts three years earlier led to the cutting of 66 jobs. Capping his argument with figures about the importance of those 474 jobs, he noted, "If you throw 2,000 people on the street—families, not just the workers—you're getting a lot of costs to the city and the state and the federal government. Our objective here is to do what's best for the community" (Fagan 1994b).

The city did not rescind or scale back Packer Plastics's tax abatement or penalize the company as a result of the job report in 1994, and the company went on to show substantial growth in employment in later years (Reeb 2007). But the questions raised in the 1994 tax abatement annual report session were a preview of boisterous times to come for this type of session.

Still, the community's dialogue about abatement in the 1992–98 period was considerably muted from what it had been before the institutionalization of a formal policy. During the 1992–98 period, the city commission issued two tax abatements that seemed to epitomize the dream that tax abatement could be used as a tool to develop investments by high-technology businesses bringing high-paying, technical jobs worthy of a university community. In 1995, the city commission unanimously approved a ten-year, 50 percent tax abatement for Oread Clinical Supplies to develop a drug manufacturing plant (Fagan 1995a). The company was a sister company of Oread Laboratories, a local company founded as a spinoff from the university's pharmaceutical chemistry research presence. The proposed bulk drug plant, which would generate small quantities of drugs for use in clinical trials and genetic drug development, promised to bring some relatively well-paying jobs, and the building and equipping of the plant would add substantially to the city's tax base. The results of the required cost-benefit analysis for the proposed plant generated the best cost-benefit ratio seen so far in the community—$2.69 in benefits for every $1.00 in costs (Fagan 1995b).

After gaining approval for an abatement for the project in 1995, the company deferred on taking up the abatement, changing its plans in 1997 to propose an even larger, $8 million plant that would be a "more technologically advanced version in response to market conditions." Ultimately, the company's plans to "be the first company in the world that can develop a drug from molecule to market" (Fagan 1997) foundered over management upheaval, and by 2000 Oread Clinical Supplies was facing the sale of corporate assets to deal with its mounting debts rather than proceeding with expansion plans in Lawrence (Fagan 2000a). But because the abatement that the city had authorized was not taken up, there was no critical rhetoric about tax abatement linked to this company's difficulties.

An even more notable tax abatement awarded at the end of this period went to Sauer-Sundstrand (which later merged with another company to become Sauer Danfoss), a maker of hydrostatic transmissions for off-highway equipment such as combines and riding lawnmowers. In this case, an 80 percent abatement was awarded for the first time in the city's history. The extraordinary abatement was given because of the scale of the project—construction of a $30 million plant, which would be the largest investment by a new company in the history of the community—and because an estimated total of 183 jobs paying on average $29,500 per year was at stake (Fagan 1998a, 1998b).

The abatement was also notable because of the other elements of the package that the city and its governmental partners put together to land the investment. To provide a suitable site for the new facility, the city and county agreed to pay the costs of site preparation and sewer extensions to an undeveloped portion of the city's business park, costs that were financed through a low-interest loan from the state of Kansas (Fagan 1998a). The state government also provided the company with income tax credits, $0.5 million in training funds, and $200,000 from its Economic Opportunity Initiative Fund (Blackwood 1999).

This tax abatement was notable for lack of controversy, despite the scope of the subsidy. As Commissioner Bob Moody noted at the time, "Stepping into a bigger than 50 percent abatement is not done lightly" (Fagan 1998a). But the vote on the abatement was unanimous. And instead of negative comments from the usual critics of tax abatements, media reports were filled with detail about the sophisticated deal, which included provisions that would empower the city to scale back to a 50 percent abatement if the company's investment turned out to be less than $30 million, as well as pleasant information about how the company had chosen Lawrence over Council Bluffs, Iowa, because of its quality of life and quality labor pool (Fagan 1998b).

Thus, the 1992–98 phase of the city's history with development incentives ended on a positive note. But as would quickly become clear, this truly was the calm before the storm. The precedent set in the 80 percent Sauer-Sundstrand abatement would be part of it.

Phase 3: Controversy over American-Eagle Outfitters Jump-Starts a New Round of Policy Change

Just as there were indications in the 1992–98 period that issues relating to economic development were still simmering below the surface calm, the city elections of 1999 made clear that these issues would play out in city politics. For one thing, Rundle, the long-term critic of tax abatements who had served on the city commission from 1987 to 1991, announced his candidacy for another term as city commissioner. When interviewed about his candidacy, he made it clear that he wanted not only to pursue "smart growth" policies but also to reexamine the matter of tax abatements. As he noted, "We use a computer model that right now only has one answer, and that's yes. . . . I think we need to be prepared to say no" (Fagan 1999a). Rundle also argued that "their [tax abatements] use borders on abuse" (Fagan 1999b).

Likewise, two other candidates for city commission indicated opposition to tax abatements, one referring to them as "corporate welfare." Several other candidates in the field of nine (from which three new city commissioners would be chosen) articulated guarded views of tax abatements, insisting that each be carefully scrutinized to ensure the benefits to the community outweighed the costs (Fagan 1999b). In the spring 1999 elections, Rundle was returned to the city commission, getting the second-highest number of votes in the field. He was joined on the commission by top vote-getter Jim Henry, who had articulated his support for tax abatements and business growth, and David Dunfield, who had taken a moderate stand on development issues, emphasizing both the potential usefulness of tax abatements and the necessity to ensure that benefits outweigh costs. These three city commissioners joined two continuing members of the city commission, both with strong ties to the local business establishment.

One year later, this new commission faced a decision about an application for tax abatement from American Eagle Outfitters, which was proposing to build a distribution center on the east side of the community. Its proposal would require the city to annex the proposed building site, 94 acres of farmland lying just outside of the city's eastside business park, and rezone it for industrial uses. Opposition to the proposal was immediately raised by individuals who objected to the conversion of prime farmland for this site and the possibility that this conversion would set a precedent leading to the loss of still more agricultural land in that sector of the county. But in April 2000, the city commission voted three to two for the annexation and rezoning, with Rundle and Dunfield opposed (Blackwood 2000a). In response, the president of Pines International, a local producer of cereal grasses, immediately withdrew from the Lawrence Chamber of Commerce, which had helped bring the American Eagle deal to the city. The company's president objected both to the conversion of precious farmland and to the unfairness of a fast-tracked process for the annexation and rezoning for American Eagle (Miller 2000).

But the real fight would come over American Eagle's request for a ten-year, 80 percent tax abatement. The city had set a precedent for such a large abatement two years earlier with its deal for Sauer-Sundstrand. Although American Eagle's proposed capital investment, like Sauer-Sundstrand's, was very large by local standards at $45 million, the wage levels of the jobs that would be created at the distribution center were considerably lower than those at Sauer-Sundstrand. This fact was immediately seized on by critics of tax abatement—and especially of an 80 percent abatement—for American Eagle (Blackwood 2000b). Opponents showed up in large numbers at the required public hearing held by the city commission, dominating input from the public with twenty-one negative statements compared to four in favor.

Nevertheless, the city commission approved the 80 percent tax abatement for American Eagle with the same split of three votes to two votes as for annexation and rezoning. In exchange, the company agreed to pay $200,000 toward necessary road improvements in the area where the distribution center would be built (Blackwood 2000c).

The controversy over this tax abatement was especially sobering for Henry, who was serving as the city's titular mayor at the time. As such, he represented the city on the committee that reviewed and made recommendations to the full city commission on abatement applications. Having "heard more public comments about American Eagle than any other issue he has dealt with as city commissioner" (Blackwood 2000d) and having made "the hardest decision he's had as a commissioner" to vote for what he dubbed "an OK abatement, not a great abatement," Henry was ready to revisit the city's abatement policy (Blackwood 2000c). One day later, with Rundle publicly stating his intent to find a way to get rid of or at least substantially limit abatements, all city commissioners agreed to form a task force that would examine economic development issues with a specific focus on tax abatements, as well as a look at the relationship between the city government and Douglas County Development Inc., the nonprofit organization formed as a public–private partnership to market the city's business park (Blackwood 2000e).

Community activists also responded to the American Eagle decision. Sparked by the disclosure that most jobs at the subsidized American Eagle distribution center would pay roughly $1,500 per month, which is only 27 percent more than the federal poverty level for a single parent and two children, activists with the Lawrence Coalition for Peace and Justice organized a living wage campaign with some small grant support from the American Friends Service Committee. That campaign was immediately opposed by the city's chamber of commerce, whose president, Bill Sepic, claimed that business perceived a living wage requirement as an "unfunded mandate" that would cause prospective businesses to shun Lawrence. Sepic made clear that he was already organizing opposition to the living wage campaign (Ranney 2000).

Less than a month later, American Eagle changed its plans to build a distribution center in Lawrence, opting instead to build the project in nearby Ottawa, Kansas. An executive with the company claimed that community opposition in Lawrence was not the reason for the change in plans. But he also indicated that because the decision-making process in Lawrence was "so drawn out," it opened the door for the company to be "inundated with offers, unsolicited, from everywhere else. People used to stand outside the commission meetings [in Ottawa] saying, 'Hey, things aren't going well [in Lawrence]. Come to our town'" (Fagan 2000b).

Despite this executive's insistence that "nobody killed the deal" and that the company's executives were "very pleased with most of the people we dealt with in Lawrence" (Fagan 2000b), leaders representing the business establishment in Lawrence and in state government seized on the incident to sharply criticize the Lawrence community and its political leaders. The chamber's vice president for economic development told the press that as a result of the American Eagle controversy, "a couple of companies [that had been looking at Lawrence for a site] have said they don't want to be fired at. . . . The word is out that we will be publicly looking at these abatements, which is not a bad idea, but some of the companies don't want to undergo that scrutiny" (Mathis 2001a).

The state's lieutenant governor, Gary Sherrer, who was involved in development activity in the state and who had suggested the Lawrence location to American Eagle executives, was sharply critical of Lawrence even before American Eagle abandoned its plans to locate there. Noting that many who were opposed to the American Eagle proposal wanted Lawrence to go after better-paying technical jobs, Sherrer indicated that he was "a little troubled by almost a job elitism attitude." In a letter that was interpreted by many as a threat to the community, he stated, "If opportunities of this type are not in keeping with the aims and objectives of the City of Lawrence, then we will not promote Lawrence as a potential site for such business facilities" (Blackwood 2000f). Once American Eagle walked away from its tax abatement deal with Lawrence, Sherrer had additional strong words for a meeting of the community's leaders: "There was nothing fatal about the American Eagle situation. . . . But you certainly wouldn't want to repeat it because then the national economic development community would sense a pattern, and that is trouble." In reference to the community controversy, he claimed, "It was the wrong signal to send" (Lawhorn 2001).

By the spring of 2001, Henry was ready to move forward on the idea of a task force to review economic development policy that had come out of the American Eagle controversy. Henry had taken some time to assemble a set of task force members to represent an array of stakeholders. There were businesspeople on the task force, including an individual whose business had received tax abatement from Lawrence; "neighborhood people"; the director of the university's Institute for Policy & Social Research; proponents of a living wage; and many others ("Tax Abatement Task Force Makeup Draws Wide Praise" 2001).

The task force labored for more than a year, taking up discussion of issues including standards for granting abatements larger than 50 percent, what to do about companies that do not deliver on the numbers of jobs or on the level of investment promised in their application, and especially the matter of a "living wage." The task force quickly reached agreement on some matters, such as having language in the city's abatement policy statement giving priority to the attraction of high-technology and research-based businesses.

However, requirements for larger-than-average abatements and wages for tax-abated companies were more difficult matters. Henry's initial idea was to give 30 percent abatements to companies that yielded barely positive cost-benefit analyses and abatements up to 50 percent for companies with better cost-benefit ratios (Mathis 2001c). But this idea failed to win many supporters, in part because probusiness supporters on the task force wanted the city to have the power to grant abatements even larger than 50 percent and in part because living wage supporters wanted provisions that more clearly tied abatements to higher wages. In July 2001, the task force settled on recommending a policy for larger-than-usual tax abatements that would reserve such abatements for companies spending at least $30 million on land and facilities and paying employees 20 percent above the average wage for Lawrence. Amid disagreement between those wanting abatements no higher than 60 percent and those wanting the possibility of abatements as high as 100 percent, the tax force declined to stipulate a maximum for abatements. In addition, the task force endorsed a recommendation that companies receiving abatements be required to yield cost-benefit analysis results of at least $1.25 in benefits for every $1.00 in costs and a recommendation that after three years in the city, a business would qualify for an additional 5 percent abatement to finance expansions (Mathis 2001b).

Living wage advocates on the task force remained dissatisfied with the recommendations. Their efforts to stipulate a specific, living wage minimum that all tax-abated companies should meet had been opposed by the manager of the Sauer-Danfoss plant, which had received the city's highest-ever tax abatement. He argued that the labor market itself would drive wages up, noting that his company had to increase wages to get the best workers in the area when they came to the community. And several other task force members were content with the existing policy of requiring tax-abated companies to pay the average wage, because from their perspective this was close to the $9.14 per hour that living wage advocates were suggesting as a living wage floor (Mathis 2001d). As it became clear that the task force would not recommend a living wage provision, members of the Kaw Valley Living Wage Alliance staged a Labor Day protest and speech-making event and claimed to have received 1,200 signatures on a petition in favor of a living wage requirement (Mathis 2001e).

In November 2001, the city commission unanimously adopted a resolution laying out its new policy on tax abatements, reflecting some of the thinking of the task force. The amount for a "normal" tax abatement was set at 50 percent for ten years. A company making investments of $20 million or more could qualify for an abatement greater than 50 percent, and no upper limit was stipulated. The new policy did not require that extraordinary wages be paid to qualify for larger abatements;

instead, it specified that for all companies receiving abatements, average wages in each employment category must meet or exceed average wages in the community (City of Lawrence, Kansas 2001)—a statement much the same as the previous policy's statement about meeting or exceeding average wages except for the specification that this be met in each employment category. Despite the community pressures for a specific living wage requirement, the new policy was therefore more responsive to the chamber of commerce, whose vice president for public policy had written to the city commission arguing against a living wage provision and stating, "I ask you to shut the door on this. . . . Send a message that the tax abatement committee did consider this issue and decided to go another direction" ("Policy Approval Doesn't End Tax Abatement Debate" 2001).

For those who wanted the city to demand more in exchange for abatements, however, the new policy stipulated for the first time that a company receiving an abatement would have to sign a performance agreement and that if the promised wages, number of jobs, and capital investments in the abatement application were not met, "then the tax exemption may be modified pursuant to the Performance Agreement as the City Commission deems appropriate" (City of Lawrence, Kansas 2001). Although eschewing any "clawback" language, this provision for the first time gave the city explicit grounds for partially or fully rescinding a tax abatement during the ten-year period for which it was granted.

The new policy also laid out a more formal annual review process through which each tax-abated company's performance with respect to capital investment, employment, and wages would be examined for compliance. Companies would also be asked to describe their achievements with respect to environmentally sound practice, "community engagement and services," and job training (City of Lawrence, Kansas 2001). To review initial applications, handle the annual reviews, and make recommendations to the city commission, a Public Incentives Review Committee (PIRC) was established. Its representation was similar to the administrative review committee that it replaced, except that more spots were provided for legislative representation from the city and county commissions and a three-year term for a community resident was added. Finally, the criterion of $1.25 in benefits for every $1.00 in costs was incorporated in the language of the policy resolution—thereby formalizing what had been an informal and loosely applied benchmark.

With its adoption of this policy, the city of Lawrence formalized its tax abatement policy even more than it had a decade earlier. Using a lengthy task force process that provided ample opportunity for the many different stakeholders to air their concerns, city officials had made progress in nailing down some details of the city's policy that had been the focus of periodic controversies. But in the process of adding strong performance agreement elements to the cost-benefit analysis requirements of its previous policy, the city had provided ample occasions for critiques of business to be aired and for pressures for a living wage requirement to build.

Phase 4: Living Wage (and Other) Issues Won't Go Away

Within a year of the city's adoption of its latest tax abatement policy in 2001, it became clear that contentiousness surrounding tax abatements was far from over. McClure, the KU professor who was a long-term critic of tax abatements, was named the citizen member of the PIRC, and from his position on that committee he was launching criticisms at the recipients of tax abatements, noting that many of them had not delivered on the investments and jobs that had been projected in their applications ("Tax Abatement Report Approved" 2002).

There were several problems with this critique from businesses' point of view. One was that the companies already holding tax abatements had all negotiated them under the previous policy regime, which did not include the language of performance agreements. As one business owner explained, "One of the things that is unfortunate is that there is commentary [at PIRC meetings] about employment levels, capital expenditures, and about wages and living wages and all this other stuff . . . [but] the fact is our abatement was approved under an ordinance that had none of that criteria" (Interview B 2008). Referring to McClure's tenure on the PIRC, he went on to note,

> He'll get quoted every year when that [report] comes out and gets reported in the press that we had X number of companies that fell below, they're not meeting their obligations. The fact is that is not true by statute. We are meeting the obligations. . . . And . . . though we do it because we want to be good community citizens, . . . we don't need to submit that wage information because quite honestly our ordinance [under which the company's abatement was

> granted] doesn't require it. But we do it because the city has asked us to do it but quite honestly we don't cower about feeling good about being a player in the market and paying a competitive wage.

Yet another business owner explained that his company was not in compliance in terms of the predictions that it made about employment at the time of its abatement application. But at the time, the company was told to "shoot for the moon" and to make aggressive predictions for growth (Interview E 2008). These aggressive predictions were clearly not seen by this business owner as part of a performance agreement for which he would be accountable, and at the time the company's tax abatement was granted, technically they were not. All of this, combined with the post-9/11 slump in the economy playing havoc with the plans of many businesses, created an awkward situation in which many tax-abated companies in the community could be claimed to be underdelivering on their promises. But from the companies' perspective, neither the legal status of their promises nor the nature of economic circumstances was adequately being taken into account by critics.

Furthermore, despite the city's new abatement policy, the process of handling individual applications was still sparking contentious debate that placed applicants in the crossfire. In November 2002, for example, the PIRC voted to recommend a ten-year, 55 percent tax abatement for Prosoco, a manufacturer of masonry and concrete cleaning solutions, to undertake a $2.5 million expansion project in the community. But from his seat on the PIRC, McClure pointedly questioned a Prosoco executive to establish whether or not the expansion would occur anyway, even without being granted tax abatement. Although he received a result of six votes to one vote in favor of tax abatement for his company, Prosoco's vice president indicated to a local news reporter after the meeting that the arguing was unpleasant and stated, "I feel, had I not already been located in Lawrence and familiar with the local politics, I could've felt put off as a business owner in coming in from the outside" ("Board Approves Tax Abatement" 2002).

Similarly, the city commission seemed to be back to a familiar pattern of four votes to one for tax abatements, with Rundle in opposition and Professor Allen Ford from KU's School of Business offering critiques from the floor. In January 2003, this pattern was revisited when the city commission took up a request from Serologicals for an 80 percent tax abatement. The requested abatement for this pharmaceutical company's planned $25 million investment in the community had many elements that community leaders wanted to see from tax abatements—a high-technology business making a large investment to build a 43,000-square-foot plant in the community's business park and hiring workers with an average wage of $47,000. As a result, four city commissioners, including one who had in previous years been critical of tax abatements, voted for the requested abatement. Nevertheless, it attracted a negative vote from Rundle, who objected to the size of the abatement, indicating that he would have voted in favor of a 50 percent abatement but that an 80 percent abatement was "not fair and equitable to the rest of the community"; echoing this, Ford exercised his opportunity at the public comment period to argue that the cost of the abatement was too much and that smaller businesses would be paying a much higher tax rate than Serologicals ("City OKs 80 Percent Tax Break" 2003).

Finally, living wage proponents had not given up on the idea of an ordinance that would commit tax-abated companies to a specific wage floor. And 2003 was a local election year, with three city commission seats up for grabs. A living wage ordinance (along with the closely related matter of "smart growth") was to be the key issue in the campaign, especially since two sitting commissioners had favored a living wage requirement in discussions surrounding the revamping of tax abatement policy in 2001. One of those sitting commissioners—Rundle—was up for reelection. If he were to win and at least one of the other two seats were to be taken by a living wage proponent, the requirement could again be placed on the agenda, presumably with greater success ("Living Wage Ordinance Divides City Candidates" 2003). This is precisely what occurred. Rundle was reelected, two others favoring smart growth and a living wage requirement joined him, and sitting commissioner Dunfield yielded to a "supermajority" in favor of a progressive economic development agenda.

The election had strongly politicized the issue, with forces in opposition to a living wage requirement becoming ever more mobilized as the prospects for a living wage–friendly city commission became clearer. At the height of the campaign season, the city's chamber of commerce had released the results of a survey showing that 80 percent of its members were "greatly concerned by the prospect of a living wage requirement" ("Living Wage Ordinance Divides City Candidates" 2003).

Three months after the election, as the new supermajority scheduled hearings on the issue and as the Kaw Valley Living Wage Alliance gathered endorsements from labor unions, churches, and neighborhood groups, the state's chamber of commerce decided to enter the fray. In a news release, officials with the state chamber accused living wage advocates of working for "Big Labor" and argued that an artificial wage requirement would lead to fewer jobs. Meanwhile, the plant director for the city's first 80 percent tax-abated company, who had served on the task force that yielded the 2001 tax abatement policy reform, told the media that a living wage requirement would have put a damper on his company's interest in the city. As he noted, "We believe the right culture in our company is to have the relationship between the company and the team members [employees] that work for the company. . . . For us, [a living wage requirement] would have sent a message this community doesn't endorse or doesn't understand the value of that relationship without a third party" ("Warmer Welcome Awaits Proposed Living Wage Ordinance" 2003). Yet another tax-abated company's chief executive went public with critical comments about the city's unfriendly environment for business, arguing, "If somebody would come to me today and ask if I could recommend them moving their business to Lawrence, I honestly would have to say no. . . . I just can't imagine why anyone should put up with this nonsense. I find it so unfriendly, I just can't emphasize that enough" ("Bogged Down in Regulations" 2003).

And as the living wage hearings loomed, the local chamber of commerce swung into action by releasing to the media results of the first business retention survey that it had ever done—results that it also presented to the city commission. The results that were highlighted reflected evidence that the community's politics and its "unfriendly business environment" were problems standing in the way of economic development ("Bogged Down in Regulations" 2003). In addition to this barrage of information about alleged problems with the city's business climate, the chamber was signaling its willingness to agree to a voluntary rather than a mandated living wage, with companies that pay substantially more than 130 percent of the poverty level for a family of three—the suggested minimum wage floor—being rewarded with a larger tax abatement (Lawhorn 2003). After some rounds of conversation between two city commissioners, including a visible living wage proponent, and key members of the chamber, chamber spokespeople shifted to support of a living wage requirement, providing that it was made part of a revamped policy resolution on tax abatement rather than a stand-alone ordinance, which some chamber members saw as potentially broader and more offputting to prospective businesses ("Living Wage: Anatomy of a Deal" 2003).

But by the late summer of 2003, many manufacturing companies in the city were taking a harder line than the chamber of commerce. Thirteen members of the Manufacturers' Network of Douglas County signed a letter to the Lawrence city commission indicating their strong opposition to a living wage requirement. These prominent manufacturers argued that such a requirement would push many of them, even those already receiving abatements, to take actions ranging from cutting workers and raising prices to thinking about a departure from Lawrence ("City to Revisit Living-Wage Ideas" 2003). Several of these plant managers or manufacturing chief executives also testified at the city commission hearing on the issue, arguing that a living wage ordinance would have deterred them from investing in the community. Still other local business executives with companies that subcontract with some tax-abated companies voiced worries that they too would be forced to pay a living wage ("City Still Fine-Tuning Living Wage" 2003).

The concerns of these manufacturing companies were undercut, however, by chamber officials' willingness to support a living wage requirement in principle, provided that it was narrowly cast so as to only apply to companies receiving tax abatements. And by a unanimous five-to-zero vote, this is what city officials enacted in the fall of 2003 ("City Approves Living Wage" 2003).

The city commission enacted a living wage requirement as an ordinance, but one that is narrow in that it applies only to tax-abated companies and specifically exempts subcontractors of tax-abated companies. The ordinance mandates that incoming companies receiving tax abatements pay all Lawrence site employees at least 130 percent of the federally set poverty level for a family of three. For companies already in Lawrence that receive an abatement to expand operations, the requirement applies only to employees whose jobs are connected to the tax abatement—that is, those hired as part of an expansion for which the company received an abatement. It also allows a sixty-day probationary period for such employees before eligibility for the living wage requirement takes hold; trainees, temporary workers, and student seasonal workers are exempt (City of Lawrence, Kansas 2003).

The ordinance also lays out some specifics about the consequences for noncompliance. Tax-abated companies that do not pay the mandated wage for two consecutive years must have their abatement revoked unless a supermajority of four city commissioners votes to waive the discontinuance because of extraordinary circumstances. And, in the first, albeit limited, form of a clawback provision in the city's history, the ordinance requires tax-abated companies to sign a performance agreement stipulating that if they fail to pay the mandated living wage floor, they will be required to pay to the city double the difference between the payroll amount that they should have paid under the wage requirement and the amount that they actually paid. The city would then disperse half of the penalty payment to current or former employees of the business in question and use the other half for economic development programs to be designated by the city commission (City of Lawrence, Kansas 2003).

Five years after the enactment of this living wage ordinance, the city's manufacturing companies were still fuming about it. One CEO of a long-term, homegrown manufacturing business saw the living wage element as "beyond unfair to the point of hypocritical" because he said he believes some jobs with city government and KU pay less than 130 percent of the federal poverty level. It is, he said, one of the most "unfair, unethical business laws" he has ever heard of. He said he feels the whole burden of offering a living wage is being heaped on eight or nine manufacturing companies currently holding abatements, a small group that in his view has "almost no political power" (Interview D 2008).

Policy-Centered Theory and the Lawrence Case

When it is applied to the public, policy-centered theory readily posits that governmental programs convey important messages to the targets of those programs—messages about their worth to and status in the community. This message sending is an essential component of policy-centered theory because it is the key mechanism through which government programs are presumed to shape individuals' understanding of their expected role in the polity and hence their levels of political engagement. Policy-centered theory is less often applied to political elites. And for one set of elites especially—members of the local business establishment—it may not be as clear to urban scholars that governmental programs *have* the power to send messages about worth and status, especially if the content of those messages is such that the privileged status of business in the community is called into question.

However, this case study shows that as city governments add various municipal controls to their tax abatement policies, their development incentive programs do send negative messages that are threatening to the status of tax-abated business owners and managers. This is not simply a matter of business elites having to confront a set of annoying barriers to getting accustomed benefits or having to adjust to a change in the bottom-line dollar value of such benefits. The passion and resentment in the reaction of tax-abated companies in this community shows that it is more personal than that. It also includes perceptions of the status and worth that are being accorded to a business owner's enterprise.

The business owners and plant managers in this community each spoke about their companies being good corporate citizens that give back to the community. They proudly pointed not only to the jobs that their companies provided but also to the numerous philanthropic activities sponsored by their companies and sometimes even to the care they took to manage the exterior appearance of their facility so that it minimized conflict with adjacent landowners and helped provide a positive image to visitors of the community.

The language that such individuals used reveals there is often a deep-seated sense that the company should be viewed as having worth to the community and that these business leaders have a personal stake in whether or not their business is considered a valued part of the community. One plant manager said, "We feel that we are a very strong part of this community" (Interview C 2008) and went on to describe the deep connections that he sees between his current employees, young people now attending high school who will need work opportunities, and the non-profit organizations with whom the organization's employees work. After describing with no small amount of pride its history as a family business built by his father, one local business owner explained that "you want to be appreciated" and for this reason it is particularly uncomfortable to be called onto the carpet at an incentives review committee hearing about underperforming on job creation. Indeed, he noted that when he first was approached by chamber of commerce officials about applying for tax abatement, he hesitated to apply because he "knew there was a lot of fighting about tax abatements" in the community and he "didn't want an abatement if it was going to cause a fight."

Given this strong need to be viewed as valued members of the community, business leaders reacted quite strongly to the messages sent by tax abatement reform. An important point in this regard is that the messages sent by tax abatement reform were embodied not only in the specific provisions of the municipal controls and other reform elements that came to be adopted but also in the critical commentary and pointed discussions that were part of the agenda-setting and policy adoption process. This is especially important to the extent that municipal controls occur in waves. Each wave of reform involves at least some reform proponents who introduce themes of corporate welfare, corporate abuse of the public trust, or other rhetoric to underscore their claim that subsidies are going to those who do not deserve them. While an unknown number of businesses looking to locate in the community might react by simply locating elsewhere, existing local business owners and managers clearly see such rhetoric as threatening not just to their monetary bottom line but to their status in the community.

But if it is clear that businesses get negative messages as development subsidy policy is subjected to waves of reform, the messages are clearly not demobilizing. If anything, there is evidence that the negative messages activate the local business community. In this sense, there is a clear difference between welfare, which chills the political participation of recipients and their friends, and added controls to "corporate welfare," which mobilizes recipients and their allies.

The various accountability controls on development subsidies are not equally capable of conveying negative messages about business. For example, in Lawrence, many businesses receiving tax abatements had little objection to the idea of having to pass the test of a cost-benefit analysis to get one in the future. Arguably, this could result from business leaders' belief that the specifics of a cost-benefit analysis could be manipulated to consistently yield favorable results. However, another reason is at least as likely. As one plant manager indicated, business leaders are steeped in the mentality of striking a good deal and are not particularly offended when city government wants evidence that tax abatement will be a good deal for the community (Interview C 2008). However, other municipal controls send more negative messages to local businesses. The case study revealed that wage requirements were viewed as particularly offensive, signifying to at least one major business owner that employers cannot be trusted to deal properly with their own employees.

The case also revealed that accountability controls expand the opportunities for business owners to experience embarrassment to which they are so little accustomed, especially if local government chooses policy design elements that maximize exposure to public scrutiny. Required annual performance reporting, for example, can either be done via a simple, low-profile filing with a designated city department, or the policy design can stipulate a highly public review of subsidy recipients' performance reports. In the context of the boisterous, critical history of tax abatements in this particular city, the choice to add the latter design element amounted to a choice that business owners would continue to be subjected to public criticism and the kinds of rhetoric that they often perceived as showing a lack of appreciation for what their business investment was doing for the community.

As policy-centered theorists have suggested, the processes through which policy generates feedback effects are quite varied. The most obvious processes—the provision of material stakes or, by contrast, the adoption of policies that threaten material stakes—are relevant when development subsidy policies are at issue. There is evidence both here and in chapter 4 of public policies shaping patterns of business mobilization along these lines. But apart from this obvious resource effect, policy feedback can be generated via several interpretive effects, such as defining membership and status in the community, delineating group divisions, shaping the way that individuals understand rights and responsibilities in the community, and influencing the ongoing salience of an issue (Mettler and Soss 2004). These subtler processes are not as easily traced in the quantitative analyses presented in chapter 4. But this case study reveals that, beyond the dollars and cents at stake, when a community adds accountability controls to its tax abatement policy, each of these interpretive effects is likely to be in play as well.

6

Policy-Centered Theory and Urban Programs

Community Effects in a Global Context

Policy-centered theory invites us to consider the possibility that public policies and the government programs that embody them may have important consequences for democracy. Government programs can distribute benefits in a way that subsequently mobilizes stakeholders or in a way that has a chilling effect on political participation; they can build civic skills and provide other assets for political mobilization, frame problems for the political agenda, reinforce the social construction of various groups, help define politically relevant identities, and either support or undermine democratic institutions (Mettler and Soss 2004, 62–63). The idea that government programs can either enhance or diminish political participation, thereby helping define the political community, is perhaps the most important insight of policy-centered theory.

Oddly enough, however, work in the policy-centered tradition has been almost exclusively dominated by a focus on the policies of the federal government and the impacts that these policies of the nation-state can have on individuals' membership and political involvement in the very large community that is the nation-state. This book has been devoted to an exploration of whether *local government* policies and programs exhibit the kinds of policy feedback effects that have been found in policy-centered studies of major social programs at the national level. From that process of exploration, the book also yields insights about modifications to policy-centered theory that are suggested by its application to government policies different from those that have been the focus of work in the genre so far. This chapter outlines these findings and insights, situates them in ongoing efforts to fine-tune policy-centered theory, and relates them to the broad issue of local adaptations to globalization challenges.

Context for Mixed Findings

Does analysis of urban programs yield evidence consistent with policy-centered theory? The answer is yes and no. That is, evidence of the expected policy feedback effects is apparent for some local government programs and policies but not for others.

Before turning to a discussion of the pattern of these findings, it is important to note that the portions of this project yielding no evidence of policy feedback effects are not the first analyses to generate such null results. Although much scholarship in the policy-centered genre yields findings of policy feedback effects, some studies in that genre, and particularly those looking for feedback in the form of change in aggregate or institution-level political patterns, report findings of policy having no feedback effects (Soss and Schram 2007; Patashnik 2008; Weir, Rongerude, and Ansell 2009).

These null results are important in two respects. As Patashnik and Zelizer (2009, 3) note, "If policy feedback is everywhere, it is nowhere." The null findings are, therefore, an important demonstration that research hypotheses drawn from the policy-centered approach are falsifiable and hence worthy of theory testing. Perhaps more importantly, the null results have sparked attention to a conditional version of policy-centered theory—that is, specification of the conditions under which policy feedback effects are more likely and less likely.

Two such efforts to outline a contingent version of policy feedback are given in some detail here and then used to interpret the pattern of findings in this book.

Proximity and Visibility as Key Contingencies

In their analysis of the 1996 welfare reform program legislated in the United States, Soss and Schram (2007) investigated whether the important changes in policy design embodied in that reform program had the anticipated feedback effects. Unlike earlier work on welfare, the focus in the 2007 article was on the program's impacts not on the recipients but on the public. Scholars and Democratic Party strategists alike expected welfare reform would diminish the negative and race-coded views of welfare recipients that had long been held by many Americans, thereby making the public more amenable to spending to help the poor, more favorably oriented toward the Democratic Party, and more likely to vote for Democratic candidates. Instead, Soss and Schram (2007, 120) found that "Welfare opponents remained just as numerous after 1996 as in the AFDC [Aid to Families with Dependent Children] era, and these individuals became no more likely to identify with the Democratic Party or vote for Democratic candidates." In short, the public was not transformed by this major welfare reform program, in terms of either their policy preferences or their political behavior.

In an effort to understand why this major reform did not have the expected policy feedback effects, Soss and Schram (2007, 121) offered a theoretical framework designed to "explain how mass feedback processes should vary across policy types and to specify the conditions under which such effects should be seen as more or less likely." Their framework may also be useful in interpreting the pattern of positive and null results found in this book's analysis of the feedback effects of local government policies. For this reason, this chapter begins with a brief summary of that theoretical framework.

The Soss and Schram framework is based on two key factors: (1) the level of *visibility* of the policy (i.e., the salience of the policy or program to the public) and (2) the *proximity* of the policy (i.e., the extent to which the program is experienced directly by members of the public, rather than being a distant object appraised on the basis of symbolic cues). Figure 6.1 shows the four types of programs possible given these two key dimensions, as well as predictions about the likelihood of feedback effects in each case. As Soss and Schram (2007, 121) noted, the typology makes sense only if we are reminded that there is not a single "mass public" but many "publics." Policies that one group experiences directly and tangibly may be known to other groups only indirectly, and policies that are highly salient to some members of the public may be virtually invisible to others.

With that caveat in mind, the type II and III policies in Figure 6.1 represent the most easily understood scenarios. Type II policies are directly experienced by a substantial portion of the American public and are highly salient. The tangible impact that these policies have on the lives of numerous individuals creates a strong potential for policy feedback in the form of resource effects, such as senior citizens' elevated political participation rates being motivated by their Social Security concerns (Campbell 2003). Because of their visibility, such programs also have a

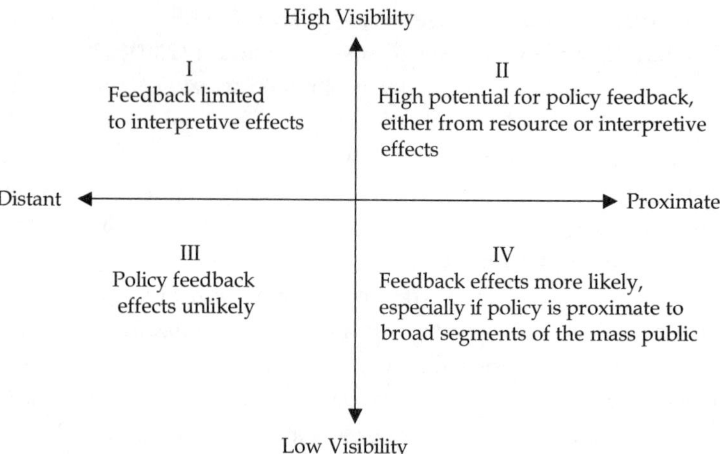

Figure 6.1. Soss and Schram framework for analyzing mass feedback processes. Source: Adapted from Soss and Schram 2007, 121.

high potential for interpretive effects via the messages that the programs send to both program recipients and broader publics about who is a valued member of the community and who is not. Whether those interpretive effects are positive and empowering or negative and demobilizing depends on the design elements of the program, including the familiar distinction between means-tested and universal programs. This type II category, with its high potential for policy feedback effects, includes major social programs that have been the focus of several foundational studies in the policy-centered tradition.

By contrast, policies that have low salience and are directly experienced by relatively small numbers of the public have a low potential for generating policy feedback effects, especially with respect to most members of the public who are by definition "unaware and unaffected" (Soss and Schram 2007, 222). Soss and Schram did not say much about the potential for feedback effects from the narrow constituency that does directly experience a type III program, such as the individuals benefitting from an obscure tax provision. However, their discussion indicated that type III programs give an advantage to status quo interests, implying that this narrow constituency would exhibit resource effects in the form of mobilization to protect benefits if the program were threatened.

Yet another scenario is found with programs that are low in salience but have tangible importance to substantial segments of the public. These type IV programs, such as worker safety regulations or the various tax benefits extended to homeowners, are little noticed much of the time, but they "shape broad patterns of belief, expectation and behavior" in the public (Soss and Schram 2007, 121). Problems in or proposed changes to such programs yield policy feedback beyond what would be expected for low-visibility programs, simply because so many people have direct experience with them.

But the type I program provided the basis for Soss and Schram's interpretation of the failure of the 1996 welfare reform program to transform the public's beliefs and political behavior in predicted ways. Type I programs are not proximate for most people. Nevertheless, type I programs are highly visible. This odd combination means that for most people, type I programs are "spectacles" that can "elicit rapt attention and powerful emotion" when elite discourse sparks media attention to them. Because most of the public has no direct experience with these programs, elite and media framing "condition mass feedback effects," which "work primarily through the expressive (symbolic) aspects" of the policy (Soss and Schram 2007, 122). The placement of welfare (both pre- and postreform) in this category provides an explanation for the failure of the 1996 reform to transform public attitudes. Because the program is not proximate to most of the public, the actual details of welfare reform were ignored even when welfare reform was a salient issue. Instead, views of welfare and welfare recipients are grounded in long-standing symbolisms, unfazed by important changes in the welfare program.

For welfare recipients, the welfare program does not fit with the type I policies. For members of this target group, welfare is proximate and salient and feedback effects are to be expected. However, because of the nature of the program's design elements, the substantial feedback effects that have been documented appear to be largely interpretive effects—that is, the demeaning, demobilizing elements of the program that depress the political participation levels of welfare recipients (Soss 1999).

As summarized in the introduction, initial theorizing in the policy-centered genre largely focused on individuals and groups that experience government programs and provided theoretical expectations about the types of policy feedback that experience with such programs might generate—most importantly, the mobilizing effects that enhance political participation and the demobilizing effects that diminish political participation. The Soss and Schram framework went beyond this in two ways: it laid out scenarios under which feedback effects are more and less likely to occur, and it placed relatively heavy emphasis on the possibilities for program-related feedback effects among individuals and groups that do not experience the program in question.

Triumvirate of Conditions Detrimental to Policy Feedback

In a recent paper, Patashnik and Zelizer (2009) took a somewhat different approach to the challenge of viewing policy feedback effects contingently. Although still focusing on national-level policies and programs, they outlined three "generic conditions that diminish the capacity for policies to generate self-reinforcing processes: weak policy design, inadequate or conflicting institutional supports, and poor timing" (3–4).

Policy design can be too weak to yield feedback if it does not "provide enough material resources to facilitate the emergence of a supportive constituency to defend the policy" (Patashnik and Zelizer 2009, 10). Although this problem affects feedback via resource effects, weak policy design can also inhibit interpretive feedback effects, particularly if the policy requires reconstructed identities or statuses that conflict with strongly held loyalties or norms (17). Furthermore, policy design can be too weak to generate resource or interpretive effects if "key segments of the public are unable to perceive what a policy does for them" (13). This aspect of weak policy design offers one point of overlap with Soss and Schram's notion of low proximity.

Inadequate or conflicting institutional supports constitute a second condition that would compromise feedback effects. A policy that is implemented in a setting of multiple institutions and policies that "are in tension with one another" rather than being "mutually reinforcing" would yield little in the way of feedback effects (Patashnik and Zelizer 2009, 19). In a related vein, if policies are simply added to existing arrangements, rather than replacing arrangements with which they conflict, feedback effects are unlikely. And when policies "are unable to call upon needed state capacities" (20), they end up being only partially implemented and hence incapable of generating feedback.

Finally, the feedback potential of public policies can be compromised by bad timing. Policies that are out of kilter with prevailing norms or policies whose support disappears due to unexpected changes in economic conditions or other historical context exemplify this problem (Patashnik and Zelizer 2009, 26–28).

Applying Policy-Centered Theory to Urban Policies and Programs

We now return to the bottom-line issues for this volume: To what extent do local government programs yield results consistent with policy-centered theory in its initial form? And where the anticipated feedback effects are not apparent, to what extent do the null results fit the interpretations offered by recent efforts to make that theory conditional? As the remainder of this chapter shows, the answer to the first question depends on the type of local government program at issue. Furthermore, the null findings that emerge are in part interpretable using either Soss and Schram's (2007) emphasis on program salience and proximity as key contingencies or Patashnik and Zelizer's (2009) diagnosis of generic conditions that diminish the potential for feedback effects. However, analysis of urban governments' activities yields additional considerations that may be as or more important than either the salience and proximity suggested by Soss and Schram or the generic conditions suggested by Patashnik and Zelizer.

Consistent Results, with a Twist

When the programs at issue are local-level versions of social programs promulgated at the federal level, analysis of feedback effects yields results highly consistent with policy-centered theory. Much of county government's social service activity involves implementation of federal or federal–state social policies, some involving means testing and some in the non-means-tested category. The political participation impacts of variation in county spending on these two kinds of programs are largely consistent with the core hypotheses of policy-centered theory.

Specifically, for those most likely to "experience" means-tested programs, higher levels of county involvement with such programs dampens political participation; for those unlikely to use means-tested programs, higher levels of county spending on such programs have no impact on political participation. This finding holds for uniquely local forms of political participation. Extending policy-centered theory to local government means considering the impact of program characteristics on forms of participation such as working on a community project; attending a political meeting or rally; signing a petition; participating in demonstrations, boycotts, or marches; and joining a neighborhood group. That we observe the disempowering effect of means-tested programs vis-à-vis *these* forms of political participation is an important piece of evidence as we consider whether policy-centered theory can be extended to local government. It also underscores that the character of social programs designed by national government has implications for civic engagement and community at the local level.

In addition, chapter 1 showed higher levels of county spending on non-means-tested social programs are linked with higher levels of engagement in locally oriented forms of political participation. This empowerment effect of universal social programs is also consistent with foundational studies in the policy-centered genre. But the empowerment effect found in chapter 1 is conditional in a way that is not apparent from existing studies in that genre—that is, the participation-enhancing effect of county spending on universal social programs is apparent *only among county residents who are unlikely to experience means-tested programs as well.* For those who are most likely to experience welfare or welfare-like programs and non-means-tested programs, the chilling effect of the former appears to trump any empowering effect of the latter.

This result is a first step toward acknowledging the layering problem that confronts the extension of policy-centered theory to local government. The layering problem has to do with residents of urban America potentially being exposed to a variety of urban government programs—programs that may have contrasting design elements and send conflicting messages to recipients. To date, policy-centered theory has largely focused on the impacts that a single, high-profile program might have on recipients. Key exceptions are recent studies by Mettler and Stonecash (2008) for the United States and Kumlin and Rothstein (2005) for Sweden, which found the expected mobilizing and demobilizing impacts of non-means-tested and means-tested programs measured as separate counts of citizen usage of various programs in each category. Still, these studies did not examine how citizens' experience with one or more non-means-tested programs might shape their reaction to the means-tested programs that they experience, or vice versa. The results reported here provide a key thesis to add to ongoing theoretical development in this area: the chilling effect that means-tested programming has on participation is more potent than the empowering effect of universal programming.

This interpretation of the lack of policy feedback from universal program spending on welfare-experiencing individuals contrasts markedly with the thrust of the Soss and Schram (2007) framework (see Figure 6.1). Presumably, the non-means-tested programs that counties fund (e.g., immunization clinics and human immunodeficiency virus testing) are at least as, if not more, important to welfare-experiencing individuals as they are to the rest of the public. Hence, although these programs may be fairly low in salience for everyone in the community, they are surely more proximate for welfare-experiencing individuals than for others. This would place welfare-experiencing individuals in the fourth category of the Soss and Schram framework, yielding the diagnosis that feedback effects are likely for this "public." They do not exhibit these feedback effects from universal programming, which perhaps has less to do with matters of salience and proximity than with the chilling effect of their simultaneous involvement in means-tested programs.

Null Findings, or Worse?

Much of what city governments do, however, involves policies and programs quite different from the social programs that are the focus of policy-centered theory. Rather than implementing programs that target specific and often monetarily significant benefits to individual clients, city governments are quintessentially involved in providing a variety of services to areal (i.e., neighborhood-sized) units. These services include street maintenance, traffic law enforcement, residential trash collection, neighborhood parks, code enforcement, and planning and zoning decisions that can affect everything from storm water runoff, to home prices, to traffic congestion and pedestrian safety.

Some cities have adopted programs that formally give neighborhood residents a say in decisions on at least some matters that would affect their neighborhood; without adopting such formal programs, other cities have made it a policy to be as responsive to organized neighborhood interests as possible across an array of activities and decisions. Either way, cities that emphasize responsiveness to neighborhoods exhibit a programmatic policy stance that on its face should empower citizen engagement, at least with respect to neighborhood-based organizations. Yet chapter 2 showed such a policy-centered theory–style expectation is not borne out. Once participation-shaping individual characteristics are taken into account, participation in neighborhood organizations is not higher when government goes out of its way to be responsive to neighborhood-based interests. If anything, it may be lower. The results are much the same when we focus on a single neighborhood-relevant government program—community policing. Attendance at community meetings is unaffected by the scope of the city's commitment to community policing activity; and in cities with more extensive community policing meetings, participation in neighborhood associations is actually less likely among whites and working on a community project is less likely among blacks.

Programs deliberately focused on encouraging citizen involvement should, in theory, send messages to citizens that their input is desirable and will be taken seriously. According to policy-centered theory, these are the kinds of messages that should, other things being equal, yield enhanced levels of citizen participation and, in the case of community policing, enhanced trust in police. Why don't they? Why, if anything, is there negative policy feedback from these programs—that is, diminished civic engagement from empowerment programs? Do these negative results constitute evidence of policy feedback, albeit feedback that is both counterintuitive and counterproductive?

The last of these questions points to an important research design issue that has a bearing on the question and should shape interpretation of the results. The research in this volume is limited to a cross-sectional analysis rather than the time series analysis featured in Soss and Schram's (2007) work, as well as some other notable pieces of policy-centered research. With a cross-sectional design, we cannot rule out the possibility that the police departments adopting more extensive versions of community policing are in cities with a history of particularly problematic police–community relations. Indeed, it is rather likely that police departments in cities with such problems would reach for community policing as a solution. Similarly, we cannot rule out the possibility that the cities that have made special efforts at outreach to neighborhoods are trying to spark civic engagement where it has been particularly lacking. If this *is* the case, what appears to be evidence of demobilizing effects from neighborhood empowerment efforts and community policing may not be evidence of such a counterproductive effect. Rather, the evidence may simply point to null results. It may show the failure of community policing to transform views of police, build social capital, and heighten civic engagement in places where police–community relations, social capital, and civic engagement were bad to begin with, and it may show the failure of neighborhood empowerment programs to get citizens involved in neighborhood associations where low levels of civic engagement led officials to take up such programs.

This takes us to the question of why these programs failed to generate the desired feedback effects. The Soss and Schram framework suggests one answer: there are no feedback effects because the programs are low in visibility and lack proximity for relevant members of the public (see type III in Figure 6.1). But is it reasonable to assume that neighborhood-responsiveness programs in general and community policing in particular are not only low-visibility programs but also programs that lack proximity to relevant groups?

With respect to neighborhood-responsiveness policy that was the focus of chapter 2, the low-proximity assumption is particularly *un*reasonable. The various matters that are the special province of neighborhood empowerment efforts—traffic problems in the neighborhood, proposed land uses that neighbors oppose, drainage problems, desires for park improvements, and so forth—may not always be salient, but these matters are close to the daily, lived experience of residents of the neighborhood. When government caves in to neighborhood opposition to unwanted land use, puts in a new park or streetlights, or begins installing new storm drains, residents are highly likely to know about it. Hence, proximity is high rather than low. In the same vein, Patashnik and Zelizer's (2009) point about policy design that is weak, in the sense that key segments of the public are unable to perceive what a policy does for them, does not apply.

Neighborhood-responsiveness programs typically belong among Soss and Schram's type IV programs, a category where feedback effects are likely. Occasionally, when high-profile matters are encountered, such as proposed redevelopment projects that would change the character of the neighborhood or incidents of flooding that highlight storm water drainage problems, the city's neighborhood-responsiveness policy is presumably proximate *and* high in salience for the neighborhood. On these occasions, neighborhood-responsiveness policy fits the type II scenario, and again policy feedback effects are to be expected.

In short, the failure of neighborhood empowerment programs to generate feedback effects in the form of enhanced neighborhood association involvement cannot plausibly be accounted for by the salience and proximity considerations that anchor the Patashnik and Zelizer framework. But as chapter 2 showed, that lack of feedback effects can be explained by collective action theory. Especially for residents who are relatively trusting of their neighbors, participating in the neighborhood organizations that are the vehicles for city hall's responsiveness to the neighborhood can be delegated to those few activists who are comfortable with and enjoy this form of civic engagement. Ironically, the more a city government demonstrates responsiveness to the neighborhood, the more institutionalized this free-rider behavior can become, thus preventing the heightened levels of neighborhood association involvement that might have been expected from neighborhood-responsiveness programs.

With respect to community policing in particular, rather than neighborhood-responsiveness policy more generally, how might we interpret the lack of desired policy feedback effects? One possibility is that the same, two-part interpretation just offered for neighborhood-responsiveness policy more generally applies to this particular program. First, policing matters are assumed to be at least proximate, if not always highly visible. Hence, the Soss and Schram framework fails to provide an appropriate interpretation for lack of feedback effects. Second, the collective action interpretation is instead appropriate for a program that is targeted to neighborhoods rather than individuals. Hence, as with other policies of responsiveness to neighborhoods, the more intense the city's commitment to community policing, the more likely free-rider behavior is to occur among residents. The typical resident, hearing that police are working with some activist members of the community to learn about the neighborhood's crime problems and engage in crime prevention projects, is more content to ride on the efforts of those neighborhood residents who enjoy that type of thing. By contrast, where police have not demonstrated greater responsiveness via ramped up community policing efforts, there is more reason for the typical resident to believe that more must be done to force authorities to pay attention to that resident's neighborhood.

Assuming that policing is at least proximate, if not always salient, such an interpretation would be perfectly suitable for understanding urban residents' responses to community policing. Certainly, it constitutes one possible interpretation of the results found in chapter 3. But what if police and their programmatic activities are not all that proximate to urban residents?

Proximity results from interaction with police when they are engaged in the kinds of community outreach activities that are the essence of community policing or from interaction with police as they carry out their traditional law enforcement role. However, relatively few residents, black or white, have either type of direct interaction with police. The evidence from case studies of community policing suggests that few "experience" community policing in the sense of attending police–community meetings or having other kinds of direct involvement with police in their community policing roles (Skogan 2004, 2006). And other kinds of direct contact between police and public are less common than we might imagine. For example, evidence from a 2005 random sample survey showed less than 20 percent of U.S. residents over the age of fifteen had face-to-face contact with a police officer in that year. Blacks had a somewhat lower rate of such contact with police than did whites (16.5 versus 20.2 percent); people age eighteen to twenty-four were the most likely to have had contact with police, with 29.3 percent reporting such contact (Durose, Smith, and Langan 2007, 2). These rates of contact between police and public suggest that for most people, policing in general and community policing in particular is not all that proximate. Unless there is something to make policing salient despite this lack of proximity, feedback effects from policing programs are, in the Soss and Schram framework, unlikely.

Acknowledgement of community policing's lack of proximity provides another interpretation—quite different from the collective action interpretation—of the lack of policy feedback from this program. In Soss and Schram's terms, the program is simply too distant and low visibility to yield either resource or interpretive effects. In a related vein, community policing is a weak policy design in Patashnik and Zelizer's (2009, 13) terms because it generates few material resources and leaves many residents with an "inability to perceive what the program does for them." And community policing often exhibits another of Patashnik and Zelizer's conditions detrimental to policy feedback: governments' insufficient capacity for policy carry-through. Both the case study of Seattle in chapter 3 and other studies of community policing reveal a program that in many communities is targeted to only a few neighborhoods; competes with ongoing pressures for traditional, crime call–response policing; and is less than fully implemented because of those pressures. These program design and implementation weaknesses help make clear why police activities can be distant rather than proximate to residents even in places that are supposedly pursuing community policing. Taken together, community policing's weak design, implementation problems, and low proximity make a lack of policy feedback effects unsurprising.

But for black residents of urban America, additional interpretations need to be entertained. Some of these interpretations are city specific. The Seattle case study in chapter 3, for example, reveals evidence of two more feedback-compromising conditions identified by Patashnik and Zelizer (2009): multiple policies in tension and poor timing. Community policing and the so-called Weed and Seed program were perceived by the community as being in tension, and the attempt to implement both at the same time clearly sent conflicting and counterproductive signals to the black community in Seattle. And there was bad timing, to say the least, in the city's adoption of a community policing program when a substantial portion of the black community was pushing unsuccessfully for something else from police—that is, greater police accountability when complaints about police misconduct are being reviewed.

Most importantly, however, is an interpretation that would diagnose the failure of community policing to yield feedback effects *for blacks* in much the same way that Soss and Schram (2007) diagnosed the failure of welfare reform to have the desired feedback effects on the public. Their diagnosis hinged on placement of welfare reform in the high-visibility, low-proximity cell (type I) of Figure 6.1—a scenario in which the public has little or no direct experience with welfare; hence, when it is made salient to them by elites, the policy is "a potent but distant symbol." Rather than reacting to the details of the program and its reform and how those affect recipients, the public values such policies as "expressions of group values." When a policy or program change "affirms dominant, widely held values, . . . rewarding individuals who live up to them, organizing practices to be consistent with them . . . and so on, one should expect it to reinforce rather than disrupt existing patterns of mass opinion and behavior" (123).

How could black residents' reaction to community policing parallel such a diagnosis? The answer lies in acknowledgement that police have a dual role in the lives of many black residents of urban America. For those who have direct, personal experience with police, policing would be proximate rather than distant. As just argued, however, this is true of only a relatively small number of urban residents, black or white—hence the overall categorization of police in general and community policing in particular as lacking in proximity.

But there is another role that police play in the lives of many black residents. Stated simply, police have a potent *symbolic* role for many black residents. Contemporary minority distrust of police is rooted in a long history of policy brutality toward minorities in the United States (Walker 1998), as well as in high-profile media coverage of contemporary incidents of police abuse or police shootings of minorities, even in other cities (Weitzer and Tuch 2002). For black residents of urban America, views of police are not simply a matter of reacting to the specifics of police activity in their own community. Instead, views of police are shaped by this broader context.

Given this second, symbolic role of police for black residents, policing regularly has high salience even if residents' limited personal experience with police provides low proximity. Soss and Schram's (2007) treatment of this high-salience, low-proximity scenario focused on the public that, in contrast with recipients of welfare, is distanced from welfare and therefore reactive to it in emotive terms. But the interpretation here of blacks' reaction to community policing emphasized that, especially for programs targeting communities rather than individuals, the program can be distant but salient *to program recipients.*

To put it another way, other policing actions—from Rodney King to Abner Louima and from some cities' aggressive order-maintenance activities to the police role as the vanguard of the drug wars that have imprisoned so many blacks—have already created strong feedback effects for blacks. These feedback effects are so strong that the particulars and details of their own city's community policing programs may not be able to penetrate the deeply entrenched symbolism of what police represent for blacks. It has been emphasized that the interpretive effects of policy involve program clients generalizing from their experience with that program's agents to government officials broadly (Soss 1999); here, we see that the failure of a program to generate such feedback effects can stem from a global stereotype driving interpretation of the local program experience. Hence, for blacks, community policing may change neither attitudes toward police nor civic engagement behavior that the program is trying to induce.

Feedback Effects in the Development Policy Sphere

Nonelite public groups are the focus of our search for feedback effects from both social programs and neighborhood-responsiveness programs that are important in the allocational policy realm. However, when we turn to developmental policy at the local level, a different kind of target group comes into focus. Local small-business owners, branch plant managers, chamber of commerce members, and indeed the entire panoply of the local business establishment constitutes an important target group for economic development policies and programs—but a target group that might be viewed more as a set of elite actors than the public groups featured in much contemporary research that empirically tests policy-centered theory. Even if they do not qualify as political elites, the local business establishment certainly constitutes a target group that Ingram and Schneider (1993) would presumably classify as "advantaged" because they are relatively powerful and typically are socially constructed as deserving and virtuous members of the community. Consistent with Ingram and Schneider's theorizing, the developmental programs targeted for this group, such as tax abatements and other incentives for industrial and commercial investment in the community, have involved relatively generous benefits with relatively few strings. But, as documented in chapter 4, many local governments and community activists have been disappointed in the results of these development subsidies, sometimes even outraged by the way in which corporations have played communities against one another to win substantial development incentives that have not yielded enough benefits for the community in the form of stable enhancements in the tax base and new jobs at good wages. At least in some quarters, critiques of "corporate welfare" have threatened the positive social construction of the local business establishment, and from the 1990s to the present, there have been waves of policy change at the local level, bringing various accountability controls to development incentive programs in some cities.

There is considerable evidence both in the chapter 4 quantitative analyses of business activity in cities across the United States and in the chapter 5 case study of Lawrence, Kansas, that business leaders have been politically mobilized by the move to add accountability controls to development subsidies. This is not to say that business interests are politically inert in the absence of this threat to unfettered subsidies. Chapter 4 showed the private sector is quite likely to be involved in economic development policymaking in nearly all large cities and in the majority of smaller cities, regardless of the nature of development incentive policy. That chapter also showed substantial private sector engagement in development policymaking does constrain cities from pursuing the adoption of accountability controls. Policy-centered theory's close cousin, state-centered theory, would have it that policy change can be driven by the states' capacity more than by societal forces such as pressures from organized interests (Skocpol and Finegold 1982). Instead, chapter 4 showed that decisions about how far to go in the direction of reining in development subsidies are driven almost entirely by how free of business influence the city is.

State-centered theory is not the same as policy-centered theory unless it explicitly incorporates some notion of not only how the states' capacity drives policy but also *how policy then shapes the character of the political sphere, providing implications for future demand making.* That is, the policy-shapes-politics link must be clear. For this reason, the investigation of possible feedback effects from city governments' pursuit of development subsidy controls is the real meat of the analysis in the development policy chapters. At the simplest level, the evidence shows development subsidy reform creates policy feedback in the form of resource effects. That is, once business subsidies have been made available in a city, more aggressive accountability controls on those subsidies elicit higher levels of business engagement in the city's economic development policymaking. The magnitude of this feedback effect does not appear to be large, and it is more apparent in smaller cities than in larger ones, but it is evident.

In some ways, this is the classic and least surprising scenario of policy feedback. A government program that provides benefits to a group thereby creates material stakes that shape incentives for political participation, especially if those material stakes are threatened. In the Soss and Schram (2007) framework (see Figure 6.1), feedback effects such as these should be expected. For local businesses, city government's policies with respect to incentives for business investment are likely to be relatively proximate—that is, broad segments of the business community would normally be quite aware of the specifics of the policy, even if those business owners are not currently recipients of tax abatements. And while this program may normally be routinized and hence low in visibility, community pressures to add accountability controls to the city's business incentive program definitely raise the salience of this program, thus placing it among Soss and Schram's type II programs, where policy feedback in the form of resource or interpretive effects is highly likely.

At the same time, it is important to acknowledge the contrasts between the feedback effects found in the realm of development incentive policy and those found for means-tested local programming in chapter 1. Although the addition of accountability controls may appear to underscore a view of development incentives as corporate welfare and an image of business claimants as potential con artists who must prove they are worthy of the subsidy, cities' adoption of these requirements *heightens* the political engagement of business leaders. It is not that business leaders are unaware of the negative messages accountability controls send about their trustworthiness, likability, and value to the community. The case study in chapter 5 indicated the many ways in which both the accountability controls and the process of adopting them send negative messages about the status of business leaders in the community; it also indicated that many members of the business establishment take such messages quite personally. However, the chilling effect that individual welfare requirements have on individual welfare recipients' political engagement is not paralleled by a chilling effect of corporate welfare requirements on corporate welfare recipients. This may be because such disempowering interpretive effects are trumped by empowering resource effects.

An alternative interpretation, inspired by the work of Schneider and Ingram (1997), raises questions about whether feedback effects truly stem directly from program design elements and the messages they send or whether design elements with negative messages affect "advantaged" target groups in ways different from the effects on "deviant" target groups. Stated another way, for those who are already politically powerful, even programs with design messages that seem to question their likability, value to the community, and worthiness may not have a chilling effect on political engagement, at least not as long as there are material resources at stake; but for those who are already socially constructed as powerless and unworthy, the demeaning messages of means-tested programs have a chilling effect. To the extent that this is the case, there will be a continuation of patterns of political engagement that favor advantaged groups despite policy reforms intended to alter their receipt of disproportionate benefits.

Big Picture Pattern of Policy Feedback Effects: From Local to Global

This book clearly provides more evidence of policy feedback effects in some spheres of local government policy than in others, as well as evidence of different kinds of feedback effects across these policy domains. As interesting as the domain-specific effects are, we cannot fail to notice the "big picture" pattern of these results. At the local level, government social programs dampen participation of the have-nots while development programs reinforce the political involvement of already-privileged business interests. Furthermore, iconic urban programs such as community policing and broader programs of neighborhood empowerment at best fail to enhance civic engagement or build social capital at the neighborhood level; at worst, they exacerbate divisions, and especially racial divisions, that undercut urban neighborhoods.

In a recent article, Schneider and Sidney (2009) reminded us that an important aspect of policy design theory and the policy-centered theory that it helped spawn is the integration of normative and empirical analysis. That is, this theoretical framework invites us to see policy feedback as "policy feed-forward" (108), shaping "patterns of political voice, power, and democratic responsiveness" (112). If the big picture pattern of policy feedback discussed here feeds forward to the reinforcement of a biased pattern of political voice, power, and democratic responsiveness, the normative impulse noted by Schneider and Sidney should push us to explore the underpinnings of this policy bias.

That brings us full circle to a consideration of how and why some urban governments have settled into the constellation of policies considered here, despite the clear bias in their impact on local democracy. Ironically, one important answer to this question moves the focus from the local level to the global. Specifically, globalization theorists point to a set of economic and social transformations that have ratcheted up the scope and pace of competition among cities in the post-1970s world (Kantor and Judd 2010). As a result, "urban elites and governments must inevitably negotiate and respond to conditions imposed on them by the disorderly, dynamic, and disruptive system of global capitalism" (Gibson 2004, 16).

In this globalized competition for investment, city governments are alleged to be even more inclined to subsidize business investment in their community; and "welfare state programs (including prolabor and redistributive policies) are increasingly viewed as liabilities" (Gibson

2004, 26). More particularly, cities in a globalized, postindustrial world are said to be competing with one another "to create the most hospitable environment for corporate investment and headquarters, 'luxury living' facilities, tourism, and retail operations" (Beckett and Herbert 2008, 106–7). Focusing on the producer service companies that are a key prize in this global cities' competition, Gibson (2004, 45) notes that global cities such as New York and London "concentrate masses of skilled service companies, but they also typically offer upper-income workers cultural amenities unavailable in most suburban strip malls and office parks." Because of the upscale cultural amenities and high quality of life required for a city to attract and retain investment in this economic sector, city governments are often alleged to have become less tolerant of crime or social disorder—manifestations of "decay and danger" that would compromise the city's image (Beckett and Herbert 2008, 109). It is out of this imperative that aggressive order-maintenance policing, the war on drugs at the local level, and other methods for the control of urban space are said to have arisen (Beckett and Herbert 2008, 109). In addition, the requirements of competing for international tourism are said to push cities in much the same direction, resulting in development policies that yield sanitized, tourist-safe enclaves that displace genuine communities (Harvey 1989; Sorkin 1992).

Therefore, in one version of the globalization argument, the continuity of policies like means-tested social programs and business subsidies that skew urban governance toward the interests of the advantaged, as well as community policing programs that fragment urban neighborhoods, can be all too easily explained by pointing to the continuation of the globalization trends that privilege these policy responses. City governments are cast in the role of promulgating such policies to compete so as to improve their position in the global hierarchy of cities.

In essence, this is not only a society-centered mode of interpretation but also one that emphasizes (1) economic imperatives over local political interests and (2) the inevitability of programmed responses to globalization over the possibility of variegated responses. In reaction, other globalization scholars have come to emphasize the diverse ways in which city governments have responded to globalization pressures, sometimes under the banner of "glocal" choices (Savitch and Kantor 2002) and sometimes via case studies that shift the emphasis from a global society-centered interpretation. Rather than blaming globalization for the inequalities and damaged communities in New York City, for example, Sites (2003) argued that the city's governing officials mismanaged the city's response to globalization by choosing policies that were ad hoc, short-term, misguided responses to global trends. Savitch and Kantor (2002) noted the variety of programmatic tactics cities can and have used to seek competitive advantage in the global marketplace and that still other cities have adopted populist policies in defiance of the pressure of global capitalism. And Judd (2003) forcefully argued against the view that globalization is forcing the postindustrial city to be "little more than an assemblage of fortified spaces colonized by global capital and affluent residents and visitors" (24). Acknowledging that some cities have developed heavily regulated tourist enclaves, Judd also indicated other cities where visitors can be "absorbed into the urban fabric" and where city officials have tempered international tourism development commitments in the light of gentrification, cultural frictions, and other impacts on resident activity (31).

As applied to urban government, policy-centered theory converges with this latter, "glocal" version of globalization theory. Policy-centered theorists have worked hard to get beyond the social science disciplinary bias toward society-centered explanation. For them, explaining continuity in policies that skew urban governance toward the interests of the advantaged is more challenging than pointing to ongoing global economic pressures. It requires first an empirical demonstration that particular public programs yield policy feedback effects that add up to a skewed pattern of political voice and power. It is that pattern of policy-induced political voice and power that can then sustain biased and destructive policies. As this book has shown, the *diversity* of policy choices that local governments make in the face of globalization pressures (e.g., more rather than less means-tested spending by county governments and more or less commitment to community policing) helps make the empirical demonstration of policy feedback effects possible. It is this policy feedback from policy and programmatic choices made by local governments that can be expected to shape what happens in local communities in a global era.

Appendix A

The Study Cities and Their 2000 Populations

CITY	POPULATION (IN THOUSANDS)
Birmingham, Ala.	243
Phoenix, Ariz.	1,321
Los Angeles, Calif.	3,695
San Diego, Calif.	1,223
San Francisco, Calif.	777
Boulder, Colo.	95
Denver, Colo.	555
Wilmington, Del.	73
Atlanta, Ga.	416
Chicago, Ill.	2,896
Baton Rouge, La.	228
Boston, Mass.	589
Detroit, Mich.	951
Grand Rapids, Mich.	198
Minneapolis, Minn.	383
St. Paul, Minn.	287
Rochester, N.Y.	220
Syracuse, N.Y.	147
Charlotte, N.C.	541
Greensboro, N.C.	224
Winston Salem, N.C.	186
Bismarck, N.Dak.	56
Cincinnati, Ohio	331
Cleveland, Ohio	478
York, Pa.	41
Houston, Tex.	1,954
Seattle, Wash.	563
Yakima, Wash.	72
Charleston, W.Va.	53

Appendix B

Additional Detail on Content Analysis Procedures and Coding Rules

Stage 1: Culling of Relevant Articles

To ensure appropriate inclusiveness, the basic search term *neighborhood* was used, generating a large pool of articles for most cities. Articles were then deleted if they used the term *neighborhood* in an irrelevant fashion (e.g., "The weather service is predicting rainfall in the neighborhood of two inches overnight"), if the article referenced neighborhood in the urban, spatial sense but with no political or governmental relevance (e.g., "Famous X, who is giving the poetry reading tonight, grew up in the Uptown neighborhood"), or even if the article referenced activity of a neighborhood association that did not reflect on the city's handling of or relationship with that neighborhood (e.g., "The Falmouth Neighborhood Association will have an ice-cream social this evening").

Articles included as relevant involved an array of matters, including reports of city officials visiting the neighborhood or holding hearings on a neighborhood problem, reports of city council deliberations on land-use proposals affecting the neighborhood (frequently with neighborhood association leaders or neighborhood residents quoted with respect to their position on the proposal), reports of grant proposals being received for the city to undertake redevelopment projects in the neighborhood, reports of various problems (e.g., loose dogs, flooding, crime, general deterioration, airport noise, or traffic congestion) that are plaguing the neighborhood and that residents want the city to handle (or to handle better), and reports of police officials working with crime watch organizations or trying to institute new block watch organizations.

Stage 2: Coding of the Character of a City Government's Dealing with Neighborhoods

In addition to the general definitions of the positive and negative codes provided in the chapter text, the following information provides further detail on typical story types that belong in each coding category.

Scenarios Warranting the Positive Code

- A past problem or deficiency in city responsiveness to the neighborhood is being tackled by the city government at a higher level of effort.
- City officials are trying to mobilize or organize residents to help tackle a problem.
- The city government or city officials are providing resources to particular neighborhoods (e.g., grant funding, community policing, historic designation, or a redevelopment project that is not a threat to the neighborhood).
- The city government or city officials are getting neighborhood residents' input on an issue, meeting with them, or both.
- The city government or city officials are providing special information resources to neighborhood residents.
- The city government or city officials are offering to collaborate with neighborhood residents to work on a neighborhood problem.
- City officials have set up a neighborhood organization or organizations to make decisions or have a special role in decision making on matters affecting the neighborhood.
- City officials are going to bat for the neighborhood against other government units (e.g., state, county, or federal) that are pursuing action adverse to neighborhood interests.
- Developers are working closely with the neighborhood on a proposed project because city government rules require it.
- Citizen volunteerism for a neighborhood project has been orchestrated via an official citywide system of neighborhood organizations (e.g., St. Paul's community councils).
- People are getting appointed to other city boards and the like based on their background in neighborhood organizations or activism.

Scenarios Warranting the Negative Code

- The city government or city officials are enacting an ordinance or making a decision that either ignores or is opposed to what residents are said to want.
- The city government is taking the next step in approving a project that constitutes a threat to the neighborhood.
- A serious neighborhood problem is being ignored or poorly addressed by city officials.
- City government actions have given some neighborhood residents the impression that they are getting less or being treated less well than other neighborhoods.
- The city government lost or is losing a neighborhood-relevant grant or grant-funding opportunity through ineptitude or other problems (not just nationwide cutbacks).
- Neighborhood organization powers are being restricted or limited from what they were, or citizen participation arrangements are being ignored or subverted.

Notes

Introduction

1. One major exception is the extensive line of work on the impacts of governing structures or institutional arrangements on citizen participation. A long line of work has suggested the depoliticizing effects of reform-style institutions such as at-large elections, nonpartisanship, and the council–manager form of government—depoliticizing effects that are evidenced partly in lower turnout rates in cities with such reform institutions as compared with nonreformed cities. To the extent that the adoption of reform-style institutions is treated as a policy choice, albeit a metapolicy choice (i.e., a policy about how policy will be made), this line of work can be said to reflect the policy-centered approach's featured emphasis on how policy affects politics. Indeed, in formulations such as Bridges's (1997) work on the history of reform in Sun Belt cities, there is a strong effort to show that the adoption of reform-style institutions and institutional arrangements was explicitly motivated by the desire to restrict the electorate.

2. Stone (2005, 257) wrote that he "does not dismiss policy from having a role in shaping political relationship." However, none of the theoretical or empirical work in the policy–centered tradition was incorporated into his essay on the politics–policy connection, and there were no suggestions about how policy shapes politics, except the broad notion that the decision to pursue a particular policy agenda means the development of new governing arrangements, which presumably define who is involved in program development.

1. The Participatory Impacts of County Governments' Means-Tested and Universal Social Programs

1. City governments are less involved in these three categories. Nevertheless, an additional $28.9 billion in expenditures in the welfare, hospitals, and public health categories came from municipal and township governments in 2001–2.

2. Several core metropolitan area counties that were in the SCBC survey are not included here because the 1997 Census of Governments does not have

financial information for them. These include, for example, Denver County and Boston's Sussex County.

3. The number of people in poverty in each county is an estimate based on the Census Bureau's report of the percentage of people in poverty in each county in 2000 multiplied by the total population estimate for each county in 1996.

4. The measure is collapsed into a dummy variable that distinguishes the 36 percent of respondents who engage in none of the forms of participation from those who engage in at least one of the forms of participation.

5. The main exception to this is Mettler's (2002) analysis, which uses a broad, composite measure of participation.

2. City Government and Neighborhoods

1. In addition to mayors, city managers, council members, zoning board of appeals members, planning commission members, police chiefs, and the like, officials from nonregional local authorities (especially public housing authorities) were treated as city officials whose actions were coded vis-à-vis neighborhood interests. However, because school districts are independent of city government in most settings, the actions of school officials were not included.

2. A research assistant independently coded a 50 percent systematic random sample of the cities. Analysis of the consistency of the author's and the research assistant's codes shows high levels of intercoder reliability (616 out of 669, or 92 percent agreement) when disagreements on mixed positive/negative codes are omitted. With all mixed codes included, intercoder reliability drops to 81.2 percent, which is still quite respectable. The analysis is primarily based on the cases that do not involve mixed codes.

3. Curiously, the collective action problem posed in Olsen's (1965) classic work is rarely raised by scholars of neighborhood organizations, even though the dilemma is a staple of studies of virtually all other interest groups. The key exception is Fung (2004, 101–106), who acknowledged this "strong rational choice" interpretation but largely dismisses it. The dismissal arises largely because, as for other scholars of neighborhood empowerment, the amount of resident participation in neighborhood associations is not the dominant consideration, as it is here. Instead, Fung (2004, 106) is concerned with the overall quality of neighborhood-level participation—i.e., the extent to which the cases he examined can be designated as instances of genuine, participatory democracy.

3. Community Policing

1. Skogan's direct observation results suggest reasons for the limited mobilization of neighborhood residents. To fulfill the promise that community policing

will enlist citizens in cooperation with neighborhood police in proactive, problem-solving efforts, beat meetings in Chicago are supposed to involve five things: problem identification, identification of proposed solutions to those problems, feedback from police officers on previous problem-solving efforts, resident feedback on the same, and a call for volunteers. However, Skogan's (2006, 143) study found only the first of these was done in virtually all beats observed. In about one-quarter of the cases, solutions were not identified and officer feedback on previous efforts was not provided. Resident feedback was given in less than half of the cases, and calls for volunteers were relatively rare, occurring in a little over a third of the meetings in 1998 and about a quarter of the meetings in 2002.

2. Schneider and Ingram (1997, 122–23) allow for the possibility that if a program goes too far in labeling individuals as deviant who do "not accept this construction of themselves," a social movement can be mobilized in reaction.

3. The SCBC survey also includes an index of informal socializing, but it is based on too many items that are not relevant to socializing with neighbors (e.g., socializing with coworkers or visiting with relatives). The survey also includes an item asking whether people in the respondent's neighborhood give them a sense of community. However, this was asked of only random half-samples of those surveyed.

4. As in chapter 2, state, regional, and large metropolitan area samples that did not generate a reasonable number of SCBC respondents from any specific city-level jurisdiction are excluded from this analysis, as were Kalamazoo, Mich., and Lewiston, Maine, for which newspaper coverage in either LexisNexis or America's Newspapers (essential for content analysis to measure overall responsiveness to neighborhoods) was not available. In addition to these, York, Pa., is excluded from this chapter, because data for this city is missing from the 1999 LEMAS survey of policing characteristics.

4. City Government, Economic Development Incentives, and Business Influence

1. The item used by Sullivan and Green (1999) to measure fiscal stress—respondent-perceived importance of raising revenues without raising taxes—was not asked on the 1999 ICMA survey and so was replaced by a pair of indicators measuring the property tax rate in the community and whether or not the community has a sales tax. Taken together, these similarly tap into the level of fiscal stress by revealing whether the property tax is already heavy and whether an alternative to unpopular property tax increases is available.

2. The 2004 survey was not used because it had a noticeably smaller response rate and hence fewer cases.

3. The 1999 ICMA survey forced a slightly different measure of corporate citizenship—whether or not private companies contribute funds to local government's

marketing efforts. The single-year 1999 results (table not shown) also suggest that a city's subsidy policy has little impact on corporate citizenship, except that cities providing no development subsidies lag slightly in corporate citizenship. The same pattern of results is revealed in a two-year analysis, with subsidy policy measured in 1999 and corporate citizenship measured in 2004.

Bibliography

Alex-Assensoh, Yvette M. 1998. *Neighborhoods, Family and Political Behavior in Urban America.* New York: Garland Press.

Ames, Lynda J. 1997. *Women Reformed, Women Empowered.* Philadelphia: Temple University Press.

Angelos, Constantine. 1988. "Trespass Law Needs Help, Say School Officials." *Seattle Times,* February 11, Zone Edition, Metro Section, page B3.

Bartik, Timothy J. 2005. "Solving the Problems of Economic Development Incentives." *Growth and Change* 36: 139–66.

Beckett, Katherine, and Steve Herbert. 2008. "The Punitive City Revisited: The Transformation of Urban Social Control." In *After the War on Crime,* edited by Mary Louis Frampton, Ian Haney Lopez, and Jonathan Simon, 106–22. New York: New York University Press.

Berry, Jeffrey M., Kent E. Portney, and Ken Thomson. 1993. *The Rebirth of Urban Democracy.* Washington, D.C.: Brookings.

Blackwood, Kendrick. 1999. "Sauer-Sundstrand Opens Doors." *Lawrence Journal-World,* May 20. http://infoweb.newsbank.com/iw-search/we/InfoWeb?p_product=NewsBank&p_theme=aggregated5&p_action=doc&p_docid=0EAEA151104F1E42&p_docnum=1&p_queryname=52.

———. 2000a. "American Eagle Gets City Commission Approval for Tax Breaks." *Lawrence Journal-World,* May 17. http://infoweb.newsbank.com/iw-search/we/InfoWeb?p_product=NewsBank&p_theme=aggregated5&p_action=doc&p_docid=0EAE9F0506460B30&p_docnum=1&p_queryname=39.

———. 2000b. "City to Take a New Look at Economic Development Policies Tax Breaks Lead to Review." *Lawrence Journal-World,* May 18. http://infoweb.newsbank.com/iw-search/we/InfoWeb?p_product=NewsBank&p_theme=aggregated5&p_action=doc&p_docid=0EAE9F0534E8EE03&p_docnum=1&p_queryname=41.

———. 2000c. "Clothier Clears Zoning Hurdle." *Lawrence Journal-World,* April 5. http://infoweb.newsbank.com/iw-search/we/InfoWeb?p_product=NewsBank&p_theme=aggregated5&p_action=doc&p_docid=0EAE9EFA421CB689&p_docnum=1&p_queryname=37.

———. 2000d. "State Official Backs Warehouse Jobs." *Lawrence Journal-World,* June 12. http://infoweb.newsbank.com/iw-search/we/InfoWeb?p_product=NewsBank&p_theme=aggregated5&p_action=doc&p_docid=0EAE9F0B1A649AD1&p_docnum=1&p_queryname=42.

———. 2000e. "Tax Abatements Have Critics and Defenders." *Lawrence Journal-World,* April 23. http://infoweb.newsbank.com/iw-search/we/InfoWeb?p_product=NewsBank&p_theme=aggregated5&p_action=doc&p_docid=0EAE9EFE85A9F6B5&p_docnum=1&p_queryname=38.

———. 2000f. "Taxpayers Mull Break for Eagle." *Lawrence Journal-World,* May 9. http://infoweb.newsbank.com/iw-search/we/InfoWeb?p_product=NewsBank&p_theme=aggregated5&p_action=doc&p_docid=0EAE9F02ACF57106&p_docnum=1&p_queryname=40.

"Board Approves Tax Abatement." 2002. *Lawrence Journal-World,* November 1. http://infoweb.newsbank.com/iw-search/we/InfoWeb?p_product=NewsBank&p_theme=aggregated5&p_action=doc&p_docid=0F71371F86D44385&p_docnum=1& p_queryname=45.

"Bogged Down in Regulations." 2003. *Lawrence Journal-World,* July 20. http://infoweb.newsbank.com/iw-search/we/InfoWeb?p_product=NewsBank&p_theme=aggregated5&p_action=doc&p_docid=0FC764A6DD128543&p_docnum=1&p_queryname=53.

Bridges, Amy. 1997. *Morning Glories: Municipal Reform in the Southwest.* Princeton, N.J.: Princeton University Press.

Brown, Ben, and William Reed Benedict. 2002. "Perceptions of the Police: Past Findings, Methodological Issues, Conceptual Issues and Policy Implications." *Policing: An International Journal of Police Strategies & Management* 25: 543–80.

Brown, Charles E. 1996. "Seattle Plans to Expand Community Policing." *Seattle Times,* November 23. http://infoweb.newsbank.com/iw-search/we/InfoWeb?p_product=NewsBank&p_theme=aggregated5&p_action=doc&p_docid=0EB5389A71EA63E9&p_docnum=1&p_queryname=2.

Byrnes, Susan. 1998. "Law Bringing Crackdown at City Parks Spurs Debate." *Seattle Times,* April 9. http://infoweb.newsbank.com/iw-search/we/InfoWeb?p_product=NewsBank&p_theme=aggregated5&p_action=doc&p_docid=0EB539364A6DE0AA&p_docnum=1&p_queryname=27.

Campbell, Andrea Louise. 2003. *How Policies Make Citizens: Senior Political Activism and the American Welfare State.* Princeton, N.J.: Princeton University Press.

———. 2007. "Universalism, Targeting, and Participation." In *Remaking America: Democracy and Public Policy in an Age of Inequality,* edited by Joe Soss, Jacob S. Hacker, and Suzanne Mettler, 121–40. New York: Russell Sage Foundation.

Chamber of Commerce of Lawrence, Kansas. 2010. "25 Largest Employers in Douglas County." Accessed November 19. http://www.lawrencekansas-economicdevelopment.com/Industries—Companies-Largest-Employers.aspx.

"City Approves Living Wage." 2003. *Lawrence Journal-World,* October 22. http://infoweb.newsbank.com/iw-search/we/InfoWeb?p_product=NewsBank&p_theme=aggregated5&p_action=doc&p_docid=0FE634810A5C7D51&p_docnum=1&p_queryname=30.

"City Crimefighters." 1995. *Seattle Post-Intelligencer,* September 25. http://infoweb.newsbank.com/iw-search/we/InfoWeb?p_product=NewsBank&p_theme=aggregated5&p_action=doc&p_docid=0EB04AB9B720E793&p_docnum=3& p_queryname=16.

City of Atlanta. 2010. "Neighborhood Planning Units." Accessed November 19. http://www.atlantaga.gov/government/planning/npu_system.aspx.

City of Lawrence, Kansas. 1991. Resolution No. 5431. A Resolution Establishing the Policy and Procedures for Tax Exemptions and Incentives for Economic Development for the City of Lawrence, Kansas. Policy document provided to author by Frank Reeb, city clerk.

______. 2001. Resolution 6343. A Resolution Establishing the Policy and Procedures for Tax Exemptions and Incentives for Economic Development for the City of Lawrence, Kansas, repealing Resolution No. 5431. Policy document provided to author by Frank Reeb, city clerk.

______. 2003. Ordinance No. 7706. An Ordinance Establishing the Policy and Procedures for Tax Exemptions and Incentives for Economic Development for the City of Lawrence, Kansas, Establishing Requirements for Companies Receiving Tax Abatements, repealing Resolution No. 6343. Policy document provided to author by Frank Reeb, city clerk.

"City OKs 80 Percent Tax Break." 2003. *Lawrence Journal-World,* January 29. http://infoweb.newsbank.com/iw-search/we/InfoWeb?p_product=NewsBank&p_theme=aggregated5&p_action=doc&p_docid=0F8E8C7CEB31431B&p_docnum=1&p_queryname=29.

"City Still Fine-Tuning Living Wage." 2003. *Lawrence Journal-World,* August 20. http://infoweb.newsbank.com/iw-search/we/InfoWeb?p_product=NewsBank&p_theme=aggregated5&p_action=doc&p_docid=0FD170642253C976&p_docnum=1&p_queryname=28.

"City to Revisit Living-Wage Ideas." 2003. *Lawrence Journal-World,* August 16. http://infoweb.newsbank.com/iw-search/we/InfoWeb?p_product=NewsBank&p_theme=aggregated5&p_action=doc&p_docid=0FD01E9586EF9A66&p_docnum=1&p_queryname=31.

"Community Policing Taking Hold in Seattle." 1994. *Seattle Times,* July 11. http://infoweb.newsbank.com/iw-search/we/InfoWeb?p_product=NewsBank&p_

theme=aggregated5&p_action=doc&p_docid=0EB53748356F8C53&p_docnum=3&p_queryname=14.

"Complaints against Cops Show Encouraging Drop." 1995. *Seattle Times*, July 24. http://infoweb.newsbank.com/iw-search/we/InfoWeb?p_product=NewsBank&p_theme=aggregated5&p_action=doc&p_docid=0EB53800ECF695D7&p_docnum=1&p_queryname=15.

Conway, M. Margaret. 2000. *Political Participation in the United States.* 3rd ed. Washington, D.C.: CQ Press.

Correia, Mark E. 2000. *Citizen Involvement: How Community Factors Affect Progressive Policing.* Washington, D.C.: Police Executive Research Forum.

Craw, M. 2006. "Overcoming City Limits: Vertical and Horizontal Models of Local Redistributive Policy Making." *Social Science Quarterly* 87: 361–79.

———. 2010. "Deciding to Provide: Local Decisions on Providing Social Welfare." *American Journal of Political Science* 54: 906–20.

Dalehite, Esteban G., John L. Mikesell, and C. Kurt Zorn. 2005. "Variations in Property Tax Abatement Programs among States." *Economic Development Quarterly* 19: 157–73.

DeLeon, Richard E. 1992. *Left Coast City: Progressive Politics in San Francisco, 1975–1991.* Lawrence: University Press of Kansas.

Dowding, Keith, Patrick Dunleavy, Desmond King, Helen Margetts, and Yvonne Rydin. 1999. "Regime Politics in London Local Government." *Urban Affairs Review* 34: 515–45.

Duffee, David E., Reginal Fluellen, and Brian C. Renauer. 1999. "Community Variables in Community Policing." *Police Quarterly* 2 (1): 5–35.

Dunsire, Charles. 1995. "In Partnership: The People and the Police." *Seattle Post-Intelligencer,* April 9. http://infoweb.newsbank.com/iw-search/we/InfoWeb?p_product=NewsBank&p_theme=aggregated5&p_action=doc&p_docid=0EB04AA36EE95A4B&p_docnum=1&p_queryname=34.

Dunworth, Terence, and Gregory Mills. 1999. "National Evaluation of Weed and Seed." In *National Institute of Justice Research in Brief* (June). Washington, D.C.: Department of Justice, National Institute of Justice, Office of Justice Programs. http://www.abtassociates.eu/reports/weedseed-rib.pdf.

Durose, Matthew R., Erica L. Smith and Patrick A. Langan. 2007. *Contacts between Police and the Public, 2005.* Washington, D.C.: U.S. Department of Justice, Office of Justice Programs. http://bjs.ojp.usdoj.gov/content/pub/pdf/cpp05.pdf.

Eisinger, Peter K. 1988. *The Rise of the Entrepreneurial State.* Madison: University of Wisconsin Press.

Evans, Peter B., Deitrich Rueschemeyer, and Theda Skocpol. 1985. *Bringing the State Back In.* Cambridge: Cambridge University Press.

Fagan, Mark. 1993a. "Abatement, Bonds Pass on 3–2 Vote." *Lawrence Journal-World,* September 8. http://infoweb.newsbank.com/iw-search/we/InfoWeb?p_product=NewsBank&p_theme=aggregated5&p_action=doc&p_docid=0EAEA016CE13CAC3&p_docnum=1&p_queryname=55.

———. 1993b. "Chamber Focuses on Local Growth." *Lawrence Journal-World,* June 9. http://infoweb.newsbank.com/iw-search/we/InfoWeb?p_product=NewsBank&p_theme=aggregated5&p_action=doc&p_docid=0EAEA00A34D4ED92&p_docnum=1&p_queryname=54.

———. 1994a. "City Grants $800,000 in Tax Breaks." *Lawrence Journal-World,* November 2. http://www2.ljworld.com/search/.

———. 1994b. "Mayor Raises Abatement Questions." *Lawrence Journal-World,* July 19. http://infoweb.newsbank.com.www2.lib.ku.edu:2048/iw-search/we/InfoWeb?p_product=NewsBank&p_theme=aggregated5&p_action=doc&p_docid=0EAEA03AC3353B26&p_docnum=2&p_queryname=1.

———. 1995a. "City Commission Decides to Give Tax Break to Oread." *Lawrence Journal-World,* November 8. http://infoweb.newsbank.com.www2.lib.ku.edu:2048/iw-search/we/InfoWeb?p_product=NewsBank&p_theme=aggregated5&p_action=doc&p_docid=0EAEA082467F251F&p_docnum=1&p_queryname=2.

———. 1995b. "Company Looks for Tax Break, New Plant." *Lawrence Journal-World,* November 6. http://infoweb.newsbank.com.www2.lib.ku.edu:2048/iw-search/we/InfoWeb?p_product=NewsBank&p_theme=aggregated5&p_action=doc&p_docid=0EAEA0827AE7E350&p_docnum=11&p_queryname=3.

———. 1997. "Oread Inc. Seeks Tax Break." *Lawrence Journal-World,* November 26. http://infoweb.newsbank.com.www2.lib.ku.edu:2048/iw-search/we/InfoWeb?p_product=NewsBank&p_theme=aggregated5&p_action=doc&p_docid=0EAEA0D7B9EB5B44&p_docnum=2&p_queryname=4.

———. 1998a. "City Grants Firm's Tax-Break Request." *Lawrence Journal-World,* February 25. http://infoweb.newsbank.com.www2.lib.ku.edu:2048/iw-search/we/InfoWeb?p_product=NewsBank&p_theme=aggregated5&p_action=doc&p_docid=0EAEA0E23554BBDA&p_docnum=1&p_queryname=6.

———. 1998b. "Sauer-Sundstrand Ready to Roll." *Lawrence Journal-World,* February 4. http://infoweb.newsbank.com.www2.lib.ku.edu:2048/iw-search/we/InfoWeb?p_product=NewsBank&p_theme=aggregated5&p_action=doc&p_docid=0EAEA0E655C54DA5&p_docnum=1&p_queryname=5.

———. 1999a. "Commission Candidates Keep Growth on Their Minds." *Lawrence Journal-World,* February 14. http://infoweb.newsbank.com.www2.lib.ku.edu:2048/iw-search/we/InfoWeb?p_product=NewsBank&p_theme=aggregated5&p_action=doc&p_docid=0EAEA13ACA80FC9A&p_docnum=1&p_queryname=8.

______. 1999b. "Mike Rundle, a Former Lawrence City Commissioner, Wants to Return to His Seat at City Hall." *Lawrence Journal-World,* February 28. http://www2.ljworld.com/search/.

______. 2000a. "Opposition Not a Factor." *Lawrence Journal-World,* November 23. http://infoweb.newsbank.com.www2.lib.ku.edu:2048/iw-search/we/InfoWeb?p_product=NewsBank&p_theme=aggregated5&p_action=doc&p_docid=0EAE9F26CDBAFCFC&p_docnum=2&p_queryname=15.

______. 2000b. "Oread Inc. Faces Second Lawsuit to Collect Debt." *Lawrence Journal-World,* August 12. http://infoweb.newsbank.com.www2.lib.ku.edu:2048/iw-search/we/InfoWeb?p_product=NewsBank&p_theme=aggregated5&p_action=doc&p_docid=0EAE9F17910758C4&p_docnum=1&p_queryname=9.

Fagatto, Elena, and Archon Fung. 2006. "Empowered Participation in Urban Governance: The Minneapolis Neighborhood Revitalization Program." *International Journal of Urban and Regional Research* 30 (3): 638–55.

Feiock, Richard C. 2007. "Rational Choice and Regional Governance." *Journal of Urban Affairs* 29: 47–63.

Fisher, Peter, Alan Peters, Dick Netzer, and Leslie E. Papke. 1997. "Tax and Spending Incentives and Enterprise Zones." *New England Economic Review,* March/April, 109–31.

Fung, Archon. 2004. *Empowered Participation.* Princeton, N.J.: Princeton University Press.

Gainsborough, Juliet F. 2003. "To Devolve or Not To Devolve: Welfare Reform in the States." *Policy Studies Journal* 31: 603–23.

Gibson, Timothy A. 2004. *Securing the Spectacular City: The Politics of Revitalization and Homelessness in Downtown Seattle.* Lanham, Md.: Lexington Books.

Goering, John, and Judith D. Feins. 2003. *Choosing a Better Life.* Washington, D.C.: Urban Institute Press.

Goetz, Edward G., and Mara Sidney. 1994. "Revenge of the Property Owners: Community Development and the Politics of Property." *Journal of Urban Affairs* 16: 319–34.

Goldsmith, Steven. 1994. "Effort to Bring Police and Community Together Produces Divisions." *Seattle Post-Intelligencer,* February 5. http://infoweb.newsbank.com/iw-search/we/InfoWeb?p_product=NewsBank&p_theme=aggregated5&p_action=doc&p_docid=0EB04A6672B0951E&p_docnum=26&p_queryname=25.

Good Jobs First. 2010. "Accountable Development: Key Reforms." Accessed November 20. http://www.goodjobsfirst.org/accountable-development/key-reforms-overview.

Grogan, Colleen, and Eric Patashnik. 2003. "Between Welfare Medicine and Mainstream Entitlement: Medicaid at the Political Crossroads." *Journal of Health Politics, Policy and Law* 28: 821–33.

Hacker, Jacob S., Suzanne Mettler, and Joe Soss. 2007. "The New Politics of Inequality: A Policy-Centered Perspective." In *Remaking America: Democracy and Public Policy in an Age of Inequality,* edited by Joe Soss, Jacob Hacker, and Suzanne Mettler, 1–20. New York: Russell Sage.

Harvey, David. 1989. *The Condition of Postmodernity.* Oxford: Blackwell.

He, Ni (Phil), Jihong Zhao, and Nicholas P. Lovrich. 2005. "Community Policing: A Preliminary Assessment of Environmental Impact with Panel Data on Program Implementation in the United States." *Crime & Delinquency* 51: 295–317.

Heclo, Hugh. 1978. "Issue Networks and the Executive Establishment." In *The New American Political System,* edited by Anthony King, 87–124. Washington, D.C.: American Enterprise Institute.

Hefetz, Amir, and Mildred Warner. 2004. "Privatization and Its Reverse: Explaining the Dynamics of the Government Contracting Process." *Journal of Public Administration Research and Theory* 14: 171–90.

Hennepin County, MN. 2009. "Your Connection to Hennepin County." Accessed February 17. http://hennepin.us/.

Hirlinger, Michael W. 1992. "Citizen-Initiated Contacting of Local Government Officials: A Multivariate Explanation." *Journal of Politics* 54: 553–64.

Hoyt, Tim. 1989. "Rundle Finds Support for Abatement Position." *Lawrence Journal-World,* December 17. http://infoweb.newsbank.com.www2.lib.ku.edu:2048/iw-search/we/InfoWeb?p_product=NewsBank&p_theme=aggregated5&p_action=doc&p_docid=0EAE9F36ECEFD833&p_docnum=2&p_queryname=1.

Imbroscio, David L. 1998. "Reformulating Urban Regime Theory: The Division of Labor between State and Market Reconsidered." *Journal of Urban Affairs* 20: 233–48.

Ingram, Helen, and Anne Schneider. 1993. "Constructing Citizenship: The Subtle Messages of Policy Design." In *Public Policy for Democracy,* edited by Helen Ingram and Steven Rathgeb Smith, 68–94. Washington, D.C.: Brookings Institution.

Ingram, Helen, and Steven Rathgeb Smith, eds. 1993. *Public Policy for Democracy.* Washington, D.C.: Brookings Institution.

International City Management Association. 2011a. *Economic Development, 1999.* Washington, D.C.: ICMA Press. http://bookstore.icma.org/Economic_Development_1999_Data_C92.cfm.

International City Management Association. 2011b. *Economic Development, 2004.* Washington, D.C.: ICMA Press. http://bookstore.icma.org/Economic_Development_2004_Data_C88.cfm.

Interview A with Lawrence, Kansas, city commissioner, November 13, 2008.

Interview B with Lawrence, Kansas, local business executive, November 13, 2008.

Interview C with Lawrence, Kansas, local business manager, November 25, 2008.

Interview D with Lawrence, Kansas, local business owner, November 5, 2008.

Interview E with Lawrence, Kansas, local business owner, November 14, 2008.

"Job Search." 1993. *Lawrence Journal-World,* June 10. http://infoweb.newsbank.com.www2.lib.ku.edu:2048/iw-search/we/InfoWeb?p_product=NewsBank&p_theme=aggregated5&p_action=doc&p_docid=0EAEA009E9953A63&p_docnum=14&p_queryname=3.

Jones, Bryan D., and Walter Williams. 2008. *The Politics of Bad Ideas.* New York: Pearson/Longman.

Judd, Dennis. 2003. "Visitors and the Spatial Ecology of the City." In *Cities and Visitors: Regulating People, Markets, and City Space,* eds. Lily M. Hoffman, Susan S. Fainstein, and Dennis R. Judd, pp. 23–38. Oxford: Blackwell.

Jun, Kyu-Nahm. 2007. "Event History Analysis of the Formation of Los Angeles Neighborhood Councils." *Urban Affairs Review* 43: 107–23.

Kaiser Commission on Medicaid and the Uninsured. 2005. "Medicaid Financing Issues: Intergovernmental Transfers and Fiscal Integrity." Accessed November 20, 2010. http://www.kff.org/medicaid/upload/Medicaid-Financing-Issues-Intergovernmental-Transfers-and-Fiscal-Integrity-Fact-Sheet.pdf.

Kantor, Paul, and Dennis R. Judd. 2010. "Cities in a Global World." In *American Urban Politics in a Global Age,* 6th ed., eds. P. Kantor and D. Judd, pp. 47–9. New York: Longman.

Kantor, Paul, Henry Savitch, and Serena V. Haddock. 1997. "The Political Economy of Urban Regimes: A Comparative Perspective." *Urban Affairs Review* 32: 348–76.

Kathi, Pradeep Chandra, and Terry L. Cooper. 2005. "Democratizing the Administrative State: Connecting Neighborhood Councils and City Agencies." *Public Administration Review* 65: 559–68.

Kerley, Kent R., and Michael L. Benson. 2000. "Does Community-Oriented Policing Help Build Stronger Communities?" *Police Quarterly* 3: 46–69.

King, Mason. 1992a. "City May Consider Limiting Tax Breaks." *Lawrence Journal-World,* November 17. http://infoweb.newsbank.com.www2.lib.ku.edu:2048/iw-search/we/InfoWeb?p_product=NewsBank&p_theme=aggregated5&p_action=doc&p_docid=0EAE9FE7CF290A07&p_docnum=2&p_queryname=5.

______. 1992b. "Commission OKs Tax Abatement Model." *Lawrence Journal-World,* January 29. http://infoweb.newsbank.com.www2.lib.ku.edu:2048/iw-search/we/InfoWeb?p_product=NewsBank&p_theme=aggregated5&p_action=doc&p_docid=0EAE9FA781966A42&p_docnum=2&p_queryname =4.

Kronebusch, Karl. 2001. "Medicaid for Children: Federal Mandates, Welfare Reform, and Policy Backsliding." *Health Affairs* 20: 97–111.

Lawhorn, Chad. 2001. "Business Climate Sprouts Worry, Lieutenant Governor Warns Leaders to Avoid Repeat of American Eagle Project." *Lawrence Journal-World,* December 14. http://infoweb.newsbank.com.www2.lib.ku.edu:2048/iw-search/we/InfoWeb?p_product=NewsBank&p_theme=aggregated5&p_action=doc&p_docid=0F071F16A23244C4&p_docnum=1&p_queryname=6.

———. 2003. "Chamber Backs Voluntary Living Wage Plan." *Lawrence Journal-World,* July 30. http://infoweb.newsbank.com.www2.lib.ku.edu:2048/iw-search/we/InfoWeb?p_product=NewsBank&p_theme=aggregated5&p_action=doc&p_docid=0FCA845CF1933196&p_docnum=2&p_queryname=7.

Lawless, Jennifer L., and Richard L. Fox. 2001. "Political Participation of the Urban Poor." *Social Problems* 48: 362–85.

LeRoy, Greg. 1997. *No More Candy Store: States and Cities Making Jobs Accountable.* Washington, D.C.: Good Jobs First. http://www.goodjobsfirst.org/pdf/nmcs.pdf.

"Living Wage: Anatomy of a Deal." 2003. *Lawrence Journal-World,* August 24. http://infoweb.newsbank.com.www2.lib.ku.edu:2048/iw-search/we/InfoWeb?p_product=NewsBank&p_theme=aggregated5&p_action=doc&p_docid=0FD2C1B56AAAF28A&p_docnum=1&p_queryname=9.

"Living Wage Ordinance Divides City Candidates." 2003. *Lawrence Journal-World,* February 17. http://infoweb.newsbank.com.www2.lib.ku.edu:2048/iw-search/we/InfoWeb?p_product=NewsBank&p_theme=aggregated5&p_action=doc&p_docid=0F94CF38956B97A2&p_docnum=1&p_queryname=8.

Logan, John R. and Harvey L. Molotch. 1987. *Urban Fortunes.* Berkeley: University of California Press.

Logan, John R., and Gordana Rabrenovic. 1990. "Neighborhood Associations: Their Issues, Their Allies and Their Opponents." *Urban Affairs Quarterly* 26: 68–94.

Lorek, L. A. 2007. "City Goes after $823,758 in Abated Taxes, Fees." *San Antonio Express-News,* state and metro edition, October 19. http://infoweb.newsbank.com.www2.lib.ku.edu:2048/iw-search/we/InfoWeb?p_product=NewsBank&p_theme=aggregated5&p_action=doc&p_docid=11C653168C28BF48&p_docnum=1&p_queryname=42.

Lowi, Theodore. 1964. "American Business, Public Policy, Case Studies and Political Theory." *World Politics* 16: 677–715.

———. 1972. "Four Systems of Policy, Politics, and Choice." *Public Administration Review* 32: 298–310.

Lyons, William. 1999. *The Politics of Community Policing.* Ann Arbor: University of Michigan Press.

MacDonald, John M. 2002. "The Effectiveness of Community Policing in Reducing Urban Violence." *Crime & Delinquency* 48: 592–618.

MacDonald, John, and Robert J. Stokes. 2006. "Race, Social Capital, and Trust in the Police." *Urban Affairs Review* 41: 358–75.

Maguire, Edward R., and Stephen D. Mastrofski. 2000. "Patterns of Community Policing in the United States." *Police Quarterly* 3: 4–45.

Marschall, Melissa J. 2004. "Citizen Participation and the Neighborhood Context: A New Look at the Coproduction of Local Public Goods." *Political Research Quarterly* 57: 231–44.

Marschall, Melissa, and Paru R. Shah. 2007. "The Attitudinal Effects of Minority Incorporation." *Urban Affairs Review* 42: 629–58.

Mathis, Joel. 2001a. "American Eagle Effect Lingers." *Lawrence Journal-World,* April 6. http://infoweb.newsbank.com.www2.lib.ku.edu:2048/iw-search/we/InfoWeb?p_product=NewsBank&p_theme=aggregated5&p_action=doc&p_docid=0EBA2B33746B5C6E&p_docnum=2&p_queryname=12.

———. 2001b. "Living Wage Group Stages Labor Day Rally." *Lawrence Journal-World,* September 4. http://infoweb.newsbank.com.www2.lib.ku.edu:2048/iw-search/we/InfoWeb?p_product=NewsBank&p_theme=aggregated5&p_action=doc&p_docid=0EE6C6A5E75EAD9A&p_docnum=1&p_queryname=27.

———. 2001c. "Task Force Approves Tax Abatement Plan." *Lawrence Journal-World,* July 18. http://infoweb.newsbank.com.www2.lib.ku.edu:2048/iw-search/we/InfoWeb?p_product=NewsBank&p_theme=aggregated5&p_action=doc&p_docid=0ED6F47F63C6DE83&p_docnum=1&p_queryname=14.

———. 2001d. "Task Force Begins to Refine Policy on Tax Abatements." *Lawrence Journal-World,* May 24. http://www2.ljworld.com/news/2001/may/24/task_force_begins/.

———. 2001e. "Task Force Revisits Wage Issue." *Lawrence Journal-World,* June 20. http://infoweb.newsbank.com.www2.lib.ku.edu:2048/iw-search/we/InfoWeb?p_product=NewsBank&p_theme=aggregated5&p_action=oc&p_docid=0ECDB9C36B0DC5F3&p_docnum=19&p_queryname=25.

Mellinger, Gwyn. 1991. "Advisory Council Urges City to Adopt Tax Break Proposal." *Lawrence Journal-World,* June 7. http://infoweb.newsbank.com.www2.lib.ku.edu:2048/iw-search/we/InfoWeb?p_product=NewsBank&p_theme=aggregated5&p_action=doc&p_docid=0EAE9F8A44AB421C&p_docnum=1&p_queryname=28.

———. 1992. "Analysis Eases Tax Abatement Controversies." *Lawrence Journal-World,* August 30. http://infoweb.newsbank.com.www2.lib.ku.edu:2048/iw-search/we/InfoWeb?p_product=NewsBank&p_theme=aggregated5&p_action=doc&p_docid=0EAE9FD600847EEE&p_docnum=1&p_queryname=31.

Mettler, Suzanne. 1998. "Dividing Social Citizenship by Gender: The Implementation of Unemployment Insurance and Aid to Dependent Children, 1935–1950." *Studies in American Political Development* 12: 303–42.

———. 2002. "Bringing the State Back Into Civic Engagement: Policy Feedback Effects of the G.I. Bill for World War II Veterans." *American Political Science Review* 96: 351–66.

———. 2007a. "Bringing Government Back into Civic Engagement: Considering the Role of Public Policy." *International Journal of Public Administration* 30: 643–50.

———. 2007b. "The Transformed Welfare State and the Redistribution of Political Voice." In *The Transformation of American Politics,* edited by Paul Pierson and Theda Skocpol, 191–222. Princeton, N.J.: Princeton University Press.

Mettler, Suzanne, and Andrew Milstein. 2007. "American Political Development from Citizens' Perspective: Tracking Federal Government's Presence in Individual Lives over Time." *Studies in American Political Development* 21: 110–30.

Mettler, Suzanne, and Jeffrey M. Stonecash. 2008. "Government Program Usage and Political Voice." *Social Science Quarterly* 89: 273–93.

Mettler, Suzanne, and Joe Soss. 2004. "The Consequences of Public Policy for Democratic Citizenship: Bridging Policy Studies and Mass Politics." *Perspectives on Politics* 2: 55–73.

Meyer, Megan, and Cheryl Hyde. 2004. "Too Much of a 'Good' Thing? Insular Neighborhood Associations, Nonreciprocal Civility, and the Promotion of Civic Health." Supplement, *Nonprofit and Voluntary Sector Quarterly* 33 (3): 77S–96S.

Miller, Joe. 2000. "Longtime Chamber Associate Withdraws Membership." *Lawrence Journal-World,* April 20. http://infoweb.newsbank.com.www2.lib.ku.edu:2048/iw-search/we/InfoWeb?p_product=NewsBank&p_theme=aggregated5&p_action=doc&p_docid=0EAE9EFD94867272&p_docnum=1&p_queryname=32.

Miller, Lisa L. 2001. *The Politics of Community Crime Prevention: Implementing Operation Weed and Seed in Seattle.* Farnham, U.K.: Ashgate Publishing.

Minkoff, Scott L. 2008. "Minding Your Neighborhood: Local Redistributive Spending in a Spatial Context." Paper presented at the Annual Meeting of the Western Political Science Association, San Diego, Calif., March 20–22.

Mossberger, Karen, and Gerry Stoker. 2001. "The Evolution of Urban Regime Theory: The Challenge of Conceptualization." *Urban Affairs Review* 36: 810–35.

Newman, Sandra J., and Joseph M. Harkness. 2002. "The Long-Term Effects of Public Housing on Self-Sufficiency." *Journal of Policy Analysis and Management* 21: 21–43.

Nevarez, Leonard. 2000. "Corporate Philanthropy in the New Urban Economy: The Role of Business–Nonprofit Realignment in Regime Politics." *Urban Affairs Review* 36 (2): 197–227.

Oden, Michael D., and Elizabeth J. Mueller. 1999. "Distinguishing Development Incentives from Developer Giveaways: A Critical Guide for Development Practitioners and Citizens." *Policy Studies Journal* 27: 147–68.

Oliver, J. Eric. 2000. "City Size and Civic Involvement in Metropolitan America." *American Political Science Review* 94: 361–74.

Olson, Mancur. 1965. *The Logic of Collective Action: Public Goods and the Theory of Groups*. Cambridge: Harvard University Press.

Patashnik, Eric M. 2008. *Reforms at Risk: What Happens After Major Policy Changes Are Enacted.* Princeton: Princeton University Press.

Patashnik, Eric M., and Julian E. Zelizer. 2009. "When Policy Does Not Remake Politics: The Limits of Policy Feedback." Paper presented at the Annual Meeting of the American Political Science Association, Toronto, Canada, September 3–6.

Peters, Alan, and Peter Fisher. 2004. "The Failures of Economic Development Incentives." *Journal of the American Planning Association* 70: 27–37.

Peterson, Paul. 1981. *City Limits.* Chicago: University of Chicago Press.

Pierson, Paul. 1993. "When Effect Becomes Cause: Policy Feedback and Political Change." *World Politics* 45: 595–628.

Pierson, Paul, and Theda Skocpol. 2007. "American Politics in the Long Run." In *The Transformation of American Politics,* edited by Paul Pierson and Theda Skocpol, 3–16. Princeton, N.J.: Princeton University Press.

Pino, Nathan W. 2001. "Community Policing and Social Capital." *Policing: An International Journal of Police Strategies & Management* 24: 200–15.

"Policy Approval Doesn't End Tax Abatement Debate." 2001. *Lawrence Journal-World,* November 14. http://www2.ljworld.com/news/2001/nov/14/policy_approval_doesnt/.

Purinton, Anna. 2003. *The Policy Shift to Good Jobs: Cities, States, and Counties Attaching Job Quality Standards to Development Subsidies.* Washington, D.C.: Good Jobs First. http://www.goodjobsfirst.org/pdf/jobquality.pdf.

Putnam, Robert D. 2000. *Bowling Alone.* New York: Simon & Schuster.

Raley, Dan. 1994. "New Police Unit Planned for Domestic Violence—Stamper Hopes to Use San Diego Model." *Seattle Post-Intelligencer,* June 24. http://infoweb.newsbank.com/iw-search/we/InfoWeb?p_product=NewsBank&p_theme=aggregated5&p_action=doc&p_docid=0EB04A77E57E2000&p_docnum=1&p_queryname=21.

Ranney, Dave. 2000. "Employment City to Debate 'Living Wages'—Lawrence Officials Differ on Regulating Companies' Payrolls." *Lawrence Journal-World,* September 4. http://infoweb.newsbank.com.www2.lib.ku.edu:2048/iw-search/we/InfoWeb?p_product=NewsBank&p_theme=aggregated5&p_

action=doc&p_docid=0EAE9F1CB3BBF0A9&p_docnum=18&p_queryname=4.

Reeb, Frank. 2007. *2007 Tax Abatement Report.* Lawrence, Kan.: City of Lawrence.

Reed, Wilson Edward. 1999. *The Politics of Community Policing: The Case of Seattle.* New York: Garland Publishing.

Reese, Laura A., and Raymond A. Rosenfeld. 2002. "Reconsidering Private Sector Power: Business Input and Local Development Policy." *Urban Affairs Review* 37: 642–74.

Sands, Gary, Laura A. Reese, and Heather L. Kahn. 2006. "Implementing Tax Abatements in Michigan: A Study of Best Practices." *Economic Development Quarterly* 20: 44–58.

Santana, Arthur. 1998. "42 Return to Community Policing—But Officer Shortage Remains, Spokeswoman Says." *Seattle Times,* September 11. http://infoweb.newsbank.com/iw-search/we/InfoWeb?p_product=NewsBank&p_theme=aggregated5&p_action=doc&p_docid=0EB53961A3AAC1B6&p_docnum =4&p_queryname=5.

Savitch, H.V., and Paul Kantor. 2002. *Cities in the International Marketplace.* Princeton: Princeton University Press.

Schneider, Anne, and Helen Ingram. 1997. *Policy Design for Democracy.* Lawrence: University Press of Kansas.

Schneider, Anne, and Mara Sidney. 2009. "What Is Next for Policy Design and Social Construction Theory?" *Policy Studies Journal* 37 (1): 103–20.

Schneider, Mark. 1987. "Income Homogeneity and the Size of Suburban Government." *Journal of Politics* 49: 36–53.

Schneider, Mark, and Kee Ok Park. 1989. "Metropolitan Counties as Service Delivery Agents: The Still Forgotten Governments." *Public Administration Review* 49: 346–52.

Scott, Jason. 2002. "Assessing the Relationship between Police-Community Coproduction and Neighborhood-Level Social Capital." *Journal of Contemporary Criminal Justice* 18: 147–66.

Sites, William. 2003. *Remaking New York: Primitive Globalization and the Politics of Urban Community.* Minneapolis: University of Minnesota Press.

Sharp, Elaine B., and Paul Johnson. 2009. "Accounting for Variation in Distrust of Local Police." *Justice Quarterly* 26: 157–82.

Sharp, Elaine B., and Steven Maynard-Moody. 1991. "Theories of the Local Welfare Role." *American Journal of Political Science* 35: 934–50.

Shukovsky, Paul, and Robert L. Jamieson. 1996. "Police to Break Up Community Teams." *Seattle Post-Intelligencer,* October 18. http://infoweb.newsbank.com/iw-search/we/InfoWeb?p_product=NewsBank&p_theme=aggregated5&p_action=doc&p_docid=0EB04AF4397DDD2B&p_docnum=4&p_queryname=23.

Sidney, Mara S. 2003. *Unfair Housing: How National Policy Shapes Community Action.* Lawrence: University Press of Kansas.

Sirianni, Carmen. 2007. "Neighborhood Planning as Collaborative Democratic Design." *Journal of the American Planning Association* 73: 373–88.

"Sit-In at Market Will Focus on Sidewalk Law." 1994. *Seattle Times,* August 31. http://infoweb.newsbank.com/iw-search/we/InfoWeb?p_product=NewsBank&p_theme=aggregated5&p_action=doc&p_docid=0EB5375F4F596CF5&p_docnum=40&p_queryname=7.

Skocpol, Theda. 1985. "Bringing the State Back In: Strategies of Analysis in Current Research." In *Bringing the State Back In,* edited by Peter B. Evans, Dietrich Rueschemeyer, and Theda Skocpol, 3–43. New York: Cambridge University Press.

———. 2007. "Government Activism and the Reorganization of American Civic Democracy." In *The Transformation of American Politics,* edited by Paul Pierson and Theda Skocpol, 39–67. Princeton, N.J.: Princeton University Press.

Skocpol, Theda, and Kenneth Finegold. 1982. "State Capacity and Economic Intervention in the Early New Deal." *Political Science Quarterly* 97: 255–78.

Skogan, Wesley G. 1994. "The Impact of Community Policing on Neighborhood Residents: A Cross-Site Analysis." In *The Challenge of Community Policing: Testing the Promises,* edited by Dennis P. Rosenbaum, 167–81. Thousand Oaks, Calif.: Sage.

———. 2004. "Representing the Community in Community Policing." In *Community Policing (Can It Work?),* edited by Wesley Skogan, 57–76. Belmont, Calif.: Thomson Wadsworth.

———. 2006. *Police and Community in Chicago.* Oxford: Oxford University Press.

Sonenshein, Raphael. 1996. "The Battle over Liquor Stores in South Central Los Angeles." *Urban Affairs Review* 31: 710–28.

———. 2004. *The City at Stake.* Princeton: Princeton University Press.

Sorkin, Michael (ed). 1992. *Variations on a Theme Park.* New York: Hill and Wang.

Soss, Joe. 1999. "Lessons of Welfare: Policy Design, Political Learning, and Political Action." *American Political Science Review* 93: 363–80.

———. 2000. *Unwanted Claims.* Ann Arbor: University of Michigan Press.

Soss, Joe, and Lael R. Keiser. 2006. "The Political Roots of Disability Claims: How State Environments and Policies Shape Citizen Demands." *Political Research Quarterly* 59 (1): 133–46.

Soss, Joe, and Sanford F. Schram. 2007. "A Public Transformed? Welfare Reform as Policy Feedback." *American Political Science Review* 101: 111–28.

Stoll, Michael A. 2001. "Race, Neighborhood Poverty, and Participation in Voluntary Associations." *Sociological Forum* 16 (3): 529–57.

Stone, Clarence N. 1980. "Systemic Power in Community Decisionmaking: A Restatement of Stratification Theory." *American Political Science Review* 74 (4): 978–90.

______. 1987a. "Summing Up: Urban Regimes, Development Policy, and Political Arrangements." In *The Politics of Urban Development*, edited by Clarence Stone and Heywood Sanders, 269–90. Lawrence: University Press of Kansas.

______. 1987b. "The Study of the Politics of Urban Development." In *The Politics of Urban Development*, edited by Clarence Stone and Heywood Sanders, 3–24. Lawrence: University Press of Kansas.

______. 1989. *Regime Politics: Governing Atlanta, 1946–1988*. Lawrence: University Press of Kansas.

______. 2005. "Rethinking the Policy–Politics Connection." *Policy Studies* 26: 241–60.

Sullivan, Daniel M. 2002. "Local Governments as Risk Takers and Risk Reducers: An Examination of Business Subsidies and Subsidy Controls." *Economic Development Quarterly* 16: 115–26.

Sullivan, Daniel M., and Gary Paul Green. 1999. "Business Subsidies and Municipal Controls." *Journal of Urban Affairs* 21: 267–80.

Sullivan, Daniel M., and Jonathan Picarsic. 2007. "Fostering Racial and Class Integration in a Gentrifying Neighborhood? The Role of a Neighborhood Association." Paper presented at the Conference of the American Sociological Association, New York, August 11.

Suttles, Gerald D. 1968. *The Social Order of the Slum*. Chicago: University of Chicago Press.

______. 1972. *The Social Construction of Communities*. Chicago: University of Chicago Press.

Taub, Richard P. 1984. *Paths of Neighborhood Change*. Chicago: University of Chicago Press.

"Tax Abatement Report Approved." 2002. *Lawrence Journal-World*, October 4. http://infoweb.newsbank.com.www2.lib.ku.edu:2048/iw-search/we/InfoWeb?p_product=NewsBank&p_theme=aggregated5&p_action=doc&p_docid=0F67F93D4F01D04C&p_docnum=7&p_queryname=12.

"Tax Abatement Task Force Makeup Draws Wide Praise." 2001. *Lawrence Journal-World*, February 21. http://www2.ljworld.com/news/2001/feb/21/tax_abatement_task/.

Taylor, John. 1989a. "City Official Calls for Examination of Tax Abatements." *Lawrence Journal-World*, November 24. http://infoweb.newsbank.com.www2.lib.ku.edu:2048/iw-search/we/InfoWeb?p_product=NewsBank&p_theme=aggregated5&p_action=doc&p_docid=0EAE9F32F9593883&p_docnum=2&p_queryname=14.

———. 1989b. "Tax Abatements OK'd, but Policy Debated." *Lawrence Journal-World,* December 13. http://infoweb.newsbank.com.www2.lib.ku.edu:2048/iw-search/we/InfoWeb?p_product=NewsBank&p_theme=aggregated5&p_action=doc&p_docid=0EAE9F375EBEFD11&p_docnum=1&p_queryname=13.

———. 1990a. "City Grants Tax Abatement for Firm." *Lawrence Journal-World,* April 25. http://infoweb.newsbank.com.www2.lib.ku.edu:2048/iw-search/we/InfoWeb?p_product=NewsBank&p_theme=aggregated5&p_action=doc&p_docid=0EAE9F4597EC3B27&p_docnum=25&p_queryname=15.

———. 1990b. "City Offers Famous Brands Half of Incentive Package." *Lawrence Journal-World,* November 21. http://infoweb.newsbank.com.www2.lib.ku.edu:2048/iw-search/we/InfoWeb?p_product=NewsBank&p_theme=aggregated5&p_action=doc&p_docid=0EAE9F65533ACF8D&p_docnum=1&p_queryname=19.

———. 1990c. "City Official Seeks Contracts with Firms Getting Tax Breaks." *Lawrence Journal-World,* October 23. http://infoweb.newsbank.com.www2.lib.ku.edu:2048/iw-search/we/InfoWeb?p_product=NewsBank&p_theme=aggregated5&p_action=doc&p_docid=0EAE9F5FCF995164&p_docnum=1&p_queryname=18.

———. 1990d. "City OKs Abatement for Davol Expansion." *Lawrence Journal-World,* June 13. http://infoweb.newsbank.com.www2.lib.ku.edu:2048/iw-search/we/InfoWeb?p_product=NewsBank&p_theme=aggregated5&p_action=doc&p_docid=0EAE9F4F31368DC3&p_docnum=1&p_queryname=17.

———. 1990e. "Tax Abatement Issue Continues to Simmer." *Lawrence Journal-World,* December 2. http://infoweb.newsbank.com.www2.lib.ku.edu:2048/iw-search/we/InfoWeb?p_product=NewsBank&p_theme=aggregated5&p_action=doc&p_docid=0EAE9F6C6AEBA9EC&p_docnum=1&p_queryname=16.

Terrill, William, and Stephen D. Mastrofski. 2004. "Working the Street: Does Community Policing Matter?" In *Community Policing (Can It Work?)*, edited by Wesley G. Skogan, 109–35. Belmont, Calif.: Thomson Wadsworth.

"Text of Letter from Famous Brands." 1990. *Lawrence Journal-World,* December 12. http://infoweb.newsbank.com.www2.lib.ku.edu:2048/iw-search/we/InfoWeb?p_product=NewsBank&p_theme=aggregated5&p_action=doc&p_docid=0EAE9F69D375F7D5&p_docnum=1&p_queryname=26.

Thacher, David. 2004. "Order Maintenance Reconsidered: Moving Beyond Strong Causal Reasoning." *Journal of Criminal Law and Criminology* 94: 381–415.

Thomas, John C. 1986. *Between Citizen and City.* Lawrence: University Press of Kansas.

Thomas, John C., and Gregory Streib. 2003. "The New Face of Government: Citizen-Initiated Contacts in the Era of E-Government." *Journal of Public Administration Research and Theory* 13: 83–102.

Thomas, John C. and Julia Melkers. 1999. "Explaining Citizen-Initiated Contacts with Municipal Bureaucrats." *Urban Affairs Review* 34: 667–90.

Thomson, Ken. 2001. *From Neighborhood to Nation: The Democratic Foundations of Civil Society.* Hanover, N.H.: University Press of New England.

Toplikar, Dave. 1993a. "Candy Plant, City Weren't a Match." *Lawrence Journal-World,* May 22. http://infoweb.newsbank.com.www2.lib.ku.edu:2048/iw-search/we/InfoWeb?p_product=NewsBank&p_theme=aggregated5&p_action=doc&p_docid=0EAEA003C83AB781&p_docnum=1&p_queryname=27.

______ . 1993b. "Wal-Mart Bypasses City with New Center." *Lawrence Journal-World,* June 8. http://infoweb.newsbank.com.www2.lib.ku.edu:2048/iw-search/we/InfoWeb?p_product=NewsBank&p_theme=aggregated5&p_action=doc&p_docid=0EAEA00A65ED81DC&p_docnum=8&p_queryname=21.

U.S. Census Bureau. 1997. *Finances of County Governments, 1997.* http://www.census.gov/govs/cog/historical_data_1997.html.

______ . 2002. *Finances of County Governments, 2002.* http://www.census.gov/govs/cog/historical_data_2002.html.

______ . 2008. "2005–2007 American Community Survey 3-Year Estimates." In *American Fact Finder.* http://factfinder.census.gov/home/saff/main.html?_lang=en.

U.S. Department of Justice, Bureau of Justice Statistics. *Law Enforcement Management and Administrative Statistics (LEMAS),* http://bjs.ojp.usdoj.gov/index.cfm?ty=dcdetail&iid=248.

Walker, Sam. 1998. *Popular Justice: A History of American Criminal Justice.* New York: Oxford University Press.

"Warmer Welcome Awaits Proposed Living Wage Ordinance." 2003. *Lawrence Journal-World,* July 13. http://infoweb.newsbank.com.www2.lib.ku.edu:2048/iw-search/we/InfoWeb?p_product=NewsBank&p_theme=aggregated5&p_action=doc&p_docid=0FC5190B801336C5&p_docnum=1&p_queryname=1.

Weber, Rachel. 2002. "Do Better Contracts Make Better Economic Development Incentives?" *Journal of the American Planning Association* 68: 43–55.

Weisel, Deborah Lamm, and John E. Eck. 1994. "Toward a Practical Approach to Organizational Change." In *The Challenge of Community Policing,* edited by Dennis P. Rosenbaum, 53–72. Thousand Oaks, Calif.: Sage.

Weitzer, Ronald, and Steven A. Tuch. 1999. "Race, Class, and Perceptions of Discrimination by the Police." *Crime and Delinquency* 45: 494–507.

———. 2002. "Perceptions of Racial Profiling: Race, Class, and Personal Experience." *Criminology* 40: 436–56.

Whitely, Peyton. 1995. "Stamper Keeping the Peace Here—After First Year, Police Chief's Marks Generally Favorable." *Seattle Times*, February 24. http://infoweb.newsbank.com/iw-search/we/InfoWeb?p_product=NewsBank&p_theme=aggregated5&p_action=doc&p_docid=0EB537B995F9DA4F&p_docnum=2&p_queryname=17.

Weir, Margaret, Jane Ronegerude, and Christopher K. Ansell. 2009. "Collaboration is Not Enough: Virtuous Cycles of Reform in Urban Transportation." *Urban Affairs Review* 44 (4): 455–89.

Wilson, James Q. 1973. *Political Organizations*. New York: Basic Books.

———. 1980. "The Politics of Regulation." In *The Politics of Regulation*, edited by James Q. Wilson, pp. 357–94. New York: Basic Books.

Wilson, James Q., and George L. Kelling. 1982. "Broken Windows: The Police and Neighborhood Safety." *Atlantic Magazine*, March 10.

Xu, Hili, Mora Fiedler, and Karl Flaming. 2005. "Discovering the Impact of Community Policing: The Broken Windows Thesis, Collective Efficacy, and Citizens' Judgment." *Journal of Research in Crime and Delinquency* 42: 147–86.

Zedlewski, Sheila, and Linda Giannarelli. 1997. "Diversity among State Welfare Programs: Implications for Reform." *New Federalism: Issues and Options for States* (Series A), No. A-1 (January). Washington, D.C.: Urban Institute. http://www.urban.org/publications/307033.html.

Zhao, Jihong, Matthew C. Scheider, and Quint Thurman. 2002. "Funding Community Policing to Reduce Crime: Have COPS Grants Made a Difference?" *Criminology and Public Policy* 2: 7–32.

Zhao, Jihong, Nicholas P. Lovrich, and Quint Thurman. 1999. "The Status of Community Policing in American Cities." *Policing: An International Journal of Police Strategies & Management* 22: 74–92.

Index

Globalization and Community Series (continued from page ii)

VOLUME 11

A Political Space: Reading the Global through Clayoquot Sound
Warren Magnusson and Karena Shaw, editors

VOLUME 10

City Requiem, Calcutta: Gender and the Politics of Poverty
Ananya Roy

VOLUME 9

Landscapes of Urban Memory: The Sacred and the Civic in India's High-Tech City
Smriti Srinivas

VOLUME 8

Fin de Millénaire Budapest: Metamorphoses of Urban Life
Judit Bodnár

VOLUME 7

Latino Metropolis
Victor M. Valle and Rodolfo D. Torres

VOLUME 6

Regions That Work: How Cities and Suburbs Can Grow Together
Manuel Pastor Jr., Peter Dreier, J. Eugene Grigsby III, and Marta López-Garza

VOLUME 5

Selling the Lower East Side: Culture, Real Estate, and Resistance in New York City
Christopher Mele

VOLUME 4

Power and City Governance: Comparative Perspectives on Urban Development
Alan DiGaetano and John S. Klemanski

VOLUME 3

Second Tier Cities: Rapid Growth beyond the Metropolis
Ann R. Markusen, Yong-Sook Lee, and Sean DiGiovanna, editors

VOLUME 2

Reconstructing Chinatown: Ethnic Enclave, Global Change
Jan Lin

VOLUME 1

The Work of Cities
Susan E. Clarke and Gary L. Gaile

ELAINE B. SHARP is professor of political science at the University of Kansas. She is the author of *Morality Issues and City Politics, The Sometime Connection: Public Opinion and Social Policy, The Dilemma of Drug Policy, Urban Politics and Administration,* and *Citizen Demand-Making in the Urban Context* and the editor of *Culture Wars and Local Politics.*